When God Speaks to My Heart

by
Rosalie Willis Storment

When God Speaks to My Heart
ISBN 978-1-936314-27-0
Copyright © 2011 by Rosalie Willis Storment

Published by Word and Spirit Resources
P.O. Box 701403
Tulsa, OK 74170

Dedication

"Heart Friends" who pray for us with love, are one of the most valuable gifts we can receive from God in this adventure of life. He has honored and blessed me with many Heart Friends near and far, around the block and around the world, who hold my arms up with love and prayer. It is to these precious Heart Friends that I dedicate this "Book of Love from God."

1

JOHN 10:27 NKJV
"My sheep hear My voice,
and I know them, and they follow Me."

My Precious One,

Ours is a close communion as between a father and his child, and you shall continue to rejoice in the freedom and ease of our relationship. Do not forsake your time with Me, for I require devotion in such a friendship. It shall continue to bring us both overflowing joy. Rejoice, for this is the beginning of an even closer, intimate relationship with Me. My children that are called by My Name shall hear My voice. It is their inheritance. Come to Me with love and peace in your heart. Open unto Me the desires of your heart, your frustrations, your weaknesses, your blessings and causes for rejoicing. Let Me share each and every response that you experience.

I Am Always with You,
Your Loving Father

Father, I love You so much! Thank You for the promise of knowing You even more intimately. Help me Father, to not only share with You my delight and excitement as You bless my life, but now to more fully share with You my frustrations and weaknesses with transparency.

Father, what areas of my life have I not readily shared with You?

_____

_____

_____

_____

_____

_____

_____

_____

_____

_____

_____

_____

_____

_____

2

ACTS 2:28 AMP

"You have made known to me, the ways of life;
You will enrapture me [diffusing my soul with joy]
with and in Your presence"

Dear One,

Cherish this time with Me. It will be like none other. I will speak to you in the day and I will speak to you in the night hours. Our time together shall be precious and well spent. Let Me direct your days, detail by detail. The enemy will try to get in, but he cannot. My power is greater, and you shall be aware of My Presence moment by moment, day by day. Cease your striving and come into peace with Me. You have come a long way, and the best is yet to come.

I Love You, Your Father

Loving Father, I do cherish this time with You, as You speak to my heart!

_____

_____

_____

_____

_____

_____

_____

_____

_____

_____

_____

_____

_____

Dear Father, I see a picture of striving, as a small child riding a tricycle. There is such a look of consternation and determination on her face, as she pedals with all of her might. Then, there is the picture of a small child, being pushed by her Father and laughing with pure joy, with legs outstretched in freedom and trust, knowing that her Daddy has everything under control! I like the second picture best! Truly, Father, the best is yet to come!

3

JOHN 16:13 TLB
"When the Holy Spirit, who is truth, comes,
he shall guide you into all truth."

My Dear One,

My guidance is yours for the asking. I delight in guiding My children. Simply walk step by step in expectation. To the one who has much, much will be given. The more revelation and awareness you walk in, the more you will receive. It is a never-ending upward spiral of joy. The one who walks in expectation receives much. Therefore, walk, expecting My guiding hand upon your life moment by moment, for it is yours. Those who expect little, receive little. Ask much, and you will receive much.

I Am Your Source, Receive!
Your Loving Father

Loving Father, You have said, "My ways are full of life and joy to the one who follows after them. It is the beginning of eternal life, gladness, joy, and peace. My people shall glory daily in the freedom that joy brings. Freedom in the Spirit brings My pure joy and freedom from bondages." Father, what freedom, gladness, joy, and peace Your guidance and revelation bring! My expectations and delight in You are high! You have never failed me! I love You, Father!

Father, here I am in Your wonderful, peaceful Presence, joyfully expecting and asking, listening intently for You to speak to my heart!

_____

_____

_____

_____

_____

_____

_____

_____

_____

_____

_____

_____

_____

_____

_____

4

JEREMIAH 33:3 NKJV
"Call to Me, and I will answer you,
and show you great and mighty things,
which you do not know."

My Child,

Your focus on Me is vital. When your focus on Me is sharp, all else falls into line. Listen quietly. Still your inner being. I can overcome the outside disturbances so you can hear My voice above the din, but it is in the stillness that real fellowship with Me is found. Communion with Me is a two-way street. It must be pursued with diligence and regularity. Do not let the trials of this world intervene. My light shall shine through all the dark corners. New areas of your life shall come to light that have not been revealed before. Fill your days with My Presence!

Listen to My Heart,
Your Loving Father

Precious Father, today I will begin to share every thought with You, my most faithful and loving friend, with a constant listening ear, knowing You will share Your heart with me.

_____

_____

_____

_____

_____

_____

_____

_____

_____

Father, the greatest desire of my heart is to be continually in Your Presence, in constant communion with You. Thank You, that You long for that kind of communion with me too. Help me, I pray, to continually walk with a pliable, humble, and repentant spirit, relinquishing all burdens to You, that I might hear Your voice clearly.

5

PROVERBS 3:26 NKJV
"For the LORD will be your confidence,
and will keep your foot from being caught."

My Child,

Depend on Me for every word, every feeling, every action, and then trust that they are from Me. Walk with a carefree assurance. Refuse to be uptight. Rebuke fear and doubt every time they show themselves. Fly like a butterfly: relaxed, free, joyful, and exuberant. Pour that exuberance out on others, with love. The joy of the Lord is your strength. Appropriate it every morning. Place your life in My hands. Go forth with confidence, knowing that I am in command and that My Spirit is within you, guiding you. Continue to prepare, storing up My Words in your heart. Much is ahead.

Hold My Hand,
Your Loving Father

Father God, just thinking of You makes me smile with joy and delight. When I allow pressures to crowd in or forget to begin the day thinking of You and listening for Your precious voice, thank You for continuing to make me more sensitive to Your gentle nudging, turning me back to the joy of the awareness of Your Presence.

Father, starting today, I will turn my thoughts toward you moment by moment.

_____
_____
_____
_____
_____
_____
_____
_____
_____
_____
_____
_____

6

PSALM 84:5 NKJV
"Blessed is the man whose strength is in You,
whose heart is set on pilgrimage."

My Child,

Quiet your spirit before Me each day. I shall lead you into what must be done. Nothing shall be left unattended. Rejoice as each day builds upon another, for in that building comes strength, fortitude, and an elastic spirit. Growth is never easy, but it is helped along with a quieted, peaceful, unperturbed spirit. Let Me quiet your spirit each day and prepare it for the events of the day to come. Then discuss each day with Me at the close of the day, and with each day we shall grow together. Now carry on with My peace within you.

Loving You,
Your Father

Father, what are the things that You long for me to share with You about my day?

_____

_____

_____

_____

_____

_____

_____

_____

_____

_____

_____

_____

_____

Father, I love sharing what is happening in my life with my Heart Friends. But You are who I should enjoy sharing the events and details of my life with the most. No human can care about the details of my life like You do. Teach me Father, I pray, to faithfully "download" and discuss the day with You at the close of each day.

7

JAMES 1:5 NKJV
"If any of you lacks wisdom, let him ask of God,
who gives to all liberally and without reproach,
and it will be given to him."

Precious One,

Presumption comes in when one bypasses a one-to-one relationship with Me. That person knows of Me, knows about Me, knows that I Am and that I am a gracious God, but has not consulted with Me to find out My will and presumes to know My will from others' previous experiences. I cannot be put in a box. My ways are higher than your ways. Again I say, "Does My Word not say, 'if one desires wisdom, just ask and I shall supply it'?" First know My perfect will in a situation through My Word and communion with Me. Then stand on that word in faith and believe.

Know Me and My Ways!
Your Loving Father

Father, I long to hear You speaking to my heart more clearly. You have said, "Precious and few are those who seek Your heart in all they say and do." The greatest desire of my heart is to be that one who hears Your heart every moment of every day, to be faithful and true in everything I say and do.

Dear Father, today I ask You for wisdom in these areas of my life:

_____

_____

_____

_____

_____

_____

_____

_____

_____

_____

_____

_____

8

1 JOHN 4:16 NKJV
"God is love, and he who abides in love abides in God,
and God in him."

My Precious One,

(**Father, what do I need to know?**) *"I love you! A deeper knowing of this is yours this night."* (**What would You have me do?**) *"Nothing, it is a gift given."* (**How do I receive, Father?**) *"Open your heart to receive with thanksgiving."* (**You are totally committed to me, Lord. Your love is unconditional. It is constant. It is filled with grace. It is totally giving. It is how You've been teaching me to be.**) *"Starting tonight, you shall more fully know the preciousness of My love, our hearts beating as one. Listen with tenacity. Listen with strength of purpose. Listen with faith to receive. Listen and believe!"*

Receive My Gift of Love!
Your Loving Father

Father, I am listening with tenacity as You speak to my heart. Thank You for Your gift of love!

_____

_____

_____

_____

_____

_____

_____

_____

_____

_____

_____

_____

_____

Loving Father, everywhere I look, there You are! Your love surrounds me with beauty! The loving Heart Friends You have put in my life sparkle with beauty! You are always there to speak to my heart with so much love, causing my heart to sing about everything. Miracles abound everywhere I look! Thank You, Father, that tonight I shall more fully know the preciousness of Your love, our hearts beating as one. I want to think Your thoughts, to listen always with strength of purpose and with the faith to receive everything You say to my heart with so much love! I love You, Father!

9

1 PETER 1:22 NKJV
"Since you have purified your souls in obeying the truth
through the Spirit in sincere love of the brethren,
love one another fervently with a pure heart."

My Precious One,

Hesitant, conditional love is the way of the world. The way of the Cross and the way of My heart, and of My love say, "Here is my heart, it is open to you. I will honor you, love you, speak well of you, pray for you, protect you and encourage you." Strength of character determines whether you will judge and uncover, or cover with My love. One who seeks to love will, on the journey, find truth. One who only seeks truth, forever seeks but never finds, thus sacrificing both love and truth, becoming an easy target for deception.

Love As I Love,
Your Loving Father

Thank You, Father, for teaching me to love with Your kind of love, to always give forth of Your Spirit through love and forgiveness, walking in strength of character that covers with Your love. You have said to not build walls of protection but to be vulnerable and transparent walking in honor in all I say and do.

Father, when I am tempted to say something negative about another, I will remember that they are one of Your treasures and I am to treasure them, too. I will lift them up to You and speak blessing over them instead.

_____

_____

_____

_____

_____

_____

_____

_____

_____

_____

_____

_____

_____

_____

10

"You will prepare and strengthen and direct their hearts,
You will cause Your ear to hear."

My Precious Child,

Teach others to be still and know Me with an assurance of My love and care. Strengthen the hearts and hands around you. Be a lighthouse of hope and freedom in such a way as to say, "You can do what He has created you to do and be. His love will set you free. Can you not see His love gives you the victory? Let Him be everything you need. His love is your security. He will fulfill your needs and cause your eyes to see His hand of blessing, proclaiming, teaching, and providing every day. His matchless love is the only way."

Be My Love, My Child!

Your Loving Father

Loving Father, cause me to know You more intimately and know Your heart of love in a deeper more complete way!

_____

_____

_____

_____

_____

_____

_____

_____

_____

_____

_____

_____

_____

_____

Oh yes, Father, this is the cry of my heart for everyone I love and meet! I want them to know they have a destiny in You! I want them to know that they can hear Your loving voice and be assured of Your love and care. I want to know that they can find hope, every kind of blessing and freedom in You! I want them to know that You are their protection, their provision, and the best friend they will ever have. I want them to know that Your love will set them free to be everything You have created them to be! Father, help me to strengthen hearts and hands around me and cause them to know You intimately and with joy!!!

11

1 JOHN 2:5 AMP
"But he who keeps [treasures] His Word,
[who bears in mind His precepts, who observes His message
in its entirety], truly in Him has the love of and for
God been perfected [completed, reached maturity]."

My Child,

Listen to My footsteps as I walk beside you or in front of you. If I am beside you, we walk, talk, and fellowship. If ahead, follow closely, for we forge new paths and you must follow closely. Hear My footsteps ahead of you now. Listen closely, follow closely. Be alert and listening for My every move. It is not hard. Listen, watch Me up ahead and follow. Speak My Words, sleep My Words, follow My Words, and be My Words. The time is now to be what I have called you to be, My lifeline of hope, peace, love, and creatively walking by My Spirit of praise and worship. I have called you to be a lighthouse of rest, by My Spirit of praise, which brings peace. Life and light spring forth from My Spirit of peace. Be a peace giver, and together we shall see lives changed, mountains moved, and My Kingdom proclaimed.

Follow Me, My Precious One!
Your Loving Father

Loving Father, this is one very special message, proclaiming what it really means to walk victoriously with You! But the key of it all is speaking Your Words, sleeping Your Words, following Your Words, being Your Words, and being a peace giver. Together we shall see lives changed, mountains moved, and Your Kingdom proclaimed! Amen!

Father, I do treasure Your written Word and Your spoken Word as You daily speak to my heart!

_____

_____

_____

_____

_____

_____

_____

_____

_____

12

JEREMIAH 31:3 NKJV
"I have loved you with an everlasting love."

My Child,

My heart croons over you a song of love, the melody sweet with the fragrance of Heaven. Can you not hear it within, eliminating all stress and fear? Listen with your spirit. Open your heart to rejoice in the love I have for you. My heart yearns after you, that you would know Me more intimately. Bask in the warmth of My love, positioned in the assurance of My promises. My love is a shield to you. My hand is upon you to bless you. The beauty of My love is real, and in Me there is a place of quiet, safe rest.

Your Loving Father

Today, I will lay all my cares aside and turn my thoughts toward God by:

_____

_____

_____

_____

_____

_____

_____

_____

_____

_____

_____

_____

_____

_____

_____

_____

Father, help me to trust in Your love for me. Bring a new understanding of Your love into my life and strength to walk in confidence, even when my heart feels uncertain.

13

ISAIAH 40:31 NKJV

"Those who wait on the LORD, shall renew their strength;
they shall mount up with wings like eagles,
they shall run and not be weary,
they shall walk and not faint."

My Devoted Child,

You have sailed many a weary, hour. Release unto Me all your fears for the future and race with Me with a boundless trust and freedom. Hold fast to My hand and face the wind with a heart full of renewed courage. You are not alone. My strength is yours, and it will carry you through unscathed. The race goes well for the strong of heart. Press forward. The way is clear ahead. You shall arrive on time. Set sail with a new determination to finish the trip to the end. It is there you will find victory.

Forever by Your Side,
Your Loving Father

Father, I hand over my concerns to You. Help me to look to You, instead of to my burdens, when I am tempted to worry. Teach me to trust in You completely, and to rest in Your guiding hand. I love You.

Father, I give these areas of concern to You this day, Lord:

_____

_____

_____

_____

_____

_____

_____

_____

_____

_____

_____

_____

_____

_____

14

Psalm 119:165 NKJV
"Great peace have those who love Your law,
and nothing causes them to stumble."

My Child,

Listen to the rustling of the trees when the breezes blow. **(Why Father?)** *It is their sighing against the pressure of the wind. They bend, but they do not break. When the breezes stop blowing, once again they stand tall and erect with strength, knowing that when the wind blows once again they are prepared for the onslaught, because they are flexible.* **(What keeps them flexible, Father?)** *They don't take the pressure of the wind personally. They don't feel that the wind is out to get them. Stand watch on your heart to remain in a state of forgiveness. Seek not acceptance for yourself, but give acceptance and reach out in love and compassion.*

With Love,
Your Father

Father, when I feel my heart becoming anxious, I will come to You, with the trust of a child and say:

_____

_____

_____

_____

_____

_____

_____

_____

_____

_____

_____

Loving Father, may I not look to others for acceptance and approval that only You can give, but faithfully reach out to others with forgiveness, acceptance, love, and compassion. Thank You, Father, that the storms of life always make me stronger and more loving when my heart is trusting You.

15

PSALM 16:11 NKJV
"You will show me the path of life;
in Your presence is fullness of joy;
at Your right hand are pleasures forevermore."

My Child,

Lighten your load even further as you come into My Presence daily. Start out with a clean slate each day by giving everything back to Me. Let Me take each day and make of it a picture and creation of My love. Sights and sounds, blessings abound, each and every day. At the end of every day, I will smile at you, My child, and say, "She did it My way! She is blessed!!!"

I Love You,
Your Father

Father, at the beginning of every day I will to give back to you all of my responsibilities, cares, unfinished business, have to's, want to's, longings, indecisions—everything—that moment by moment You might lead me into what You want me to do and accomplish that day.

Father, what other ways can I totally relinquish each day to You?

_____

_____

_____

_____

_____

_____

_____

_____

_____

_____

_____

_____

_____

_____

_____

_____

_____

16

GENESIS 15:1 AMP
"I am your Shield, your abundant compensation,
and your reward shall be exceedingly great."

My Child,

Be still and know that I am God. The child who trusts and obeys his parents enjoys many more privileges. So it is in the Kingdom of God. The child who digests My Word and obeys it walks in much more from Me than the child who lets things come and go as they may. I am the rewarder of those who diligently seek Me. Much is coming. You must prepare. Continue digesting My Word. Walk with the assurance, My child, that I am with you this day. My love will surround you as you go forth. Praise from your lips shall show others the way. My people shall walk with Me as they see you walk with Me. Enter into My blessings. Walk fully in them. Listen for My voice. You shall know My voice.

I Love You, My Child,

Your Father

Father, You always have a strategy. How would You have me study, absorb, and enjoy Your Word now?

_____

_____

_____

_____

_____

_____

_____

_____

_____

_____

_____

Loving Father, I love the way You have taught me, reading Your Word cover to cover, version after version. Every day, a feast, as I've delighted in the treasures from Your heart given to me through Your Scriptures, Your Word! But the most wonderful time of all was reading the whole Amplified Version cover to cover, straight through, out loud. When one hears Your Word, sees Your Word and hears Your voice at the same time, it brings enlightenment! Nothing compares!

17

PSALM 42:1 AMP
"As the heart pants and longs for the water brooks,
so I pant and long for You, O God."

My Child,

Blessed is the one whose heart pants after Me in anticipation and desire to know Me better. Their spirits shall be like well-watered plants, thriving in the sunshine. You are blessed, My child. Let your blessings flow out to those around you through the laying on of hands and the laying on of prayer. Your requests shall be made known and acted upon. Many shall the blessings be, and many shall bless My Name because of your faithfulness. Minister and give forth in the spirit of love and forgiveness. Press on into My Kingdom, giving forth My blessings.

I Love You,
My Faithful Child.

Father, I pray for more confidence to let Your blessings flow out to those around me by the laying on of hands and the laying on of prayer, knowing that You will answer with Your heart of love! May I pray for others as easily as I breathe!

Loving Father, my heart is listening with anticipation and joy!

_____

_____

_____

_____

_____

_____

_____

_____

_____

_____

_____

_____

_____

_____

_____

_____

18

"If you abide in Me, and My words abide in you,
you will ask what you desire, and it shall be done for you."

My Beloved Child,

Search the Scriptures and know the intricacies of My Word. Let Me point out to you the nuances that shall delight your heart and cause you to grow. My Word is truly an open door to you that cannot be closed. Loose yourself from the trials of life by laying hold of My Word to you. Seek and you shall find; knock and the door shall be opened unto you. Yes, a new day has begun, and the trials that you have known shall fade away into the distance, as the vista of the new day opens before you.

You Are Blessed beyond Measure,
I Love You, Your Father

Loving Father, what wonderful intricacies and nuances from your Word do You want to share with me today? I am listening with delight!

_____
_____
_____
_____
_____
_____
_____
_____
_____
_____
_____
_____
_____

Father, one of the first things You ever said to me was, "Make of your heart a storehouse for My Word. My Word will guide and comfort you. I will lead you, My child, gently and with care. Do not ever fret. Patience! It has to be wrought in the spirit, step by step. Worry not with the minute, but keep your eye on the big picture. Everything through a praising heart comes out joy and gladness." And so I have made of my heart a storehouse for Your Word. Now, what joy, as You point out to me the nuances and wonderful intricacies of Your Word, to delight my heart and cause me to grow even more. You are ever faithful, my loving Father!

19

"Your word is a lamp to my feet and a light to my path."

My Precious Child,

Will to know My Word. It is an open door for you that will never close. My Word is nourishment, it is strength, it builds faith, and is the source by which questions are answered. It is the source of all wisdom and knowledge. Grow in it. My Word is the instrument through which you shall grow steadily, and others shall be drawn right along with you. My Word is the source of life, eternal and abundant. Glory in it. Know that I am your God. I love you. You need not ever be afraid. I am always with you, in every thought, word, and action. The things of this world will fade away, but My Word abides forever. Walk fully in it.

I Am with You Always,
Your Loving Father

Dear Father, reading Your Word has caused me to know You as a faithful and loving Father, whom I can trust with all my heart. And then to know that You long to speak to us, Your children, the same as You spoke with those who wrote Your Word long ago, brings overwhelming joy to my heart. I love reading and singing Your Word, and I love hearing Your words to my heart. Thank You, Father, for being such a loving God!

Father, what would You have me learn from Your Word today?

_____
_____
_____
_____
_____
_____
_____
_____
_____
_____
_____
_____
_____
_____

20

PSALM 19:11 AMP
"Your word have I laid up in my heart,
that I might not sin and against You."

My Child,

My love and My Word are inseparable. One cannot fully be manifested without the other. Those who try, fail! Love, given without My Word, does not bring life. It is incomplete and brings frustration and pain. My Word, without My love brought forth, brings forth legalism, death, and pain. It is the union of both My love and My Word, that brings the forth life, fulfillment, peace, and My perfect joy. Be a restorer of My love, brought forth through My Word. Bring forth life in its fullness.

Be My Word and My Love,
Your Loving Father

Father, thank You, for opening new realms of Your Word and Your love to me today. My heart is open to receive.

_____
_____
_____
_____
_____
_____
_____
_____
_____
_____
_____
_____
_____
_____

Loving Father, one of the first things You said to me as I began my adventure with You was, "Stay in My Word! It imparts faith! The Word of God will not benefit you unless its hearing is mixed with faith, and faith leads to action. This then is eating My Word. Real food mixes with the juices in your stomach (faith) and is turned into energy (actions)." So, Father, faith in Your Word leads to the greatest action of all, loving with Your love, which brings life! Thank You, Father, for the gifts of Your Word, Your love, abundant life, fulfillment, peace, and Your perfect joy.

21

PSALM 118:14 AMP
"The Lord is my Strength and Song;
and He has become my Salvation."

My Child,

Stake your claim by My Spirit, and stick to it like glue. Seek Me daily for My Word and promises and let them be your pillar of strength. My strength is your strength, and My Word is that strength. Stand on it, My child, unwavering, and strength shall be yours. To take away my Word is to take away your strength. Let it saturate your being. Let it be the meat that energizes and moves you. My Word—your life and being! Rejoice in the Word that is in your heart. It is there to stay and causes you to grow in strength, each day. Go forth in the strength of My Word!

I Love You,
Your Father

Precious Father, Your Word truly is my life and very being! It brings me strength when there seems to be no strength. Your promises bring me hope. But most of all, having intimate communion with You, is life! Thank You for always being there for me! I love You, Father!

Father, what would You have me meditate on from your Word today?

_____

_____

_____

_____

_____

_____

_____

_____

_____

_____

_____

_____

_____

_____

_____

_____

22

JOHN 10:16 AMP
"And they will listen to My voice and heed My call."

Dear One,

My people shall hear My voice. More and more they shall walk in My way. My way shall shine forth as a beacon of light upon My people, and those tottering on the borderline shall find themselves drawn to that light. Continue to shine forth as that beacon of light. The words that you speak are not as important as the love and light of My smile that pours through you to them. Feed on Me and My Word and keep your heart full to overflowing. The overflow will catch them like honey.

I Love You,
Your Father

Beloved Father, teach my ears to hear even more clearly, I pray, as You speak to my heart!

_____

_____

_____

_____

_____

_____

_____

_____

_____

_____

_____

_____

_____

Loving Father, it is so exciting every time another one of Your treasures finds out it is possible for them to hear Your loving voice of encouragement and wisdom, love and hope! You have said that the fruit of my life would always be a blessing to me and to others, and so it is that they then turn around and bless me, as You bless them! You are so wonderful, Father!

23

PROVERBS 15:23 AMP
"A man has joy in making an apt answer,
and a word spoken at the right moment—how good it is!"

My Child,

Be a communicator of My Words through thought, word, and deed. Stand tall in My Spirit, flanked on either side by the strength of My love. You shall inherit the blessings of My Kingdom in full measure, pressed down, and running over. Be a processor of My Word! (A processor takes the film that cannot be seen or understood and makes it into beautiful pictures that can both be seen and understood.) Beauty for ashes, a heart filled with love has been My gift to you. Release it to others.

Be My Love,
Your Loving Father

Loving Father, You have always said that the purity of heart (*thoughts*) and actions (*deeds*) always speak louder than words! But Father, thank You for also anointing my words to bring forth beautiful pictures of Your wonderful love and care for Your people! Thank You for helping me to stand tall in Your Spirit, flanked on either side by the strength of Your love!

Father, help me to be an even more effective processor of Your Word, reflecting who You are in everything I say, think, and do! I love You, Father!

24

PROVERBS 15:8 AMP
"The prayer of the upright is His delight!"

My Precious One,

Prayer is much like My Word. It must be consumed with faith and comes out belief. Presumption comes in when one bypasses a one-on-one relationship with Me. That person knows of Me, knows about Me, knows that I Am and that I am a gracious God, but has not consulted with Me to find out My will and presumes to know My will from others' previous experiences. I cannot be put in a box. My ways are higher than your ways. Does My Word not say, that if one desires wisdom, just ask and I shall supply it? First know My perfect will in a situation through My Word and communion with Me. Then stand on that Word in faith and believe.

You Are My Delight!
Your Loving Father

Faithful Father, there is so much on my heart to share with You and to hear Your heart and wisdom about!

_____

_____

_____

_____

_____

_____

_____

_____

_____

_____

_____

Loving Father, thank You for teaching me Your ways! Daily, I desire wisdom! Thank You that when I ask, You graciously supply wisdom and the knowledge of Your perfect will in a situation through Your Word and communion with You! Standing on Your Word is not always easy, but when You see the desire and determination of our hearts to stand, You lovingly supply the faith and strength to stand! You are so wonderful, Father!

25

1 CORINTHIANS 13:2 NKJV
"And though I have all faith, so that I could remove mountains,
but have not love, I am nothing."

My Child,

It is a fine line between faith and presumption. Faith calls forth those things that have been proclaimed by the Spirit of God. Presumption calls forth that which has been proclaimed by the heart of man. Be the friend of faith and the foe of presumption. (Father, how do I know the difference?) *The heart knows. Listen to your heart and respond appropriately. Steer clear of those who proclaim My ways without My heart. It is a mixed word, incapable of being leaned on with all your weight. The Spirit of the Lord proclaims truth through love. If love is lacking, so is truth. You cannot have one without the other. First comes love, then comes truth. Reversed, truth is not revealed, but a heart that needs love. Be sure of this very thing, that one cannot mock love without mocking truth. They go hand in hand.*

Walk in My Love!
Your Loving Father

Loving Father, Your Words of Wisdom bring such joy and understanding to my heart! You said, "Days and nights shall become as one, as you seek to know my will for you. At times you shall say, 'I wonder,' but in the next breath you shall say, 'I know!'" And so it has been, dear Father, that as I seek You for answers, You present them to me with clarity and understanding, that I might continue to learn Your ways and truth, through Your love!

Loving Father, may I only call forth in faith those things that have been proclaimed by Your Spirit of truth and love as You speak to my heart!

_____

_____

_____

_____

_____

_____

_____

_____

_____

26

PSALM 107:7 AMP
"He led them forth by the straight and right way."

My Child,

Master the art of maintaining open-ended plans, that My plans might always become and remain paramount in your life. Close-ended plans stagnate and cease to function. My plans for you are as the butterfly, free and unrestricted by your views of them. Stymie not and seek not to mold them into your own conformity of sight. Let loose of your plans and let Me take hold of the helm. Blessed is the one who sees the plan, yet does not dictate the outcome, but leaves that to Me. Follow with dexterity and delight, with a loose grip on the future. Let Me lead in all things. Let Me bring forth creatively and freely.

Fly Free My Child!

Let Me Lead!

Father, my life is in Your loving, protective hands! Your plan for my life is the plan I want to live by! Thank You, Father, for speaking to my heart, as we walk that plan out together!

_____

_____

_____

_____

_____

_____

_____

_____

_____

_____

_____

_____

Loving Father, when You said, "Master the art of maintaining open-ended plans," it brought such freedom to my heart! What a wonderful way to live, following You with dexterity and delight, with a loose grip on the future, no longer being bound by close-ended plans that stagnate and cease to function. Free to fly like the butterfly, letting You take hold of the helm! What a wonderful way to live! I love You, Father!

27

PROVERBS 10:9 AMP
"He who walks uprightly walks securely,"

My Precious Child,

Set a standard for life! Set a standard for love: unconditional. Set a standard for peace: a peace unruffled by circumstances. Set a standard for joy: My radiance brought forth by My Presence! Set a standard for wisdom: wisdom brought forth by the guidance of My Spirit. Set a standard for life, brought forth through communion with Me!

I Am with You Always,
Your Loving Father

Loving Father, You said, "Many shall come to know of My leading and guiding power through the relating of My guidance to you. Brighten the lives of others by My Spirit within you. Heighten their awareness of Me through your relationship to Me. Many I shall send to you to warm and direct toward Me. The stream of humanity shall be endless, but My Spirit shall guide you in every instance. Do not let not go of My hand. Fasten your gaze on Me and move forward as I shall lead. Glorious shall the journey be and delighted shall you be and those around you. Give forth of My love to you. Give forth with a gentle, loving, and understanding heart, filled with the blessings of My love to you."

Beloved Father, thank You for the preciousness of communion with You, as You speak to my heart!

_____

_____

_____

_____

_____

_____

_____

_____

_____

_____

_____

_____

_____

_____

_____

_____

_____

_____

_____

28

ISAIAH 26:3 NKJV
"You will keep him in perfect peace
whose mind is stayed on You,
because he trusts in You."

My Child,

Radiate My peace! All seek My peace. All search for its richness and fulfill-ment. Make it readily available and easily read on your countenance and in your life. My peace is the bait held forth in joy, and with promise. Liberally give it forth in My Name. All that come in contact with My peace shall be affected by it, warmed and softened by it, that My love might be received. Light the fires of understanding in many, through your constant and persistent peace.

With Love,

Your Father

Faithful Father, what else would You have me hear from Your heart this day?

_____

_____

_____

_____

_____

_____

_____

_____

_____

_____

_____

_____

_____

Father, thank You for teaching me to walk in peace, day by day and moment by moment. Thank You for forgiving me when I become anxious. Help me to remember to climb right back into Your lap, to come right back into that place of peace, calm, and trust, so that I can continue to radiate Your peace. Thank You for Your laughter and joy, bringing a perpetual smile to my face.

29

PHILIPPIANS 4:7 NKJV
"And the peace of God, which surpasses all understanding,
will guard your hearts and minds through Christ Jesus."

My Precious Child,

Peace, peace, wonderful peace, coming down from My heart of love. Stand strong in My peace and keep the light of praise burning. Sacrifice one and you sacrifice the other. Enter into My peace through the avenue of praise. It is a sure way into My Presence. Understand and comprehend this truth with steadfastness, for it is a light unto your feet. Relinquish it not and let not the flame be extinguished. Go forth, strong in the foundation of My truth and My love. The peace of the Lord is your strength. It comes down upon you as a magnificent blanket of purity, to wash away the contaminants of the world.

Be at Peace My Precious Child,
Your Loving Father

Beloved Father, the love of my life! I praise You with honor and devotion, and thank You for Your all-encompassing wonderful peace, which is my strength! Thank You that Your peace is a magnificent blanket of purity, to wash away the contaminants of the world! But most of all Father, thank You for Your precious Presence! I love You, Father!

Father, thank You that I can enjoy Your Presence 24 hours a day! Thank You for speaking to my heart!

_____

_____

_____

_____

_____

_____

_____

_____

_____

_____

_____

_____

_____

_____

_____

30

PSALM 9:1 AMP
"I will praise, You, O Lord, with my whole heart;
I will show forth [recount and tell aloud]
all Your marvelous works and wonderful deeds!"

My Precious Child,

The more you praise, the more you love. The more you love, the more you praise. It's like saying, "Which came first, the chicken or the egg?" They reproduce each other. Love is a total thing, no areas reserved. Praise shall flow from your lips as streams of living water, watering the dry land. Those walking in the desert shall be drawn to Me through your praise and through the love that praise shall produce. Praise Me! Praise Me!

You Are My Treasure,
Your Loving Father

I love You, Father, and my desire is to love as You love! Thank You for daily pouring into me Your wisdom and Your love, as I listen to You speak to my heart!

_____

Loving Father, I praise You, love, honor, bless, and thank You for Your life poured out on me and through me to others! Long ago, You said, "To brush away a tear, to lend gentleness and strength is your calling. Be my messenger of love. Maintain a gentle, loving, peaceful, joyful spirit, filled with thanksgiving and praise!" Thank You, Father, that those walking in the desert shall be drawn to You through that praise, and through the love that praise shall produce. Father, I love to recount and tell aloud Your marvelous works and wonderful deeds! I will praise You, O Lord, with my whole heart forever!

31

EPHESIANS 3:17 AMP
"May Christ through your faith, [actually] dwell [settle down, abide,
make His permanent home] in your hearts!
May you be rooted deep in love and founded securely on love."

(Lord, help me to love with *agape* **love.)** *It is going to be fun, an adventure. See Me place the desire in your heart and be encouraged as you see it come to pass. Stand encouraged. Now is the time to rejoice and go forward in the fullness and radiance of My Spirit. It is truly a new day with new ways. Release unto Me your spirit to soar, for I have given you a spirit of delight, and you shall again delight in all that I bring to you and cause that spirit of delight to be birthed in others. Be refreshed, My little one, and continue on in this journey of life, with renewed vision and vigor. I love you!*
You Are Precious to Me,
Your Loving Father

Precious Father, You bring such delight and joy to my heart. Thank You for the fun and adventure of learning to love with Your *agape* love! Thank You, Father, for renewed vision and vigor and encouraging my heart to soar with You!

I love You, Father! Thank You for speaking to my heart!

_____

_____

_____

_____

_____

_____

_____

_____

_____

_____

_____

_____

32

"You will not need to fight in this battle.
Position yourselves, stand still
and see the salvation of the LORD, who is with you."

My Child,

Forbearance is still a virtue to be pursued. But with forbearance must be love and wisdom. Love will steady forbearance, and wisdom will guide it. Stand steady and firm and let not up your steady stance of strength, strength built upon the strong foundation of My Word. Whisk confusion out the window. Steady strength and assurance are your portion. I will deal with inconsistencies. You be consistent in Me. I calm the storm and still the angry seas and bring justification and vindication. Fear not, but continue on day by day. I am with you!

I Love You,
My Child!

Dear Father, I love Your precious Presence!

_____

_____

_____

_____

_____

_____

_____

_____

_____

_____

_____

Thank you, Father, for keeping me steady and secure when everything around me is unsteady and insecure. Your love steadies me and makes me feel secure when the storms blow. Thank You for teaching me patience, forbearance, in the midst of the storm. And Father, thank You for Your Word, that makes me strong!

33

PSALM 126:2-3 AMP
"Then were our mouths filled with laughter,
and our tongues with singing.
Then they said among the nations,
'The Lord has done great things for them.
The Lord has done great things for us! We are glad!'"

My Child,

Fill your life with My music, joy, and song and splash it onto others with freedom and liberality. A life filled with joy and song has no room for criticism and negativism. Laughter pushes out darkness. (I see a lake teeming with fish. Lord, please explain the parable.) The fish are My blessings, jumping out at you with joy and freedom. The lake is you, your life. Your life is filled with blessings, jumping with joy, freedom, and abundance. Join in the joy, freedom, and abundance and know that all is within My timetable and care. Be still and know that I Am God, and I Am the rewarder of those who diligently seek Me. Stand fast upon My Word and rejoice in the fulfillment of that Word.

You Are Blessed!

Your Loving Father

Father, You have done such great things for me, day after day, year after year. When 1 find myself feeling weak and tired, all I have to do is laugh and strength amazingly pours in. Laughter is such a gift from You. Thank You Lord, for giving me Heart Friends who love to laugh with me, another priceless gift that only You can give. Thank You, Father, for answering my prayer long ago, to surround my life with loving Heart Friends who love with Your love.

Loving Father, You have blessed me so much! How can I bless You today?

_____
_____
_____
_____
_____
_____
_____
_____
_____
_____
_____

34

"I will praise, You, O Lord, with my whole heart;
I will show forth [recount and tell aloud]
all Your marvelous works and wonderful deeds!"

My Blessed Child,

A songbird chirps and sings, welcoming the new day with song. It proclaims and calls forth the new day with joy, exuberance, and faith that it will be a great day, filled with the love and blessings of a benevolent and loving God and Father. So are you to chirp and sing, proclaiming My loving works to a sleepy world. Continue to chirp and sing, calling forth the blessings of the new day. Birds are unafraid and confident in their freedom, for they fly high in the sky where predators do not go. Sound forth My love and faithfulness. Sound forth My ability to heal and save. Go forth in My Name, proclaiming to all that there is a place of quiet rest, safe in the arms of God!

Be Confident in My Love!
Your Loving Father

I will praise You, Father, with my whole heart and tell of all Your marvelous works and wonderful deeds! Thank You for speaking to my heart with such love!

_____

_____

_____

_____

_____

_____

_____

_____

_____

Loving Father, the lights in my heart just turned on! It is so exciting! No wonder I love to start each new day with music, for it proclaims and calls forth the new day with joy, exuberance, and faith that it will be a great day because of Your love and faithfulness! Thank You, Father, that You have created Your songbirds to be unafraid and confident in their freedom, knowing there is a place of safety and quiet rest in Your arms of love! I love You, Father!

35

EXODUS 20:1 AMP
"I am the Lord your God,
Who has brought you out of the land of Egypt,
out of the house of bondage."

My Blessed Child,

Sunshine and flowers, beauty and grace; it's going to be a wonderful place! As you seek My face every day, I will show you the way, and you will traverse the way with great delight. What seems out of sight now will come clear and rise up to meet you. So be joyful, My child. It is all under My control. I've been making you complete and whole enabling you to rise to every occasion with strength of character, peace, wisdom, and love. Strength of character, yes; strength of purpose, yes; and the strength of My love permeating your being. Stand fast and know heart-peace wherever you go.

I Take Pleasure in You, My Child,
Your Loving Father

Father, You have said, "Stand still and know that I Am God. Be ready and eager, but moved only by Me. Little by little, every obstacle shall be removed, every piece put neatly in place. Place your hand in Mine, and step by step we shall see the vision come into focus and into fulfillment. You are blessed, My child, to see and know the joy of step by step fulfillment, brought forth by Me, with loving attention to each and every detail." And so, Father, it has been, to the joy and delight of my heart! Even when the way is dark, You are there, lighting my way. I love You, Father!

Loving Father, my heart sings to You a song of love with thankfulness and praise!

_____

_____

_____

_____

_____

_____

_____

_____

_____

_____

_____

_____

_____

36

"Behold, I stand at the door and knock; if anyone hears and listens to
and heeds My voice and opens the door,
I will come in to him and will eat with him,
and he [will eat] with Me."

My Precious One,

Relax in My Presence and lift up your heart to Me with steadfast love and adoration. Let Me be your place of habitation, just as you are Mine. I am your steadfast rock of protection. There is a cleft in that rock for you. Nestle into that cleft with trust and love, as a child snuggles into its parent's lap for warmth and affirmation. I long to be that quiet place of rest and affirmation for you. Rest in Me, child. Rest in Me. Take one step at a time. When you have rested and learned of that quietness in Me, then we can proudly step out together in service and in love. Learn of My love for you, child. Rely on and perceive deeper levels of that love. It is yours. Receive, and then become a restorer, an instrument for restoring that love to the brethren. It is yours, My child. Reach out and receive it.

You Are Precious to Me,
Your Loving Father

Precious Father, my heart reaches out to You with love and adoration, thanksgiving and joy!

_____

_____

_____

_____

_____

_____

_____

_____

_____

_____

Loving Father, there is no place I would rather be than quietly snuggled next to Your heart, listening to Your heartbeat, trusting You with the trust of a child, and listening to Your loving words of affirmation to my heart. Thank You, Father, for drawing me daily to that treasured place. Thank You for teaching me daily, deeper levels of Your all-encompassing love.

37

ECCLESIASTES 3:11 NKJV
"He has made everything beautiful in its time."
Also He has put eternity in their hearts."

My Child,

Look out at the panorama before you. Soak in its beauty. See the ups and the downs, the hills, mountains, and valleys, and the areas clouded by haze, but it is all beautiful. So is your life. Every day, every hour, every minute, every second is a beautiful product of My perfect plan for your life. Some meanings are hidden by the soft haze, but they, too, are important and beautiful in My sight. The ups and downs, the hills, mountains, and valleys form the beauty that is so pleasing to the eye. So it is with you. I am forming beauty in your life, beauty that will last forever and will be a blessing forever. Relish and enjoy the formation. I am imprinting My beauty upon your body, soul, and spirit. Enjoy the process through faith, love, peace, joy, and trust. My very best is yours to enjoy. Continue on, My child, with My grace sustaining and leading you. My peace leads you forth to victory.

I Am with You!
Your Loving Father

My Father, truly as I look out over the panorama before me, it is a perfect description of the beauty of every day of my life. The beautiful mountains and valleys, the clouded and hazy areas, all come together to make a beautiful whole. Each night as I talk over the events of each day with You, I am in awe at the intricacy of each one, and my heart reaches out to You with gratefulness and love. Thank You Father for Your loving care!

Father, today I will focus on seeing Your beauty in each and every occurrence of the day, listening closely to Your voice speaking to my heart.

_____
_____
_____
_____
_____
_____
_____
_____
_____

38

ROMANS 12:9 AMP
"[Let your] love be sincere (a real thing)."

My Child,

Let love be your aim in all things. Release your burdens, rejections, disappointments, and disunities unto Me. Let Me carry them. Don't hold any of them to yourself. Drop them into My arms in an eternity of forgetfulness. Live only in the joy of this moment with Me, with My love; for what is past is past, totally past, and what is in the future is in the future beyond your reach. All you have is the loving, peaceful, and pure present, if you allow it to be. What others think of you does not matter. It is what you think of them that matters, if you have given all over to Me, and love them with a pure, undefiled love. Sincerity comes from a pure, undefiled heart, from which all contaminants have been released unto Me. So go forth this day, resting in the assurance of My love, freely bestowing that same love upon others, unrestricted by the past or the future.

Love with My Love, My Child,
Your Loving Father

Father, I give You every rejection that I have held onto, even unknowingly, and put them in a basket, like dead leaves, and give the basket to You!

_____

_____

_____

_____

_____

_____

_____

_____

_____

_____

Loving Father, what a wonderful way to live, releasing every burden, rejection, disappointment, and disunity unto You, and letting You carry them! That makes it possible to see and love everyone with purity of heart, with no history of hurts or disappointments, simply loving each one as You love them, unrestricted by the past or the future, which leaves simply the loving, peaceful, and pure present. How freeing to know that what others think of me does not matter. It is what I think of them that matters, and I choose to love. What a wonderful, loving, exciting life You give us to live, Precious Father!

39

JAMES 1:4 AMP

"But let endurance and steadfastness and patience have full play
and do a thorough work, so that you may be [people]
perfectly and fully developed [with no defects], lacking in nothing."

My Child,

Faith that is firm is also patient! Have I not spoken of patience before? Let patience have its way in your life. Let faith stand tall in your heart, statuesque and immovable, for have I not planned and shall I not carry it out to the "nth degree"? Lift those up to Me whom I give to you with perfect trust and a patient heart, for I shall move upon them and I shall perform all that I have decreed, but none of it can you bring to pass. Only I can bring to pass all that I have decreed. So stand firm, stand fast, stand tall, with the assurance that My will shall come to pass in My time, not thine. Frantic hurriedness brings mistakes and failure. Patient plodding brings My victory and My success. Be that patient plodder in My Kingdom, for together we shall win!

I Love You, My Child,
Your Heavenly Father

Father, this word gives me such peace of heart. In the past, You said, "Remove the spirits of impatience, uncertainty, and doubt, for I have led you in the past and will continue. Forever be on your guard against frenzied activity. My way is with a quiet assurance, confidently walking one step at a time. Steadfastly and firmly, My Son walked this earth, with love and compassion; so are you to walk."

Loving Father, the sound of Your voice brings such peace and turns my heart, once again, to walk in trust and patience. I have quieted my spirit within me to listen to Your heart.

_____

_____

_____

_____

_____

_____

_____

_____

_____

_____

40

"For the vision is yet for an appointed time
and it hastens to the end [fulfillment]; it will not deceive or disappoint.
Though it tarry, wait [earnestly] for it, because it will surely come."

My Child,

Let go of the past! Walk into the future with great joy and freedom. My strength is with you for foreordained exploits. Strain not to see too far in the distance. Walk in peace with Me this day, fulfilling My call upon your life in small ways each day that build upon themselves to create all that I have proclaimed. Little bits each day create the finished creation. The door shall open on time and you shall go through each one at its appointed time. Confer with Me often and in the times to come, for My Wisdom shall come forth to confirm and establish you in all that you should do and pursue.

I Go before You,
Your Loving Father

Father, what is on Your heart for me to know today?

_____

_____

_____

_____

_____

_____

_____

_____

_____

_____

_____

_____

Loving Father, no wonder You have always stressed peace and strength of character, that I might be content to let You add little bits, each day, to perfect the finished creation of my life and destiny, not to bolt and run ahead of You. It gives me such peace and joy to know that You have foreordained exploits for me and that Your wisdom will confirm and establish me in all that I should do and pursue. I love You!

41

HEBREWS 11:1 NKJV
"Now faith is the substance of things hoped for,
the evidence of things not seen."

My Child,

By faith man walks with Me. The carnal mind seeks to box Me in, to figure out each detail. The carnal mind seeks to anticipate My moves and to crow about them. The humble inherit My Kingdom. Far better be it to walk with a constant awareness of My Presence and My guidance than to seek Me as one would a horoscope or a fortune teller. With faith one walks with assurance, without fear or apprehension. So are you to walk.

I Am Guiding You, My Child,
Your Loving Father

Loving Father, You have said, "Lean not unto your own understanding, but reach out for My understanding and wisdom. Resort not to blind decisions. Reach out to Me for My direction in all things. Be sensitive to the nudging of My Spirit. Run not in circles." Thank You, that when I walk in constant awareness of Your Presence and Your guidance, I can walk without fear or apprehension, with faith that You are always with me, helping me to make the right decisions. When I find myself running in circles, I will know to slow down and once again come into Your Presence with peace.

Father, I am coming into Your Presence once again today, quieting my heart, loving You!

_____
_____
_____
_____
_____
_____
_____
_____
_____
_____
_____
_____
_____
_____
_____

42

PSALM 140:13 NKJV
"Surely the righteous shall give thanks to Your name;
The upright shall dwell in Your presence."

(Father, I want to be faithful to start each day right by bringing it to You, and to end each day right, by discussing it with You at the end of the day.) *You will, for it will amplify the sweetness of the day and give you a greater understanding of the day from My perspective. Trials will be averted and your life mission amplified. A tale of two cities will be told. One was weak but then became bold. You will be known by tenacious boldness. Stick with it My child. The rewards far exceed the struggle and I am with you every step of the way! My delights shall fill your heart with joy and My Presence shall continue to fill your heart with love.*

I Love You!
Your Father

Dear, dear Father, I lift this day up to You.

_____

_____

_____

_____

_____

_____

_____

_____

_____

_____

_____

Father, You are so precious to my heart. You are always so encouraging and loving. Thank You, Father, for the peace and the joy rising up in my soul, with a new sense of strength, life, beauty, and contentment. Thank You, Lord, I am so grateful!

43

ACTS 2:28 NKJV
"You will make me full of joy in Your presence."

My Child,

What is pleasure to you? (It is having people in my home that are really loving each other and loving and enjoying Your Presence. Father, what is pleasure to You?) *Being in My people's homes that really enjoy Me and My Presence. What do you see when you see Me?* (I see love, gentleness, passion, beauty, faithfulness and grace. Lord, what do You see when you see me?) *I see a face that glows with My love. I see a reflection of Me! What does steadfastness mean to you?* (Continuing step by step in the way You are leading no matter what the circumstances because of peace and joy persistently walked in.)

I Love You, Father!

I Love You, Too, My Child!

Nothing is more pleasurable in life than having these times with You, Father! Truly in Your Presence is fullness of joy. My heart sings with the pleasure Your Presence brings. Thank You for Your gentleness, passion, beauty, faithfulness, grace, and especially, Your love. Thank You for such a peaceful habitation in Your heart.

Father, when the struggles of life try to overcome me with their loud demands, I will remember moment by moment to stay in Your Presence dear, where peace and joy remain steadfast and secure, as I learn to trust in You by:

_____

_____

_____

_____

_____

_____

_____

_____

_____

_____

_____

44

PSALM 100:2 NKJV
"Serve the LORD with gladness;
Come before His presence with singing."

My Child,

Stay awhile. Let Me enjoy the warmth of your smile. Blazing new trails isn't easy, I know, but I am with you wherever you go, saying, "Go here, go there, it's a plan, the outcome secure." You know there is nothing to fear. Continue to stand in peace to know you are safe wherever you go. For My love surrounds and makes known, "Don't mess with this one—she's not alone!" So be at peace and you will continue to hear My Words of love upon your ear. Sing My Words of love to you, to keep your spirits high in all you do. Songs of love sustain the soul, that you may remain secure and whole.

My Love Surrounds You,
Your Loving Father

Father, when I feel anxious, I will find that place of loving peace and rest close to Your heart....

_____

_____

_____

_____

_____

_____

_____

_____

_____

_____

_____

_____

Father, You give such loving confidence! You have fashioned me to snuggle close to Your heart with peace and undistracted love, with the trust of a child. When I snuggle in close to Your heart, my whole body, soul, and spirit comes to peace and rest and I know that all will be well as I take it step by step without fear or apprehension. You give peace, not as the world gives peace, but as a loving Father gives peace to His treasured, adored child, who trusts in Him with all her heart.

45

JAMES 1:4 NKJV
"But let patience have its perfect work,
that you may be perfect and complete,
lacking nothing."

My Child,

What do you think is the purpose for waiting and patience? **(Learning to trust Your love and goodness to me, to know that You won't drop the ball in my life, or let me miss Your best for me. That Your timing is everything, and that what You have promised will come forth in Your timing. You will give me Your best, not second best and You will fulfill what You have promised.)** *Do you believe this?* **(Oh yes, Father, I do. You have always been faithful to me and enveloped me with Your love and blessings.)** *Patience gives way to strength and strength makes a way for truth. I am changing you from the inside out. The cares of this world are becoming less and less important, for you are learning that it is not what you do, but what I do for and with you that matters.*

I Love You, My Child.

Father, it's an adventure of a lifetime walking moment by moment with You. Thank You that every detail of my life is important to You. Thank You Lord, that You have taught me that time is my friend, and will continue to be until the end. I don't need to worry about the how, when, or where, because You will continue to lead and guide me every step of the way. That every day is a treasure to behold, to hold loosely in my hand, delighting in every facet of its sparkle and glow.

Father, my heart overflows with joy and love for You. Thank You for helping me to always bring my impatience to You, knowing Your timing is perfect.

_____

_____

_____

_____

_____

_____

_____

_____

_____

_____

46

JOHN 15:11 NKJV
"These things I have spoken to you, that My joy may remain in you,
and that your joy may be full."

My Child,

Joy is your portion. I have proclaimed it to be so. (Thank You Father for the joy You give to me) Time and time again you have said, "Joy, oh joy, where have you gone?" and yet joy is ever there for you to pick up and enjoy with abandonment and freedom. It is ever My gift to you, always there to put on and enjoy. Joy walks hand and hand with peace. Peace and joy, the signature of the knowledge of My love.

You Are Loved!
Your Father

How can I bring more joy to You, Father?

_____

_____

_____

_____

_____

_____

_____

_____

_____

_____

_____

_____

_____

_____

_____

_____

Loving Father, You have said that our lives are to be "Word Pictures of Your Love." My desire is to consistently walk in Your joy and peace no matter what is going on in my life, trusting You with the outcome in every instance. Thank You for helping me to choose to walk in joy, with abandonment and freedom. Your Joyful Child!

47

"Oh, let me be weighed in a just balance…
that God may know my integrity!"

My Child,

I am bringing balance to your life! Balance for the journey, for the road traveled. Balance to know that your expectations rest in Me and not in others. Balance to know that your peace rests in Me and My ability to come through. Balance to have no need to fear or worry. Balance to know that in your joy is your strength. Balance to always enjoy the ride without expectations, good or bad. Balance to be able to laugh in all circumstances. Balance to be able to walk in trust and faithfulness at all times. Balance to remain safe and secure in My arms of love. Worry and doubt will always be far removed from you, as you each day take the stand to trust, believe and freely receive My Spirit of love as a part of everything you think, do, and say.

I Love You,
Your Father

Loving Father, thank You for bringing balance to my life so that I can get off the roller-coaster ride and trust You completely. No longer to be plagued by emotions that go up and down, that don't find a safe place to land. Balance to know that I can trust You for every detail of the journey of my life. I love You!

Father, when I find myself once again on that roller coaster ride of unsettledness, I will turn to You with trust, saying, "Lord, speak to my heart, I am listening."

_____

_____

_____

_____

_____

_____

_____

_____

_____

_____

_____

48

JEREMIAH 24:7 NKJV
"Then I will give them a heart to know Me,
that I am the LORD;
and they shall be My people and I will be their God."

My Child,

Do you sense something different about today? (Oh yes, Father, today has been a day of reflection. Something new is in the air. What is it Father?) *You are coming into a total acceptance of My love for you. A total acceptance of My love in all that you do.* (Yes Father, what You long for is that we want to talk to You, spend time with You, hear Your voice and get to know You more every day.) *It's called intimacy. Without it there is no relationship. An open heart invites intimacy and causes the walls to come down in others. An open heart is a loving heart. An open heart has no fear. Be My open heart to My people. Let them come in and they will recognize the pain and fear they have let come in, causing them to build walls, which also keeps love out. Resting in your heart of love they'll begin to realize what My love is all about. They will begin to feel and see what it really means to be secure and free.*

Love Them to Me!

Your Loving Father

Father, how would You have me more effectively open my heart to those You bring to me?

_____

_____

_____

_____

_____

_____

_____

_____

Father, every day You bring such joy to my heart and excitement for the understanding You give of how we are to live. There is nothing on earth that I enjoy and love more than intimate conversations with You. Thank You for putting such a love in my heart for Your treasures, Your people. Thank You for teaching me to love them as You do.

49

1 Corinthians 13:8 nkjv
"Love never fails."

My Child,

Continue listening with your whole heart. (Lord, I think what You mean is to love with my heart wide open, unafraid of repercussions, just loving for love's sake, with no fear.) *Yes, My child, it's the only way to live. It's the only way to give, loving with no expectations. With that kind of love, no rejection, bitterness, anger, hurt, or judgment can grow. That kind of love is free and pure, filled with joy and contentment in the giving. Nothing negative can stick to that kind of love. It brings honor, healing, and joy wherever it goes.* (So Lord, the criteria for every action is, does it honor God and does it honor the person or dishonor the person.) *Freedom rings and sings in a heart that is pure and loving, as I love.*

Love As I Love!
Your Loving Father

Father, it is so hard to love without expectations, but so worth it to have no residue of bitterness, anger, hurt, judgment, or rejection. Whenever I am tempted to feel any of these things, I will look to You and remember, I am loving, in partnership with the Creator of the Universe, who loves me unconditionally, and so am I to love. Thank You for loving me so much!

Father, what else would You have me know about loving others as You love?

_____

_____

_____

_____

_____

_____

_____

_____

_____

_____

_____

50

JOHN 13:35 NKJV
"By this all will know that you are My disciples,
if you have love for one another."

My Child,

I have placed in your heart the seed that thrives and grows—the seed of love. There can be no love without honor—honor for one's God, oneself, and for others. Love without honor is manipulation, control, lust, or fear. Without honor, expectations are met with disappointment. Let only words of love, honor, blessing, appreciation, and truth come from your mouth. Speak only words that uplift and bring hope, words that bring blessing and not a curse, words that reverse the curse, words that bring healing to the heart, body, and soul, words that complete and make whole. Speak words that make the heart sing. My child, be not only a word picture of My love to the world, but also a word picture of honor that transforms the world through love.

Speak Words of Honor and Love,
Your Loving Father

Father, when I am tempted to say words that are not from Your heart, please stop me in Your own precious way, that I will recognize.

_____
_____
_____
_____
_____
_____
_____
_____
_____
_____

Dear Father, I pray that only positive, uplifting words of blessing come from my heart and mouth. Words that bring healing, that complete and make whole. Words that edify and make the heart sing; words of honor, appreciation, and truth. May I speak only as You would speak, whether it be with meekness or boldness, that they would be only words from Your heart. I love You!

51

PROVERBS 15:33 NKJV
"The fear of the LORD is the instruction of wisdom,
and before honor is humility."

Dear One,

It is called honor! Honor your God's wishes! Honor those around you and honor yourself! Seek to walk in honor in all that you do and say. Dishonor destroys. Honor brings life and wholeness. Discernment is recognizing dishonor. Trials come from dishonor. No longer will dishonor sneak up on you to entrap you. You shall recognize it for what it is. Lack of love! Lack of love for God, for you, and for themselves.

You Are Loved,
Your Father

Father, thank You for giving me added discernment for the journey of life. My desire is to honor others as You have honored me. You love me, not because I deserve Your love, but simply because You love me. Thank You for teaching me to recognize dishonor in all its forms. Father, I love You!

Thank You Father for increased wisdom and discernment as I come to You each day. How would You have me respond to dishonor?

_____

_____

_____

_____

_____

_____

_____

_____

_____

_____

_____

_____

_____

_____

_____

_____

_____

52

PHILIPPIANS 4:6 NKJV
"Be anxious for nothing,
but in everything by prayer and supplication,
with thanksgiving, let your requests be made known to God."

My Child,

Express your needs and your views more clearly and precisely to Me. In this way we can more fully work together, building trust and faith as we go. Do not be afraid of your negative feelings, for as you express them to Me, I can respond with the answer you need. Negatives held within remain negative, and increase in their negative power. Negatives brought to the surface and expressed to Me can then be turned to positive, and will continue to grow in their positivity. So anger expressed to Me can be turned from "My anger at You God" to "Thy will be done." Negative to positive. So, do not hide your feelings from Me. Express them that they might be dealt with to your help and to My Glory.

Share Your Heart with Me,

Your Loving Father

Father, this is what I want to bring to You today:

_____

_____

_____

_____

_____

_____

_____

_____

_____

_____

_____

Father, the desire of my heart is to stretch out my arms to You in total submission, speaking freely what is on my heart—my doubts, needs, and feelings. Help me Lord to meet my inadequacies and misdirected feelings head on with You, speaking them to You, unadorned, that they might all be turned from negative feelings to positive answers. Father, thank You that I can share anything and everything with You. I love You so much!

PSALM 55:22 NKJV
"Cast your burden on the LORD
and He shall sustain you...."

Dear One,

Tie your shoelaces, that you trip not on the unimportant. The dangling shoelaces are as dangling burdens, cares, and details of everyday life. Keep them continually tied in neat bows, lying at My feet. Only when you allow them to become untied and dangling in disarray will you trip and fall over them and become entangled. My peace abides in an ordered life whose focus is on Me. As long as the details of everyday life are tied in bows before My Presence, your spirit is free to soar and fly with Me. Done in reverse, the spirit is tied, and the natural life lies in disarray and confusion.

Walk in Peace,

Your Loving Father

Father, many times You have said that my peace is the barometer by which I can judge how well I am walking in Your Presence. Whenever I feel disarray and confusion and feel weighed down by the cares and details of life, thank You for helping me to remember to quiet my heart and once again come into Your Presence dear, with the trust and confidence of a child. Thank You Lord, that day by day You are teaching me to discern the difference between the important and the unnecessary.

Father, I never want to forget the wonderful truths You so painstakingly are teaching me day by day. How can I be a better student of Your ways?

_____

_____

_____

_____

_____

_____

_____

_____

_____

_____

_____

_____

_____

_____

54

MATTHEW 11:28 NKJV
"Come to Me, all you who labor and are heavy laden,
and I will give you rest."

Dear One,

Take your rest as one who has walked the highways and byways and trod the weary miles. Be not ashamed of spending time quietly without the pressures of tasks crying to be accomplished. Let Me refresh your spirit and your body through this time of peaceful, refreshing solitude and rest. Rest in Me. Enjoy the quiet. Enjoy the smallest of blessings around you. Resist the temptation to lock yourself into one activity after another.

I Carry You next to My Heart,
Your Loving Father

Father, how would You like for me to enjoy my time with You today?

_____
_____
_____
_____
_____
_____
_____
_____
_____
_____
_____
_____
_____
_____

Father, seasons of change have rearranged everything I have known, but it has been a liberating process, complete and filled with Your favor. You have said to relinquish not the sweetness of our time together, but to simply continue on step by step into this new realm of relationship with You. I get my comfort and love from You, Father. Thank You for always being there for me.

55

2 Thessalonians 5:17 NKJV
"Pray Without Ceasing."

My Child,

As you reminisce over our time together, you will find it has been precept upon precept, line upon line, a progressive walk with Me. Now you will truly see what it really means to be free. Free of self doubt, free to express what it means to be free, loving and walking with Me. Long ago you said, "If I can't know and walk with God, I might as well be dead," and so you read and read and read. Praying without ceasing was your goal that you might live through your spirit, not your soul. I heard that prayer, for I was there, and together we have traveled this long and arduous road. Do you remember when you decided that you would find out what it meant to pray without ceasing? (Yes, Lord, like it was yesterday.) *Because of that decision, your life has become a prayer.* (Father, I wanted You to be my best, trusted friend, having conversation going on continually with You. No wonder communication is so important to me.)

Together Forever,
Your Loving Father

My Father, that was the best decision that I have made in life. It took me from knowing about You, to the wonderfulness of knowing You. And how I long to know You more, day by day in every way. I never want to be satisfied with yesterday's blessings. I want to let my heart soar in continual communion with You, keeping my eyes, ears, heart, and mind continually focused on You. You are my Treasure!

Today IS the first day of the rest of my life. I will spend it loving You!

_____

_____

_____

_____

_____

_____

_____

_____

_____

_____

_____

56

MATTHEW 11:29-30 NKJV
"Take My yoke upon you and learn from Me,
for I am gentle and lowly in heart, and you will find rest for your souls.
For My yoke is easy and My burden is light."

My Precious Child,

Relax and enjoy the time that I have given to you. Redeem the time with faithfulness, but come to Me with a relaxed, joyous heart. Resist the temptation to reject as unworthy, time spent quietly and peacefully. Times of tranquility bring peace to the spirit. Many of My children have spent their lives so busy "redeeming the time" that they have never taken the time to get to know Me, to share with Me their time, joys and fellowship. Do not let yourself fall into that rut. Work is never ending. If you wait until it is done to find the time for Me and My Word, and the little joys of life in My Kingdom, you will never find the time to truly have a walk with Me. Do not let work and responsibilities rule you. Reach out and take My hand, letting Me direct the work, the play and the rest.

I Love You,
Your Father

Precious Father, how can I more effectively let You direct every facet of my life?

_____

_____

_____

_____

_____

_____

_____

_____

_____

_____

Thank You, loving Father, for the peace Your Spirit brings. Thank You for joy and laughter and the beauty of Your Creation. But most of all thank You for the moment, by moment wonderment of being Your child. Every day You surprise me anew with something to delight my soul.

57

COLOSSIANS 4:2 NKJV
"Continue earnestly in prayer,
being vigilant in it with thanksgiving."

My Child,

Ministry is a sacred trust that can only be maintained through constant communion with Me. Constant awareness is the key to constant success. As our communion together wanes, so does all else that is of importance in the life of the Spirit. Constant vigilance that secures a continual focus upon Me in worship and prayer keeps the spirit ever rising to new levels of effectiveness. Know that it is possible for the spirit and mind to be in constant prayer and worship, even while engaging in the affairs of the day. Continually strive for this. Do not let up. Keep your thoughts on Me, and you shall not waiver or draw back. Determine your course and stick with it with diligence.

Your Faithful Father

Dear Father, thank You for Your faithfulness and love in my life. When I am weary and tired, or when I am excited and feel blessed, in all circumstances I determine with tenacity and vigilance to always be found in Your Presence, communing with You!

Father, the desire of my heart is to have a continual focus on You in worship and prayer throughout the day and night. Father, I love You! Let me count the ways:

_____

_____

_____

_____

_____

_____

_____

_____

_____

_____

_____

_____

_____

_____

_____

58

PROVERBS 16:9 NKJV
"A man's heart plans his way,
but the LORD directs His steps."

My Child,

Eye hath not seen nor ear heard the wondrous works the Lord brings forth for those who love Him. Restrict not your thinking as to what you can see. Let your thinking scan the far vistas of My creative power. Handle each situation as it arises with confidence and assurance. There shall be a way for each task that I lay before you. Through trust and perseverance, each task shall be completed well, and in My time. Go forth renewed and refreshed in spirit and alive to My ways and leadings. Respond with alertness, trust, peace, and joy. And so shall your days fall one upon the other as a patchwork quilt is sewn together to make a perfect whole. Just as each square of the quilt is different, so will each day be different, but complete in every way. So rest in My love, protection, and perfect will for you, and rejoice as you see each day added to make you whole and complete.

You Are Blessed,
Your Loving Father

Father, what areas of my life am I right now holding onto with too tight a grip?

_____

_____

_____

_____

_____

_____

_____

_____

_____

_____

Father, help me always look to You and not assume that we are going to continue to do things the same way as always. Help me to be flexible and be willing to release when You say release, always knowing that Your way is the best way. Lord, my desire is to always trust You with every detail of my life. My desire is to follow You with dexterity and delight, with a loose grip on the future.

EPHESIANS 2:8-9 NKJV
"For by grace you have been saved through faith,
and that not of yourselves; it is the gift of God,
not of works, lest anyone should boast."

My Precious Child,

Do not let piety rob you of your strength and purpose. Piety is a spirit that comes in through rejection, the desire to be accepted by trying to be good enough, to try to deserve to be accepted. A child of God does not have to try to be good enough. He is counted as worthy because of My Son's death on the cross. This is your covering, your righteousness. You could never make yourself good enough by your strivings. The spirit of piety seeks to gauge a person's worth through the eyes of other people. True piety from Me, not Satan's counterfeit, seeks to please Me, and is not motivated by approval from man. Look to Me for your approval. Keep your eyes off man. Stand straight as an arrow, looking neither to the right nor left, but straight up.

I Love You,
Your Father

Dear Father, it is so easy for me to seek the approval of those around me and to forget that when I have Your approval, all is well. Feeling unacceptable truly does drain one of strength and purpose. When my eyes are on You, I know that You love me unconditionally, and take delight and joy in me. That I don't have to prove anything to You, because You know and understand every facet of my being, and still, You love and treasure me. The reality of it is too wonderful for words! Thank You, Father!

Father, I bring my insecurities to You. What areas am I not even aware of that need Your healing?

_____

_____

_____

_____

_____

_____

_____

_____

_____

_____

60

Ephesians 4:31-32 NKJV
"Let all bitterness, wrath, anger, clamor, and evil speaking
be put away from you, with all malice.
And be kind to one another, tenderhearted, forgiving one
another, even as God in Christ also forgave you."

My Child,

Trust not in humans. Put your trust in Me. Do not expect what they cannot give. Repent and go on. The wages of sin (bitterness) is death. Repentance brings life. Repent and rejoice in Me. Lighten your load as you go along. Carry not that which was not meant to be carried. Take it not to yourself. Repent for the immediate hurt and give it to Me. Then, go on your way rejoicing. It is no fun to poke at someone who refuses to be hurt. When you turn on them with like responses, they are justified. That is why I say, love and turn the other cheek. Anger cannot feed on such an environment. It can feed upon itself but not upon you. Keep your spirit pure before Me. Do not give anger or bitterness a moment to breed.

You Are Blessed,
Your Father

Father, please show me the areas that I have hidden in my heart of anger and bitterness, that need to be brought to the light.

_____

_____

_____

_____

_____

_____

_____

_____

Father, every time my spirit gets agitated because of the actions of others, I chose to forgive, bless, repent for the immediate hurt, give it all to you and go on rejoicing with no expectations. Father, the desire of my heart is to have a pure heart in all I say and do before You.

61

ISAIAH 61:3 NKJV
"That they may be called trees of righteousness,
the planting of the LORD,
that He may be glorified."

My Child,

Beware of intruders into your life: intruders of despondency, rejection and unbelief. Stand firm and tall for you are a full grown oak that cannot be toppled, unless you allow intruders to invade like termites. Your faith is strong and sure. Stand like the oak, both feet solidly planted and both arms outstretched in blessing and praise. I water and refresh the outstretched arms, and the oak, in turn, gives blessing, shade and refreshing to those who come within its outstretched boughs. Receiving and blessing. Receiving and blessing. The oak in its strength is a blessing to many. So shall you be.

With Blessings,

Your Father

Dear Father, when intruders of despondency, rejection, unbelief or any other invading negatives of life present themselves, I will sing to You love songs with outstretched arms in blessing, thanksgiving, and praise. Thank You for alerting me to their presence and Father thank You for refreshing me and shading me with Your love and blessings. Father, the joy of my heart is that You bring Your treasures to me that I might be a blessing, too.

Father, Your loving-kindness overwhelms me with such joy. How can I overwhelm You with joy today?

_____

_____

_____

_____

_____

_____

_____

_____

_____

_____

_____

62

PSALM 23:1 NKJV
"The LORD is my Shepherd;
I shall not want."

My Precious Child,

The Lord is your Shepherd. You shall not want for any good thing. My Glory shall shine about you as the noonday sun. You are being established and well grounded. Your way has been made straight. You shall be the Pied Piper along that straight and narrow path. Walk jubilantly! In proportion to your liberality of praise expressed will be My generosity in infinite magnitude. Labor not to analyze each need. Leave diagnosis and mechanics in My hand. Complexities exist only in your mind from the enemy to dull your faith. Ignore them. You be, and I will do. I shall lead you! Fear not, for the foundation upon which you stand is Me! Delight this day in that assurance and go forth radiating that assurance to others.

You Are Precious to Me!

Your Loving Father

Father, what walls have I built around my heart that keep me from fully being a "Word Picture of Your Love" to those around me?

_____

_____

_____

_____

_____

_____

_____

_____

_____

_____

_____

_____

Father, often You have said that You have created Your people to *be* the manifestation of Your love upon the earth, a "Word Picture of Your Love." That if we will be Your children who love with Your love, with thanksgiving and joyful praise, then You are free to *do* all that You have purposed in Your heart to do through us and for us. I delight in You, Father!

63

JOHN 9:31 NKJV
"If anyone is a worshiper of God
and does His will, He hears him."

My Child,

Worship Me in spirit and in truth, for it is through worship that real fellowship with Me is found. Worship opens up the human spirit to Me. Worship takes down the walls that would keep Me out. True worship brings right standing with Me, for it breaks down all the barriers and opens the door for communion and fellowship on a one-to-one basis. Raise up your voice in singing to Me and I shall hear and rejoice in you. Raise up your voice in praise and thanksgiving. Make a joyful noise and rejoice!

I Rejoice in You,
Your Loving Father

Father, I long to show my love for You through ever-deepening, extravagant worship. You have said that true worship is intimately loving You with all of our being. I pray that there would never be walls between us that would keep you out. Father, when You said that worship was simply coming into Your Presence and loving You, it made the "lights go on" in my heart and released a joy within me that I had not known. Thank You so much!

Father, how can I bless You even more as I worship You?

_____

_____

_____

_____

_____

_____

_____

_____

_____

_____

_____

_____

_____

_____

64

PSALM 104:33 NKJV
"I will sing to the LORD as long as I live;
I will sing praise to my God while have my being."

My Precious Child,

Sing as a bird. A bird does not sing for love and approval. It sings for the pure joy of singing, for the pure joy of being a part of My creation. Therefore, the joy and beauty of My creation pours through it. Thus will you now truly sing as My songbird, for the pure joy of My love within you and for the pure joy of being Mine. That pure joy and love will pour through you, and others will seek the joy of being Mine too. You shall find My praises flowing from your lips as a waterfall, to water a dry and thirsty land. In perfect trust, you shall sing forth My praises. Take a lesson from the birds. Continually sing My praises. Then you will always be prepared.

Sing with Joy!
Your Loving Father

Father, please give to me a "new song" from Your heart to sing to You today.

_____

_____

_____

_____

_____

_____

_____

_____

_____

_____

_____

Father, every morning the birds sing with such pure exuberance and beauty. They bring such joy to my heart. I can only imagine what joy we bring to Your heart when we sing praises to You, with that same pure exuberance, joy, and beauty, in perfect trust and delight in being Yours. Surely creation must sing with us, if we could only hear the symphony of praise that we join, singing praises to You!

65

JOHN 16:33 NKJV
"These things I have spoken to you
that in Me you may have peace.
In the world you will have tribulation; but be of good cheer,
I have overcome the world."

My Child,

Inner beauty is brought forth through pressure to teach one to respond to pressure with peace. It is a process that must be lived step by step. Rejoice in the becoming. Relax and know My will for you, to have a loving and pure heart. My ways are unperceivable to those floating on the sidelines, but many times I have shown you the beauty of My Kingdom and you have been delighted. Now I shall show you what it means to be My disciple, steadfast, immovable, and unafraid. You shall see more than you have seen in a lifetime and you shall remain unruffled in the shadow of My wing, for My pinions shall protect you, uphold you and show you the way. Many shall be the upheavals, but nothing shall cause you defeat. Resting in the power of your Maker and Friend shall bring you through and you shall know the sweet savor of victory!

You Are Blessed,
Your Loving Father

Father, thank You for Your faithfulness, protection and loving care over me and those I love. Thank You for directing my every step and the peace to know that even through upheavals and storms, You are there holding my hand and bringing me through to victory. You mean everything to me Father!

Father, today I place my hand in Yours with the trust of a child. What areas in my life would You have me release completely to You?

_____

_____

_____

_____

_____

_____

_____

_____

66

JOHN 15:12 NKJV
"This is My commandment, that you love one another
as I have loved you."

My Child,

Warmth and affection are vital to growth in My Spirit. Be an example of the warmth and love that is Me. Be not sparing. There is always more than enough for each and every one, and you receive double what you give. Give without fear. Simply give. Giving lightens the load of receiving. My gift of love manifested in one of My children becomes magnified as they go forth sharing it and bestowing it with ever-increasing intensity and strength of purpose. Be a magnifier of My love to you. Give forth as I give forth, without reservation, without fear, without thought of oneself and how the love you share it is being accepted.

Love with My Love,
Your Father

I love you so much Father! My heart sings to You today.

_____

_____

_____

_____

_____

_____

_____

_____

_____

_____

_____

_____

Loving Father, nothing is more wonderful than Your love except Your Presence, which is Your love. Oh, I get it—how exciting! We are to be in Your Presence, and carriers of Your Presence at all times, and when we do, we are Your love!

67

1 JOHN 4:12 NKJV
"If we love one another, God abides in us,
and His love has been perfected in us."

My Dear Child,

Carry My love forth into the cold and barren places that I shall lead you to. Pour forth the streams of My living love. There are two kinds of love, mechanical, natural love that lacks warmth and life, and My living love that brings healing and completeness to the receiver. Be a restorer of My living love. You have received, now give. Give forth with abundance. Give forth with no reservations. Give forth with exuberance. Give forth with quiet strength. Just give forth. Place your hand in Mine and give forth as you draw forth from Me.

Your Loving Father

Dear Father, Your love has transformed my life. What an adventure to see others' lives transformed in the same way through Your Presence and the warmth and joy of Your living love. Your love brings healing and restoration. Thank You for trusting me with Your love. Thank You that the sky is the limit to impart Your love and healing into each aching heart. I love You Father!

Father, help me to be alert and to move when You move, keeping my focus on You so that I don't let Your "divine appointments" pass me by.

68

ROMANS 5:3-4 NKJV
"We also glory in tribulations, knowing that tribulation produces perseverance; and perseverance, character; and character, hope."

My Child,

The race goes to those with steady persistence, not to those who run in agitated spurts! Do not struggle with the whys and wherefores. I have been with you the whole way, lighting your path with truth. Let that light shine now with brilliance. Straightforwardness is still a virtue. Nothing shall be lost, destroyed or mislaid along the path, nor accepted that is not from Me. I have protected you, led you, and brought you to a wide place of blessing. Lest you say "I am worthy," I have brought you through troubled and mired waters, and yet the mire has fallen away and left only My truth and blessing. Pride causes the mire to stick.

Trust in Me!

Your Loving Father

Father, I bring these areas of struggle to You, that Your truth and blessing may shine upon them and give me peace:

_____

_____

_____

_____

_____

_____

_____

_____

_____

_____

_____

Thank You Father, that I can trust You to lead me day by day along the pathway You have chosen for me. When I struggle with the whys and wherefores I will choose to remember that when I trust You and persistently walk with You, Your truth and blessing always prevail in my life.

69

JEREMIAH 15:16 NKJV
And Your Word was to me the joy and rejoicing of my heart;
for I am called by Your name."

My Child,

The joy of the Lord is your strength and it shall continue to be so. Linger over and delight in the joys I bring your way, as a child handles a beautiful jewel, turning it over and over in its hand, not trying to figure out its facets, but simply reveling in its timeless beauty, in the awe of its sparkle and life. Be a communicator of that sparkle and life. Its reflection shall shine forth to others and they shall be warmed by the glow. Life grows in warmth. You shall reflect warmth to those who are new, and warmth to draw new life and strength to the seasoned veterans. Now, take it a step further. My Word is that jewel that reflects the light, the glow. Be a reflector of that light as you continually look into it, turning it over and over in your hand, reflecting its warmth and life-giving glow. The Word, the Word, the Word, your life is in the Word, and the life you pass on to others is from the reflection of that Word. Magnify the Word, rejoice in the Word, and reflect the Word!

You Are Precious to Me,
Your Father

I love You Father! I love the sparkle, beauty, warmth, life, and joy of Your love, of Your Word, which is You! Such joy You bring to my heart every day. Thank You for filling my heart with Your words of love. Thinking of You always causes me to smile with delight. Father, I love You!

Thank You for Your Word, Father. What would you have me learn from Your written Word and Your spoken Word to my heart today?

_____

_____

_____

_____

_____

_____

_____

_____

70

1 PETER 3:8 NKJV

Finally, all of you be of one mind, having compassion for one another;
love as brothers, be tenderhearted, be courteous;
not returning evil for evil or reviling for reviling,
but on the contrary blessing, knowing that you were called to this,
that you may inherit a blessing."

My Child,

Light shall be the burden carried of My compassion and love. It shall go forth from you as gently and easily as the breath of My Spirit. Forbearance is still a virtue to be pursued and obtained. It is captured through constant and vigilant love and acceptance, unconditional love, given and received, untainted by performance orientation. No need to perform to your standards to receive your unconditional love. Unconditional love given brings forth unconditional love received. Give it forth liberally and unrestricted, to the joy of your heart and to the joy of My heart. You shall see and experience more love than you have ever known. Reach out with acceptance and love.

With Unconditional Love,
Your Father

Father, I just want to hear Your words of love to my heart today.

_____

_____

_____

_____

_____

_____

_____

_____

_____

Father, long ago You said that I was to live my life with patience, which is forbearance. That I was to love unconditionally without thought of return, for the greatest love of all is always from YOU. Father, time has shown that Your way is a wonderful way, the only way to live, bringing such joy and fulfillment. Thank You Father for Your love.

1 PETER 4:8 NKJV
"And above all things have fervent love for one another,
'for love will cover a multitude of sins.'"

Dear Child,

Learn to manage your emotions through forbearance. Acceptance in the midst of trials is truly riding the high road. The road is sparsely traveled but prepared for you. Follow it with diligence. Forsake disgust, dismay and dissatisfaction. Follow discipline, diligence, and delight in the road followed. Cover their lack and need with your love. The world waits to condemn. You accept, encourage, and love. All else slows their progress and stunts their growth in Me. Let Me rebuke, let the world criticize, but you accept, encourage, and love.

Accept, Encourage, and Love!

Love As I Love!

Father, we cannot earn Your love any more than we can earn the love of our friends and family, and yet we try. But freely You give us Your love by grace and so we are to be givers of love and blessings, restricted not to those who seem to deserve them. Help us, Father, to judge not, that we not be judged. Thank You, for helping us, by Your grace, to simply, love.

Father, when I am tempted to do or say something that is not loving or honoring, I choose to bring blessing instead by:

_____

_____

_____

_____

_____

_____

_____

_____

_____

_____

_____

_____

_____

_____

_____

_____

72

GALATIANS 5:13 NKJV
"Through love, serve one another."

My Child,

How do you bake a cake? (You add the ingredients one by one, mix them, bake the cake, and serve it.) I prepare My servants the same way and then serve them to the world as a sweet aroma, drawing the world to Me. Be prepared to go forth with joy, for I have prepared you. I have baked you to perfection in the oven of My love. You shall bless and refresh, heal and restore. Yours shall be the family of God!

I Love You!
Your Father

Father, when I'm tempted to get out ahead of Your plan for me I will remember to listen to Your loving voice saying to me:

_____
_____
_____
_____
_____
_____
_____
_____
_____
_____
_____
_____
_____
_____

Father I cherish what You have done for me, day by day, year by year, adding the ingredients, one by one as I see glimpses of Your plan for me coming together. The Law says I will go do something for God. Grace says, I will simply love the Lord with all my heart and He will do whatever He wants through me, for I am willing!

73

PROVERBS 3:5 NKJV
"Trust in the LORD, with all your heart,
and lean not on your own understanding."

My Child,

Remain in my peace, no matter what the situation. My peace is like a warm blanket and is maintained through trust in Me. Fear and anxiety is the opposite of trust. Walk in peace, joy, and trust, which is faith. Real love moves when the peace within says, "now is the time to act." Typically it is called love, but it is pressure of the other side, to try to do the right thing, the unselfish thing, to do something, anything, to show that you care. This causes frustration, anxiety, resentment, and stress, and is ineffective. Love must come through the vehicle of peace, knowing that I am in charge and all will be well. Give freely, as I lead you to give in peace, not as pressure leads you to give through guilt. Be a giver of the strength of my Word, through peace.

Remain in My Peace!
I Love You!

Father You've always said to listen to my heart. That Your Word and Your peace reside there. When I find myself walking in fear and anxiety, I will once again wrap myself in the warmth of the blanket of Your love and peace, and trust You.

Father, how can I trust You more today?

_____
_____
_____
_____
_____
_____
_____
_____
_____
_____
_____
_____
_____
_____

74

1 JOHN 4:8 NKJV
"He who does not love does not know God,
for God is love."

My Child,

Contained within your heart is the knowledge of My love. It is a love unhindered by time and space. It goes beyond the limited confines of the mind. It must be understood from the heart. Limited is the understanding brought forth by logic. My love is limitless. Love as I have loved you. Be My love. Manifest My love. Be a reflection of My love to others. Grow in My love day by day. The more you understand of My love and walk in My love, the more you can give of My love. You can only give what you have. Walk in My light that you might turn the darkness around you to light. Darkness cannot abide in the Presence of light. My light and My love are one.

Love As I Love,
Your Loving Father

Father, Your love keeps life simple, not complex. Today and every day the desire of my heart is to love with Your love. Today I will reflect Your love by:

_____

_____

_____

_____

_____

_____

_____

_____

_____

_____

_____

Father, You love me just because I'm me, not because of what I can do for You or how good I can be or how holy I can be. You just love me. You bless me and give me Your best, what is best for me, not necessarily what would be best for somebody else. You teach me to walk unafraid, confident and secure. You give me Your peace and Your joy and teach me that worry and anxiety are sin because You are in control, working all things together for my good. Nothing will slip by You. I will never "miss it" because You are always there to help me.

ECCLESIASTES 10:12 NKJV
"The words of a wise man's mouth are gracious."

My Child,

I am in control of your destiny and each page shall turn at its appointed time. Continue to walk in My grace and continue to hold it out for others. Grace is a gift gently held in the hand and gently given as a gift to others, that they might receive it with thanksgiving and joy. Frustration turns that gift of grace to law and turns it to condemnation instead of joy. Then truth is turned to pain that cuts, instead of blessing, which heals. Bear not the burden for My plan. Let it flow by the power of My Holy Spirit through you. Let the majesty of My love flow through you uncomplicated and uncontrived. Be simply the revolving door through which My love, joy, and Spirit flows out to My people.

I Love You and Direct Your Paths,
Your Loving Father

Father, may my words be always words of patience, love, and grace, uncomplicated by frustration or condemnation. I love the vision of the revolving door through which Your love, joy, and Spirit flows out to Your people through me. Lord, help me not to be tempted to take responsibility for Your plans for my life or for others' lives. But to simply trust You to bring them to pass, as I fulfill my part, being Your obedient child with a loving, joyful, trusting, peaceful heart.

Father, what is Your direction for me this day?

_____
_____
_____
_____
_____
_____
_____
_____
_____
_____
_____
_____
_____
_____
_____

76

1 CORINTHIANS 13:7 NKJV
"Love bears all things, believes all things,
hopes all things, endures all things.
Love never fails."

My Child,

There are all kinds of love. Love that rejoices in the fetes of others, love that sticks close through failure and pain, love that makes light of wrongs endured, and love that persists against all odds, for the Word spoken believed. This is the love I have given you to give. Let not up when odds seem slim and defeat seems to prevail. Turn defeat into victory by claiming My truth and standing on that truth undaunted by the passing scene, for My Word stands and My promises are sure. Be not faint-hearted, but strong in your faith and belief, and strong in the love I have given you to give. Be a giver, not a taker. Give your love to others without thought of return, taking only from Me, My love, and you will never lack.

I Love You,
Your Father

Father, who would You have me love with Your love today?

_____

_____

_____

_____

_____

_____

_____

_____

_____

_____

_____

_____

Father, many times You have told me to love unconditionally with no expectations or thought of return, knowing through You, I will never lack. Many times defeat seemed to prevail and yet always, defeat was turned into victory, many times in ways I could have never dreamed. You are such a creative God, and when I stand strong, undaunted by the passing scene, the outcome always strengthens my faith and love for You. Thank You for the adventure of life and Your faithfulness and love!

77

ISAIAH 65:14 NKJV
"Behold, My servants shall sing for joy of heart."

My Child,

Let your life sing within the perfection and beauty of the framework of the symphony I have created you to be. Enjoy the beauty, the perfect timing, and the music of your life that I have created, and others shall enjoy it also and be blessed. Be the symphony I have created you to be through trust, contentment, love, peace, and joy in Me, and faith that I have written the score to perfection. Blessed is the one who allows Me to create of their lives a symphony.

Be Blessed This Day!

Your Loving Father

Father, may I always allow You to create, write, and conduct the beautiful music of my life. How wonderful to know that I am a symphony created by the Creator of the Universe. It saddens me to think that I might try to take the pen from Your hand and add to the perfect score You have written through lack of trust and impatience. I choose to let my life sing within the perfection, beauty, and perfect timing of the symphony You have created me to be.

Father, thank You for singing through me and with me. Today I worship You and bless You with songs of praise, with love and gratefulness.

78

"[Growing in grace] they shall still bring forth fruit in old age:
they shall be full of sap [of spiritual vitality] and rich in the verdure
[of trust, love, and contentment.]"

My Child,

Regard in your heart, take notice of and pay special attention to the times and the seasons of My visitations to you. First was the planting of the seed. Then was the tender care and nourishment of the seed and the joy over its growth. Next came the fruitfulness and joy that fruit brought. Then came the pruning and the elimination of contaminants. This period was grievous but necessary. A quiet season followed where the tree grew strength and fortitude for the storms of life, that it would stand tall and straight, unmoved. Whereas it could give fruit before now it can also give shade, peace, comfort, and protection. If a tree is allowed to produce too much fruit, it ruins the tree, breaking limbs with the weight and destroying its beauty and its ability to give shade, peace, comfort, and protection. The tree must have seasons of quiet and unfruitfulness that it might draw in its strength, drawing on the Son and nourishment to grow full, strong, and beautiful.

Holding Your Hand As You Grow,
Your Loving Father

Dear Father, what season of growth am I in now and how shall I proceed?

_____

_____

_____

_____

_____

_____

_____

Father, thank You for Your provision, faithfulness, and gentle care every step of the way. When I think that it is just too hard to proceed, You bring encouragement and let me know that You are right there with me. Thank You Father for the pleasure of Your company throughout all the seasons of growth. I love You!

79

1 Corinthians 15:57 AMP
"But thanks be to God, Who gives us the victory,
[making us conquerors] through our Lord Jesus Christ."

My Child,

My heart sings for you. I have planted, protected, and lovingly provided for your growth and care. You have developed and grown, and together we have rejoiced as each victory was won. I have stabilized you and brought forth from your being, gifts and attributes of My Spirit. I am well pleased with My creation. There is more to be added, more to be subtracted, but together we shall rejoice as each day brings forth new growth and new victories.

You Are Blessed,
Your Loving Father

Father, there is such joy in finding treasures that You have put within me that I didn't even know were there. Giftings, callings, talents, anointings, and blessings, just waiting for You to call them forth, to Your joy and to my delight. Father, every day is an adventure with You! I love You!

Father, what would You have me know about You today?

_____
_____
_____
_____
_____
_____
_____
_____
_____
_____
_____
_____
_____
_____
_____
_____
_____
_____

80

ISAIAH 40:1 NKJV
"Comfort, yes, comfort My people!"
Says your God.

My Child,

Trials and testing magnify My faithfulness and love, and enlarge the heart to give. Comfort My people! Lasting happiness is yours as you bless and comfort My people. See, I have led and comforted you that you might become a wide, resting place for others. Trials and tribulation strengthen the character, giving the strength and tenderness necessary to comfort My people. Know that I will bless and comfort you.

Your Loving Comforter

Father, how can I bring comfort and blessing to Your people today?

_____

_____

_____

_____

_____

_____

_____

_____

_____

_____

_____

_____

_____

Father, through every trial and testing, You are always faithfully there to bring comfort and strength to my heart, always letting me know the importance of passing every trial and testing through trusting You and letting You lead. As a child my prayer was, "Father, I want to be happy." Now as an adult, truly there is such happiness found in blessing and comforting Your people, just as You comfort and bless me.

81

1 THESSALONIANS 5:16 AMP
"Be happy [in your faith] and rejoice
and be glad-hearted continually."

My Child,

Unmarked trails are ahead, waiting for your footsteps, ready to reveal My truth. Rejoice in the present, for it is mine. Rejoice in the past for it has brought forth the present in all its glory. The future is mine to bring forth as I will, but know that I love you and I do all things well. Be assured that what I have planned is good and will come forth at its appointed time. Peace, My peace, I give unto you. Not as the world gives peace, but My peace is solid and undisturbed by places, people, or things. Place your trust in Me, unmovable and unperturbed, for I shall bring you to a solid place of My making. Release unto Me your fears for the future.

Trust Me!
Your Loving Father

Thank You Father, for teaching me that You don't look back on any part of my life with regret, because You are redeeming and using every portion of it to create a beautiful picture of Your love on the canvas of my life. When I tend to drag behind me portions of the past that You have already moved on from, or fear for the future, or am frustrated with the present, help me once again to turn to You for truth and peace.

Father, what portions of my life am I still dragging along behind me that I need to let go of?

_____

_____

_____

_____

_____

_____

_____

_____

_____

_____

_____

_____

82

"[Most] blessed is the man who believes in, trusts in,
and relies on the LORD,
and whose hope and confidence the LORD is."

My Child,

Liken your life unto a beach ball. It bounds along where I take it with joy and trust, anticipation and exhilaration for what is next. Suddenly it punctures and the air goes out of it. It is shocked and vulnerable, but totally repairable by the Father. (It was such a pretty ball—idolatry) (Will it be pretty again—lack of faith.) (When will it be repaired—self pity) Receive again the bouncing ball, that I might take it again where it pleases Me.

I Will Not Fail You,
Your Loving Father

Father, today when I am tempted to be anxious and doubt, I will hand you back my life (the beach ball) with trust, and listen to Your words of love to my heart.

Father, so often life seems like a roller coaster ride. Like the bouncing beach ball, one moment I'm up and the next moment I'm down, wondering what just happened. Father, I choose, with all my heart to honor and trust You. To know that truly, my life is in Your hands and that I can trust You. Thank You for Your faithfulness to me! I love You!

83

PSALM 23:3 AMP
"He refreshes and restores my life."

My Child,

Stand in the awareness of My love and protection. Stand in the awareness of My fulfillment in your life. I shall not fail you. Be refreshed. Be revived, and be at peace. (It has been a beautiful day of refreshment, Lord.) It shall be ever thus. Tucked into each day I have placed places of refreshment. Look and you shall see and experience My refreshment on a continual basis.

I Love You,
Your Father

Father, Your beauty and peace can be found anywhere when I slow down and look and listen, and brings instant refreshment and joy. Your love shining through a friend's face, the song of a bird, a kind word, a hug, a gentle touch, but most of all hearing words from Your heart and the awareness of Your Presence. Thank You for Your protection, fulfillment, and love active in my life every day.

Father how would You like to use me today to bring Your refreshment to others as You have brought refreshment to me?

_____

_____

_____

_____

_____

_____

_____

_____

_____

_____

_____

_____

_____

_____

_____

84

PHILIPPIANS 2:13 AMP
"[Not in your own strength]
for it is God Who is all the while effectually at work in you
[energizing and creating in you the power and desire] both to will and
to work for His good pleasure and satisfaction
and delight."

My Child,

Your words, as brought forth by Me, shall bring forth the miracles you wish to see. Stick to basics. Keep your eyes on Me. My will shall prevail. Leave the melodramas to others. Keep it simple and unencumbered. Proceed with simplicity. Respond with clarity and go forth with assurance. Magnify My Word and minimize problems. Sit in the Heavenliness with Me, undisturbed, unperturbed, and unafraid, resting in the peace of My love.

You Can Trust Me!

Your Father

Father, today I bring to You everything that causes me to feel disturbed and anxious that I might walk in Your peace and trust You!

_____

_____

_____

_____

_____

_____

_____

_____

_____

_____

_____

_____

_____

So often, Father, You have said to keep it pure and simple. How exciting to realize that when I rest in Your peace and keep my heart undisturbed, unperturbed and unafraid, speaking Your Words with my eyes focused on You, that You bring forth the miraculous as I truly reside in Your Presence. What an exciting way to live Father! I love You so much!

85

GALATIANS 5:22 AMP
"But the fruit of the [Holy] Spirit,[the work which His Presence within us accomplishes] is love, joy, (gladness), peace, patience (an even temper, forbearance), kindness, goodness, (benevolence), faithfulness."

My Child,

Light the fire of joy in your heart. Light the fire of hope, springing alive through peace. Light the fire of forgiveness and love. Light shall be the burden carried of My compassion and love. It shall go forth from you as gently and easily as the breath of My Spirit. Go forth with joy, go forth with peace, go forth with love, go forth with the gifts of My Spirit. Stand tall in My love and in standing tall, shade others with My love.

Love As I Love,
Your Father

My Father, thank You for teaching me to love with Your love. The rewards of learning to love with Your love far outweigh struggles to learn, and bring forth the greatest joys in my life. Thank You Lord for trusting me to love Your treasures, Your people.

Father, I bring to You those who have been harder for me to love unconditionally. Please show me how You see them, so I can love them as You do.

_____

_____

_____

_____

_____

_____

_____

_____

_____

_____

_____

_____

_____

86

COLOSSIANS 1:11 AMP

"[We pray] that you may be invigorated and strengthened with all power according to the might of His glory, [to exercise] every kind of endurance and patience, (perseverance and forbearance) with joy."

My Child,

What do you think the purpose is of learning forbearance and patience? (It is to cause me to trust You and to find peace in the midst of every storm and circumstance.) *Peace and patience keeps one from taking offense.* (Father, when faced with dishonor and anger, it is so hard not to take offense, but to respond with compassion and truth.) *My child, situations shall continue to come and go, but through your life I can continue to sow blessings and life, confidence, comfort and joy to My people. Don't you know that My love goes before you preparing the way each and every day? Now rest, My child and know My healing power in your life and in the lives of those you love.*

Be Loving and Patient!

Your Loving Father

Father, when I'm tempted to respond negatively I will remember how You treat me with such love and patience.

_____

_____

_____

_____

_____

_____

_____

_____

_____

_____

Father, You have wondrously surrounded me with prayer and love, and have said when one strikes out who feels neither, that I'm to respond with compassion, for Your truth will win out and Your compassion will rule and bind up hurts and fears. That I'm to reach out unafraid of repercussions. Simply to reach out, love, and let You take care of the results. Father, may I always respond to rejection and offence with Your love and acceptance that heals broken hearts and sets captives free.

87

PHILIPPIANS 4:4 AMP
"Rejoice in the Lord always
[delight, gladden yourselves in Him];
again I say, Rejoice!"

My Child,

Rejoicing in the present lets My Spirit reign, for rejoicing relies on trust and faith, which are the bulwarks of My peace. No wind of trial shall diminish you or knock you over. The tempest shall blow, but you shall remain firm and strong, able to withstand and remain steady. My word to you this day is, remain steadfast in My love. Wrap it around you as a cloak. Let Me handle the details. You handle the rejoicing.

You Are Loved, My Rejoicing Child,
Your Father

Father, thank You for teaching me to trust You through the many trials and tests of life. To know that I'm always made stronger and more resolute to trust Your love when I determine to rejoice in the present and let Your Spirit reign. What a wonderful gift You give to Your people, Your peace that we can delight in, in the midst of trials and storms, with the absolute awareness of Your total love.

Father, when I am tempted to panic with the events of the day, I will begin sharing with You the many ways You bring joy and delight to my heart.

_____

_____

_____

_____

_____

_____

_____

_____

_____

_____

_____

88

COLOSSIANS 3:13 AMP

Be gentle and forbearing with one another and, if one has a difference
(a grievance or complaint) against another, readily pardoning
each other; even as the Lord has [freely] forgiven you,
so must you also [forgive].

My Child,

See me, not in the corporate, but in the individual. Be mindful of My love for you. (You love me the way I want to be loved.) Love others in the same way. Don't point out wrongs and slights. Pray. Be a praise giver, not a slight harborer. Be a restorer. Be a waterer and the bearer of blessings. Be My love and My light to the brethren. Be assured of My love and you will not lack for their love.

Love As I Love,
Your Father

Father, today I will focus on thinking and speaking positive words of blessing, love, and encouragement.

_____

_____

_____

_____

_____

_____

_____

_____

_____

_____

Father, over and over You have said to reach out with love, compassion, and forgiveness. That the words that I speak are not as important as the spirit and love by which they are given—Your Spirit and Your love. That as I reach out with unconditional love and encouragement, You will use my words to cover their lack and need with Your love. Thank You Father, for nudging me when I start to speak negatively about one of Your treasures.

89

LUKE 21:19 AMP
"By your steadfastness and patient endurance
you shall win the true life of your souls."

My Child,

Strength of character comes forth through patient waiting. Patient waiting has become the vehicle through which My blessings shall come forth. Change is not easy, but necessary to bring forth growth. It comes forth slowly, developing patience and faith. Welcome change with open arms. It is a friend. When it seems that change will overwhelm you, stand back and rejoice. Be at peace, for I am with you, comforting, consoling, directing, and loving. I have fashioned the fabric of your life into a tight weave that none of my blessings might fall through. All shall come to pass at My appointed time and in My appointed way. Be at peace and rejoice, for with my perfect timing it shall all come together, nothing lacking, with perfection. Rest in that assurance.

I Will Never Leave You or Forsake You,
Your Father

Father, when I become impatient for Your promises to be fulfilled in my life, I will stop and remember all the wonderful blessings You have bestowed upon me already, blessings upon blessings upon blessings. Your love and blessings overwhelm me with their magnitude, and my heart sings with gratefulness.

Father, I repent for being impatient in the following areas of my life:

_____

_____

_____

_____

_____

_____

_____

_____

_____

_____

_____

_____

90

PSALM 16:9 AMP
"Therefore my heart is glad
and my glory [my inner self] rejoices;
my body too shall rest and confidently dwell in safety."

My Child,

Lean into My arms and commit your whole being unto Me. That is called "rest." Rest from the fear of things left undone. Rest from the fear of "missing it." Rest from the clamoring of "to be." For my Spirit in and through you is "all in all." Rest, My child, in Me, completely removed from the passing scene. My Presence shall become precious to you in new ways, undreamed of. Be content in Me. Release unto Me all cares and worries. My hand is over you to prepare you for what is to come. Relax in My hand and lean on Me with confidence and trust. All shall be accomplished in My time and at My pace. Rest in Me child. Be at peace and know Me. Be saturated in My love. Tranquility of heart shall be the fruit. Nothing shall push or pull you in any direction but Mine.

Rest in Me, My Child!

I Love You!

Father, today I release unto You all of the cares and worries that have kept me from resting in Your love.

_____

_____

_____

_____

_____

_____

_____

_____

_____

_____

_____

Father, what a wonderful place to be, being fashioned by Your own hand of protection and creation. When I become impatient, help me to remember that I am Your special creation in process. When I see imperfections, You see progress. Father, I long to know Your Presence in a more intimate and precious way. Thank You Father, that this is the desire of Your heart too, and it becomes a reality as I learn to rest in You. I love You, Father.

91

1 JOHN 5:18 NKJV
"There is no fear in love; but perfect love casts out fear, because fear involves torment.
But he who fears has not been made perfect in love."

My Child,

It is My love that sets one at liberty to set others free. All you have to give is My love. Everything else is a byproduct of that love. There is no freedom where fear resides. "Perfect love casts out fear." Be a carrier of My perfect love which casts out fear, and opens the door to freedom. Perfect love equals love, acceptance, and forgiveness. Those who walk in perfect love (God's kind of love) must treat those who don't with honor. Dishonor is never a part of perfect love.

Love As I Love,
Your Father

Father, please help me to remember it doesn't matter what others do, it only matters how I respond, and I choose to respond with honor, love, forgiveness, patience, and blessing.

Father, today, when I am tempted to think or speak of someone with dishonor, I will repent and instead, think or speak words of honor.

_____

_____

_____

_____

_____

_____

_____

_____

_____

_____

_____

_____

92

PSALM 117:2 AMP
"For His mercy and loving-kindness are great toward us,
and the truth and faithfulness of the Lord endure forever."

My Child,

Listen with your heart. You are fashioned for warfare—a warfare that comes from love and faithfulness, against which nothing can overcome. Strength of heart stands firm and is fearless because of trust in My love and faithfulness. You always walk above distractions when you walk in love, with a singleness of heart and mind. Your trust in Me becomes the boundaries and love fills in the picture. Faithfulness maintains the truth and the love.

Listen with Your Whole Heart!

Your Loving Father

Father, what else is on Your heart for me to know today?

_____

_____

_____

_____

_____

_____

_____

_____

_____

_____

_____

_____

_____

_____

Father, thank You for helping me, day by day, to stand firm and fearless with strength of heart, because of my trust in Your love and faithfulness. When I feel distracted, help me once again to focus on You and listen with my whole heart to Your words of truth and love to my heart.

93

1 JOHN 4:19 NKJV
"We love Him because He first loved us."

My Precious Child,

Rest in My love. Fear not the storms that gather, for just as surely as the clouds gather overhead, they will be blown away, the sun will shine brightly again and the storm will have left life-giving rain to nourish My children in ways they know not of. Be refreshed each day, whether the sun shines or if the clouds are overhead, for either way, I bless you daily and bring forth My perfect will in your life, and in the lives I give you to love. I bless you My child, each day I bless you. My eye is upon you to bless you.

Rest in Me, My Child,
Your Loving Father

I love You Father! Thank You that I can trust You each moment of each day, to protect me and to protect those that I love. Thank you for bringing peace to my heart as I walk through the storms of life securely held close to Your heart.

Father, what else is on Your heart to share with me this day?

_____

_____

_____

_____

_____

_____

_____

_____

_____

_____

_____

_____

_____

_____

_____

_____

94

JOHN 8:32 NKJV
"And you shall know the truth, and the truth shall make you free."

My Child,

I have many things to tell you, many truths for you to learn. Day by day I reach out to you and place a nugget of truth in your hand for you to ponder and mull over, turning it over and studying it as it molds your life. Take each nugget, each day and let it work it's weight in gold. (**Father, sometimes it seems that I am juggling nuggets.**) *I never give you more than you can handle. Thanksgiving and praise help the truths to absorb more quickly. Negative words spoken harden the heart against the absorption of truth. Flee anything negative, complaining, criticism, condemning, the three C's constricting, and emphasize the positive, cheerful, joyful, loving, and praiseworthy good report.*

You Are A Treasure to My Heart!

Your Loving Father

Father, You are such a "Treasure To My Heart" too! I long to hear Your words to my heart, all the day long and through the night! My heart is open to You.

_____

_____

_____

_____

_____

_____

_____

_____

_____

_____

_____

Father, it's my desire that only words of love, honor, blessing, appreciation, and truth come from my mouth and from my thoughts, with joy. When I'm tempted to speak negative and condemning words, thank You for helping me to have a will and the heart to speak words that uplift and bring hope. Help me Father, to always ask myself, "Do the words I am about to speak bring honor to the one spoken of?"

95

JAMES 4:6 NKJV
"But He gives more grace.
Therefore He says 'God resists the proud,
But gives grace to the humble.'"

My Child,

Grace multiplied is the goal, causing grace given, causing grace given, causing grace given, etc. The opposite becomes condemnation given, causing condemnation given, causing condemnation given, etc. It is like a pebble thrown into the water, causing the ripple effect. Sow good seed for the harvest. Good seed is motivated by pure love, with no agendas or motives. This makes discernment easy. Is it motivated by grace and love or by condemnation.

Give As I Give,
Your Loving Father

Father, every day is a gift from your heart of grace and love to Your people. You are the gift. The desire of my heart is to also become the gift, in Your likeness, with no agendas, motivated by pure love, sowing good seed for the harvest. May my life be a reflection and picture of Your grace and love. You are my greatest treasure! I love You!

Father, I love hearing Your words to my heart.

96

LUKE 18:17 NKJV
"Assuredly, I say to you,
whoever does not receive the kingdom of God
as a little child, will by no means enter it."

My Child,

There is a place in the Spirit where all things are made new every day. That place is as a small child, coming into My Presence with wonder and delight, untouched by the passing scene. Continue to be as that small child, lacking in nothing, content and at peace in My Presence. My heart is with you, My child, to stay in that place with wonderment and joy, with nothing lost, but all gain, continuing step by step, your destiny to fulfill. My heart is with you this day. Rejoice and go forth singing in My Presence with delight and joy. Each day is a testament of My love. Each day is a revealing of My plan.

I Love You!

I Love You, Too, Father!

Father, how can I bring delight to You today?

_____

_____

_____

_____

_____

_____

_____

_____

_____

_____

_____

_____

Father, the joy of being Your child is beyond words, every day a treasured gift from You. When I find myself caught up with the cares of life, all I have to do is think of You and my whole being smiles with delight, and peace once again descends. I love You so much Father!

97

PSALM 16:1 AMP
"Keep and protect me, Oh, God,
for in You, I have found refuge, and in You do I put my trust
and hide myself."

My Child,

Security comes by knowing and trusting Me. I shall not fail you, but preserve you. Purpose in your heart to be secure in this place, this place of much grace. Purpose in your heart to know that I, Your loving Father will not let you down. Purpose in your heart to be at peace in this place. I have said it doesn't depend on you, it depends on Me, and I see the beginning from the end. Struggle versus the sweetness of My love are two opposite ends of the spectrum. Struggle is the warning bell to come into My Presence, into the sweetness of My love, to diffuse the struggle, and bring peace. It is a moment by moment decision to come into My peace and fellowship with Me, where the absence of fear, agitation, and doubt is secure.

You Are Secure in Me,
Your Loving Father

Father, the desire of my heart is to always remember to start the day in Your Presence, and to moment by moment, spend the rest of the day in fellowship with You, listening to Your instructions and sharing my heart with You. And then at the end of the day, to go over the details of the day with You for Your wisdom and understanding of what has transpired. Father, I know that this is Your desire for me also.

Father, today I purpose in my heart to stay in the peace of Your Presence, enjoying the sweetness of Your love. My heart is listening for Your voice:

_____
_____
_____
_____
_____
_____
_____
_____
_____
_____
_____

PSALM 31:1 AMP
"In You, O Lord, do I put my trust and seek refuge."

My Child,

Safe and secure! I have made you safe and secure in My arms of love, depending on Me for your every breath and all that pertains to your life. I have lavished My love and favor upon you as a doting father lavishes his love and provision upon his favored child. Every moment of every day is a banquet of love, peace, and joy, with your Father and Friend. The freedom of My heart is yours. Let go of preconceived ideas and go forth unfettered by the past and its inconsistencies. My heart is with you to rejoice in the now. It contains all you will need for the journey to come. Go forth with abandon! Go forth with uncontained joy! Go forth with the unfathomable knowledge of My love!

Your Father and Faithful Friend

Father, is there anything from the past, that I am still hanging on to?

_____

_____

_____

_____

_____

_____

_____

_____

_____

_____

_____

_____

Father, thank You for helping me to lay down all preconceived ideas, sorrows, and inconsistencies from the past, so that You are free to create of my life a beautiful symphony of Your love. Thank you Father, for helping me to live in the present, and to leave the past behind in peace. I love being Your child, Father!

99

PSALM 23:4 AMP
"Yes, though I walk through the [deep, sunless] valley
of the shadow of death, I will fear or dread no evil,
for You are with me."

My Child,

Have you noticed that the storms leave debris and disruption in many areas? You have been through many storms that have touched every area of your life. Restoration and cleanup is a step by step endeavor. Just seeing the areas needing attention brings forth reconciliation and order. Fear not the storms of life. My grace is there to protect and restore. All that is needed is a willing heart. Time is still your friend. See to it that you don't rush ahead to accomplish that which is not eminent, but needs time. See Me in every word you speak, in every thought you make, and in every action you take. I am with you in everything you do, say, and think. Feel not alone, but know My staying power within you. Nothing passes by Me. Relax in My love. Lasting peace I give to you to wash away the debris!

I Am Always with You,
Your Father

Father, thank You for Your protection, provision, and Presence during the storms of life. Thank You Father, that each time I come out of a storm, I find myself stronger, more grateful for Your love, loving and trusting You more. Thank You that I am never alone. I love You!

Father, You light up my life! How can I bless You today?

_____

_____

_____

_____

_____

_____

_____

_____

_____

_____

JOHN 13:34 AMP
"Just as I have loved you,
so you too should love one another."

My Child,

I have shown you many problems in My Kingdom that need My Spirit of love and deliverance to set the captives free. I have placed you in positions to directly give My love that delivers. Restrict not its delivery. Let it flow unhindered by frustration, fear, or judgment. Let it flow liberally, that I might use it to bring freedom to others and defeat to the enemy. Remember, give advice when asked for, give love as naturally as you breathe, and you shall see victory on all fronts.

Love As I Love You,
Your Loving Father

Father, are there any areas in my life where I'm holding back love because of unforgiveness, frustration, fear, or judgment?

_____

_____

_____

_____

_____

_____

_____

_____

_____

_____

_____

_____

Father, what an adventure it is each day, seeing how Your love delivers and sets the captives free, bringing defeat to the enemy. And what freedom to just let it flow unhindered by frustration, fear, or judgment. To keep remembering it is not about me, it is about You, and how much You love Your people, and how much I'm to love them too. What freedom and what joy!

101

GALATIANS 5:1 NKJV

"Stand fast therefore in the liberty by which Christ has made us free,
and do not be entangled again with a yoke of bondage."

My Child,

See the birds, how they fly with such freedom? The vastness of My universe is theirs to enjoy. They sing victoriously in their freedom with great joy and trust. There is strength in freedom. Singing brings joy to the hearer. Freedom with wisdom brings life. Restraints with fear bring death. Measure your life by My Spirit of freedom within your heart. Freedom to love, freedom to rejoice, freedom to receive My Words of life, freedom to give My Words of life, freedom to walk in faith and trust, freedom to thank Me in all things, and freedom to **be** *all that I have created you to be. Be close to My Father heart, My child, and let Me continue to help you walk in the Glory of My freedom.*

Be Free My Child,

I Love You

Father, some days I wake up with Your light of hope and freedom shining in my heart with all of its brilliance and truth. Anxiety, stress, and doubt cannot live in such a brilliant light. On those days, I fly with You like the eagle with such great joy and delight. Other days, You still have to remind me to fly. My goal is to fly every day with You Father, in the Glory of Your Presence, letting the freedom of Your Spirit ring in my heart with great abounding joy. I love You so much, Father!

Father, what keeps Your Spirit of freedom from residing with power in my heart?

_____

_____

_____

_____

_____

_____

_____

_____

_____

_____

_____

_____

102

PSALM 31:15 AMP
"My times are in Your hands."

My Child,

Lay down your abilities before Me and let Me develop them to their fullest. Let Me promote or let those abilities lay dormant along the way, for I shall prosper and bring forth your talents at the appropriate time, and there shall be no limits put upon My assigned blessings and in the use of your talents. Fear not for their use. Let me use them for My Glory, and I shall bring forth an abundant harvest from each talent at the appointed time and place. Remain under the constant care and abiding love of My outspread wing of protection and direction. Fear not, My little one. Let Me lead and bring forth an abundant harvest in your life with nothing lacking.

Trust My Love,
Your Father

Father, I lay before You my impatience in the following areas…

_____

_____

_____

_____

_____

What areas in my life have I not been faithful enough in?

_____

_____

_____

_____

_____

Father, knowing that You direct the times and seasons of my life, and open or shut the doors of opportunity along the way, brings such peace. When I look back over my life, I can see Your hand of direction and blessing throughout. You have said, it would always be said of my life that it was stranger than fiction, and truly it is. You certainly keep it interesting. I love You Father!

103

PHILIPPIANS 4:1 NKJV
"Stand fast in the Lord, beloved."

My Child,

Stand straight and tall and be a sturdy ambassador of My Kingdom, undaunted by blight, persecution, unloveliness, or criticism, for I guide your ship. I set the wheels in motion that propel you along, and I set the boundaries beyond which you will not go. You answer to Me and Me only, and I have set your course for victory and blessing, blessings for you and for those whose lives you touch. Fear not their reactions, their neglect, their failures, or their critical spirits. Be gracious and loving. Give them space, for I am molding them and I am responsible for their growth also. Be flexible and resilient in My hands, and watch Me bring forth a beautiful life—yours! Be a beacon light of love, compassion, and gentleness, with a forgiving, spacious spirit, and a light and joyous heart.

You Are My Treasure,
Your Loving Father

Father, You always have such simple answers for complex questions and I am grasping the essence of Your message: love given for its own sake, not for its return. That to give that sort of love, I must be totally secure in Your love. As I stand secure in Your love, I will have the joy of watching the mountains fall in others' lives, by the power of Your love.

Father, I love the sound of Your voice and Your words of love falling on my ear!

_____

_____

_____

_____

_____

_____

_____

_____

_____

_____

_____

_____

104

"The Lord has heard my supplication;
the Lord receives my prayer."

My Child,

Tell them. Tell them for Me, that I love them. Loose them from their boxed-in feelings of worthlessness and impotence. Let them know that with My love, they are powerhouses. Change their fears to "can do's." I have heard their cries in the night and I am releasing them to be My love, unhampered by tradition and negative words. Show them, My Child, by your words of victory brought forth by My love, the realms of victory in store for them as they walk victoriously into and through the freedom of My love. Go to it, My Child, for I am with you to direct your words and your thoughts, and together we shall see the bound set free.

I Am with You,
Your Loving Father

Father, what else is on Your heart for me today?

_____

_____

_____

_____

_____

_____

_____

_____

_____

_____

_____

Father, nothing is more rewarding in life than loving You, loving others, and having intimate fellowship with You. Thank You Father, that together with You, I get to see the bound set free! What joy!

105

COLOSSIANS 2:2 NKJV
"That their hearts may be encouraged,
being knit together in love."

My Child,

Enlargement and encouragement are two words that compliment each other in their power and scope. As you encourage others, there is an enlargement of their vision and scope. It enlarges their vision to see beyond their pain and discouragement, beyond their limited vision of truth. I have broadened your scope of truth and brought you from limited vision to a place of enlarged vision, to see the pain in others beyond their pleasant exterior. Many shall they be, those that I shall show you, those who have need of love and encouragement to penetrate their outer shell. Watch for them as I bring them your way, and you shall know, and you shall discern, and you shall set them free. Have I not said "Freedom! Set My people free!" And you shall set My people free from the bondages that beset them and keep them from a victorious walk with Me. Set them free! Set them free! Be free, My child!

I Love You, My Child,
Your Father

Father, You have set me free in the most miraculous and wonderful ways and I will be eternally grateful. What joy to be a part of seeing others set free in the same wonderful and miraculous ways. It is so exciting to be able to encourage and love others in the same way that You have encouraged and loved me. I love You!

Father, what are some of the areas in which I am still not walking in freedom?

_____

_____

_____

_____

_____

_____

_____

_____

_____

106

EPHESIANS 4:15 AMP
"Let our lives lovingly express truths [in all things,
speaking truly, dealing truly, living truly]."

My Child,

Discover the nuances and intricacies of My Kingdom by acutely listening and watching. See My hand in every situation. (Lord, You are teaching me that I don't want to be bound by the fearful judgments of other people, that I hear from others' mouths every day.) Truth is your friend and protector. Fear not, but continue to march forth undaunted and unafraid, gleaning truth from the north, south, east, and west. Keep a watch upon your mouth to speak truth in love, compassion, and forbearance, void of guile, resentment, or bitterness. Speak the positive in truth and love. Leave the negative unspoken.

Be My Love,
Your Loving Father

Father, how can I please You today in word, thought, and action?

_____

_____

_____

_____

_____

_____

_____

_____

_____

_____

_____

_____

_____

Father, help me always, I pray, to judge the words that I speak by whether they bring blessing and healing, or condemnation. The desire of my heart is that my words always carry Your Spirit of truth and love.

PSALM 96:9 AMP
"O worship the Lord in the beauty of holiness."

My Child,

Worship allows My heart to capture your heart. Freedom is a state of mind loosed by the heart focused on Me, in the freedom of worship. I would not have you weighed down with earthly concerns. I would have you move through them, hardly noticing—only long enough to lift them up to Me. Let your concern be for freedom of intimacy with Me. Concerns will melt away and be met in the power of My Presence. Shackles fall away in the absolute beauty and freedom of My Presence. Stagnation cannot rest upon a warrior in My Kingdom. Celebrate! Celebrate! I am a celebrating God—One who celebrates My coming in fullness in you.

You Are Loved,
Your Father

Precious Father, You have captured my heart! I long to come into greater depths of intimately loving You through the freedom of worship. Through worship, my whole being sings and celebrates the joy of loving You!

Dear Father, please teach me more about intimacy with You today.

_____

_____

_____

_____

_____

_____

_____

_____

_____

_____

_____

_____

_____

_____

108

MALACHI 3:2 AMP
"For He is like a refiner's fire."

My Child,

The spirit of heaviness is being replaced by My pure joy, fashioned in the fire of adversity. It shall come forth unabated and resounding with My power and grace, for you shall rise up and sing forth My power, authority, and healing to those who are weary from the battle. You shall recognize them, for you too have been through the fire and are coming through with the brilliance of My Spirit upon you. See not the smoke. See the brilliance of My light. Dance in the midst of the fire.

Dance and Sing, My Child!
Your Loving Father

Father, You make my heart sing with pure joy. How can I bring joy to Your heart today?

_____

_____

_____

_____

_____

_____

_____

_____

_____

_____

_____

_____

Father, truly I can say it has all been worthwhile, every struggle, every pain, every test and trial. Thank You that the spirit of heaviness is being replaced by Your pure joy. What joy to recognize others coming through the fire, singing forth Your power, authority, and healing to those weary from the battle, that we might come through together with the brilliance of Your Spirit upon us.

109

PSALM 109:1 AMP
"O GOD, my heart is fixed
(steadfast, in the confidence of faith)."

My Child,

Leadership is based on the ability to lead My people into the Promised Land, the land flowing with milk and honey, which is the Holy of Holies, which is a place of fellowship with Me; deep, intimate relationship with Me. Contrary to popular belief, I am not found in the rushing brook, in the morning sunrise, or the majestic mountain. I am found in the human heart. It is there that I reside in power. It is there that I take the crooked and make it straight, and set the captives free!

You Are Blessed,
Your Loving Father

Dearest Father, my desire is to spend every waking and sleeping hour in Your Holy of Holies, that place of intimate fellowship with You. Thank You for the beauty of Your rushing brook, morning sunrise, and majestic mountains, but I am so glad that You reside in my heart, making my crooked places straight and setting me totally free!

Father, how can I be more totally open to Your loving Presence in my heart?

_____

_____

_____

_____

_____

_____

_____

_____

_____

_____

_____

_____

_____

_____

_____

_____

_____

JOHN 1:9 AMP
"There it was—the true Light [was then] coming into the world
[the genuine, perfect, steadfast Light]
that illumines every person."

My Child,

I have mined and brought forth nuggets of precious jewels for you to pick up and turn around in your hand, seeing My Light glisten on them. And as you are standing there looking at the different facets and the Light glistening on them, others will come around and look over your shoulder and the Light of My Presence will reflect onto their faces. They won't see that reflection happening, but it will be happening, because it is My Light and My Presence and it is doing what I sent it forth to do. You are simply standing there, holding My Presence, holding My Light, and letting it beam off that jewel into their faces, into their very beings. So it is as I've always said, "You simply be the reflection of My love, and I will do what needs to be done in their hearts."

You Are Blessed,
Your Loving Father

Father, what is on Your heart for me to hear today?

_____

_____

_____

_____

_____

_____

_____

_____

_____

_____

My Father, many times You have said that You can always be found amongst Your treasures—Your people—and that is where I'm to be found, also. You have put such a love in my heart for Your people that nothing gives me greater joy, except You. Thank You Father!

111

PSALM 40:10 AMP
"I have proclaimed Your faithfulness and Your salvation.
I have not hid away Your steadfast love
and Your truth from the great assembly."

My Child,

A picture is worth a thousand words. Be a picture of My faithfulness and love. Let Me paint the picture clearly in your life. Straight as an arrow shall the message be for all to see, a picture of Me, seen through thee! The sky is the limit, My love to impart into the niches and crevices of each aching heart. Be diligent, be faithful, My Glory you will see, as you minister My love to every need.

Be My Love,
Your Father

Father, every day that goes by, Your love becomes more precious to me. And every day that goes by brings a deeper love for Your treasures, Your people. Thank you, Father, for sharing with me such wonderful gifts of love.

Above all Father, You are my treasure! How can I walk closer to Your heart today?

_____

_____

_____

_____

_____

_____

_____

_____

_____

_____

_____

_____

_____

_____

112

JOHN 4:24 AMP
"God is a Spirit [a spiritual Being]
and those who worship Him must worship Him
in spirit and in truth [reality]."

My Beloved Child,

Religion verses lavish worship! Religion is man bypassing God. Worship is man coming to God in intimacy. Avoidance verses intimacy. Religion, the letter of the law, brings death. Worship by the Spirit brings life. Religion is the form, worship is the substance. Worship brings My Glory, My Presence, and My goodness. Religion brings deadness, separation, and My wrath. Be a carrier of intimate worship, praise, thanksgiving, and intimacy with Me, through your steadfast love, faithfulness, and grace extended, never taking offense. More and more, lavish worship and freedom, love, and joy that worship brings, shall draw others into the light of My love. Freedom is rare and beautiful to behold.

You Are Blessed,
Your Loving Father

Father, speak to my heart that I might further learn Your ways.

_____

_____

_____

_____

_____

_____

_____

_____

_____

_____

_____

Father, Your steadfast love, faithfulness, and goodness daily bring such joy to my heart. Thank You, Father, that You not only love me with an unfathomable love but that You also encircle me with a family of friends, who love me with Your unfathomable love. Your ways are so wonderful to me!

113

JOB 10:12 NKJV
"You have granted me life and favor,
and Your care has preserved my spirit."

My Precious Child,

Settling in on you is a greater sense of your destiny. Liken it to a child, who knows her daddy loves her and all he has is hers. But as she grows up, the awe of all that is set before her begins to dawn on her and become plain, the responsibility, favor, and open doors. It is all yours, My Child, and the ramifications are endless. See the past merge into the present with peace and favor. See My light rest upon you to accomplish all I have set before you, with love, favor, and joy. The ministry of grace has filled this place and placed you on solid footing for the things to come. You shall not miss it. It is yours to explore and delight in with all your heart.

My Child,
I Love You!

Father, many times You have said that I will not miss the wondrous things You have in store for me, because I trust You. And Father, I have learned that no matter how things look, I can trust you. Thank You Father, for merging the past into the present, with peace and favor. Thank You, Father for the pure delight of being Your child! I love You!

Thank You Father, for giving me a sense of destiny. What is on Your heart for me to know today?

_____

_____

_____

_____

_____

_____

_____

_____

_____

_____

_____

_____

114

HEBREWS 12:1 AMP
"Let us run with patient endurance
and steady and active persistence the appointed course
of the race that is set before us."

My Child,

My plan for your life has seemed slow, laborious, and greatly lacking in detail. But know that within My framework of time, much has been accomplished and much shall stand the passage of time. Here a little, there a little, each day compiling a masterpiece of great beauty. Continue your quest for the gold. It is a quest worthy of My love and the fulfillment of My Word. It seems to be a marathon that you are running for the gold, but know this: the quest is worth the effort to run the race. You are surrounded by My love and protection as you run.

I Am Proud of You, My Child,
Your Loving Father

Father, speak to my heart, I'm listening.

_____
_____
_____
_____
_____
_____
_____
_____
_____
_____
_____
_____
_____
_____
_____

Loving Father, what joy to know You are proud me. And Father, thank You for teaching me that every day is complete in You. That at the end of the day, I can go to bed with peace, knowing that another portion of Your masterpiece has been compiled, because You lead, guide, and direct my steps.

115

2 Corinthians 2:15 AMP
"For we are the sweet fragrance of Christ
[which exhales] unto God."

My Child,

Put your hand to the plow and don't look back. Seek Me at every turn. The day is as the night to Me. Languish not in the application of My Word to you. Latch hold of the fragrance of the hour. Just continue to move forward with grace and truth, ever mindful of My unconditional love for you, and then pour it out on others. Be strengthened this day from the rigorous trials. You have stood your ground and maintained your stride. Continue forward with renewed vision and strength. Trials come and go, but they leave in their wake a fragrance that cannot be matched any other way. Be blessed this day. You have come a long way. Bask this day in the warmth of My love.

You Bring Me Joy,
Your Loving Father

Father, Your words of encouragement and unconditional love give me strength to go forward, knowing that You are always with me for every challenge that comes my way. Thank You for that assurance. I love You, Father!

Father, today I just want to pour out my love on You and bless You!

_____

_____

_____

_____

_____

_____

_____

_____

_____

_____

_____

_____

_____

_____

116

MATTHEW 7:7 NKJV
"Ask, and it will be given to you:
seek, and you will find;
knock, and it will be opened to you."

My Child,

Stay close to My heart and you won't fall apart. Mighty and tremendous are the plans I have for you. Don't worry about what you cannot see. Mistakes are made by stepping forth too soon. Make sure every detail is completely in tune. Justifying this and that is a sure and costly trap. Seek My face each day. It's the only secure way. Costly trials are averted this way, when you let Me have the final say. Stay close to My heart. Let Me be a part of every thought and action proclaimed, each and every day as you walk My way.

You Are Loved,

Your Father

Father, please speak to my heart as I share my heart with You.

_____

_____

_____

_____

_____

_____

_____

_____

_____

_____

_____

_____

Teach me Father, I pray, to stay closer to Your heart, that I not get caught up in the events of the day and miss the words that You would say to my heart. I don't want to miss a single word of direction, instruction, love, encouragement, friendship, and fellowship. I love You Father, so much!

NEHEMIAH 8:10 NKJV
"The joy of the LORD is your strength."

My Child,

The joy of the Lord is your strength and your song, your protection all the day long. Never despair! Never give up! For I see the end from the beginning, bathed in the light of My love. Victory shines forth brilliantly in My eyes. Share the knowledge of that victory in Me, for it is yours to share in all its fullness of joy. The choice is always yours. Rejoice and be glad, for I have told you the outcome is victory, or languish and be sad for lack of commitment to My Word, which always brings victory. Walk in the light of My love. It brings joy. Go forth singing, laughing, praising, rejoicing, and standing on My Word of victory.

Walk in the Joy of My Love!

Your Loving Father

Father, no wonder the joy of the Lord is my strength, for when I sing, laugh, praise, and rejoice in You, I walk in Your victory! It is only when I let negative emotions creep in that I lose sight of Your vision and victory for my life. I delight in You, Father!

Father, You fill my heart with such joy. Let me count the ways....

_____

_____

_____

_____

_____

_____

_____

_____

_____

_____

_____

_____

_____

_____

_____

118

EPHESIANS 5:2 AMP
"Walk in love, [esteeming and delighting in one another]
as Christ loved us and gave Himself up for us."

My Child,

Many times you have stood in the breach, unaware, being that bridge, drawing those from a place of distance to the light and truth of My love. Fear not to be that bridge. A bridge does not take on the characteristics of those who pass over it, but of the One who created it. Continue to look to Me, your Creator, for your truth and your very being, and freely give of the love and faithfulness I have given. Have I not told you, "You simply be, I'll do?" You be My love to My people, and I'll do within My people what needs to be done." I have not told you to choose. I have simply told you to love. Let others judge, condemn, and reject as unworthy of their time and love. You with faith and trust in Me to protect you, simply love!

Love As I Love You,
Your Loving Father

Father, teach me even more how to walk in the light and truths of Your love!

_____

_____

_____

_____

_____

_____

_____

_____

_____

_____

_____

_____

Father, there is such joy in simply loving; speaking Your words of encouragement and truth and watching You work miracles in lives. And Father, You have shown me that when others judge, condemn, and reject as unworthy, that they, too, need to be loved, so that You can work Your miracles in their lives.

119

1 THESSALONIANS 3:12 AMP
"And may the Lord make you to increase
and excel and overflow in love for one another
and for all people, just as we also do for you."

My Child,

Be My love! Manifest My love! Be a reflection of My love to others! Radiate My love! Be a transmitter of My love! Receive it and transmit it continuously by My Spirit. Be a life-giver. Stand in the gap for My precious ones. Let them learn by your example. Peace and joy open the door to My rest, brought forth by love. Grow in My love day by day. The more you understand of My love and walk in My love, the more you can give of My love. You can only give what you have.

Love As I Love You,
Your Loving Father

Father, Your love is straightforward, honest, gives wisdom, discernment, knowledge, peace, joy, warmth, comfort, and truth. It restores and blesses. Your love keeps life simple, not complex. It turns darkness into light. Your love puts people on solid ground, for they know they are accepted and acceptable. This is how I want to love also, Father. Thank You for teaching me Your ways.

Father, what would You have me learn today from Your heart of love?

_____
_____
_____
_____
_____
_____
_____
_____
_____
_____
_____
_____
_____
_____
_____

120

HEBREWS 4:12 AMP

"For the Word that God speaks is alive and full of power [making it
active, operative, energizing, and effective]; it is sharper than
any two-edged sword, penetrating to the dividing line
of the breath of life (soul) and [the immortal] spirit."

My Child,

My Word penetrates deeply into the inner being, bringing about results of My making. My Word molds, shapes and produces fruit that is sweet to the taste, giving life, stamina and hope to those languishing on the sidelines. Let My Word continue to bubble forth with abundant life. Hearken to the sound of My voice in the still of the night, in the evening hours, in the cool of the day, and in the midst of your daily activities. Tune your heart to listen, to establish unbroken communication between Me and thee. My Spirit waits for an invitation to commune.

Listen with Your Heart My Child,
Your Loving Father

Thank You, Father, for speaking words of wisdom to me today, through Your written and spoken words to my heart.

_____

_____

_____

_____

_____

_____

_____

_____

_____

_____

_____

Father, Your written Word and Your spoken Word are both such treasures to my heart. They are the foundation of everything worthwhile in life, bringing understanding, hope, and abundant life everlasting. Such a sense of destiny pervades my spirit as I walk with You, loving Father!

121

JAMES 3:18 NKJV
"Now the fruit of righteousness is sown in peace
by those who make peace."

My Child,

Minister My peace and love to others as I have ministered My love and peace to you. See them through My eyes. Let Me love them through you, judging not, but accepting them on their ground; accepting them totally and letting Me take care of the unnecessary props. I bring forth righteousness in each one. That is not your part. Your part is to accept and love them where they are. My peace I give to you, that you might love without condemnation, frustration, or confusion.

I Love You!
Your Father

Father, thank You for helping me to love others unconditionally, as You love, with honor, faithfulness, and forgiveness. And Father, I am so grateful to You that as I am learning to love with Your love, You fill my life with friends who are learning to love in the same way. Father, You are so wonderful!

Loving Father, I can hardly wait to hear what else You have to say to my heart today.

_____

_____

_____

_____

_____

_____

_____

_____

_____

_____

_____

_____

_____

_____

_____

JUDE 24 NASB
"Now to Him who is able to keep you from stumbling,
and to make you stand in the presence of His glory
blameless and with great joy."

My Child,

Rest My child, in the Glory of My Presence. Weighed down by doubt and unbelief, one cannot soar, but loosed through song and worship, one can soar in the Heavenlies with Me. Soar, My child, soar, and let Me soothe frayed wings that have been battered by the winds that have blown unabated. Be at peace, My child. Rest in My love. People, places, and things are the building blocks of a life. Love, faith, and honor are the building blocks of the spirit. All are given by My hand. All are received by choice, by you. Trust Me to give them all to you and trust Me to help you to receive.

Trust Me, My Child,

Rest in Me

Father, today I bring my questions to You from my heart.

_____

_____

_____

_____

_____

_____

_____

_____

_____

_____

_____

_____

_____

Faithful Father, once again I put my life in Your hands, knowing that I can trust You to create of my life a beautiful symphony of Your love. That as I trust You, You are free to direct my feet in the way You have chosen for me to go. And that as I seek the answers from You, You bring clarity and truth to my life, so that I can soar in the Heavenlies with You.

123

EPHESIANS 5:19 AMP

"Speak out to one another with psalms and hymns and spiritual songs, offering praise with voices [and instruments] and making melody with all your heart to the Lord."

My Child,

Fill your life with song. Come into My Presence with singing. Glorious and magnificent song brings joy and life to My children who languish in the heat of the battle. Restrain not the song of praise in your heart. Let it sing with glorious abandon. Let My peace reign in your heart as I replace frustration and confusion with joy and light, as you sing your praises to Me. Go forth now, unencumbered by doubt, guilt, and confusion. Go forth in trust and faith that what I have begun in you, I will complete. I will not abandon you. You are safe within My loving hand, and what you see as failure, I see as growth. Go forth, My child, with abandon, in the safety of My love. Languish not, for I see, restore and hasten to lift you up when you lose your footing. Get right back up in confidence.

I Will Never Leave You or Forsake You,
Your Loving Father

Thank You Father, for Your tender loving care. It is so wonderful to know that what I see as failure, You see as growth. That I can live in abandoned trust and faith in You, because what You have begun in my life, You will complete. My heart sings to You, Father, with such joy and love!

Loving Father, I will come into Your Presence with singing this day.

_____

_____

_____

_____

_____

_____

_____

_____

_____

_____

124

EZEKIEL 34:26 AMP
"There shall be showers of blessing
[of good, insured by God's favor]."

My Child,

Amongst My flowers grow thorns, but they cannot affect the beauty and blessing of those flowers, for My sun, rain, and soil cause them to flourish, grow, and shine forth My Glory. Trust Me to continue to nourish, love, and protect you, causing you to grow and flourish. Be not concerned about the thorns among the flowers. Let Me deal with them. You keep your face raised to the sunshine of My smile and soak up the rays of the sun. Let the rain of My Spirit refresh you and the soil of My love enfold You, causing you to flourish and grow. Be at peace in the sunshine of My love. Sing in the sunshine!

I Care for You,

Your Loving Father

Loving Father, I speak to You my words of love with abandon.

_____

_____

_____

_____

_____

_____

_____

_____

_____

_____

_____

_____

_____

Loving Father, You take such good care of me. The wonder of it all is how You delight in me just as I delight in You. The sunshine of Your smile is daily evident in my life. I am so grateful! You truly nourish, love, and protect me, causing me to flourish and grow. Your love is too wonderful for words, and yet You treasure my words of love to You, just as I treasure Your words of love to me.

125

PSALM 51:10 AMP
"Create in me a clean heart, O God, and renew a right,
persevering, and steadfast spirit within me."

My Child,

Stand guard on the portals of your heart, that they not betray you, that evil not be allowed to enter through frustration, fear, or injustice. Keep a clean heart, no matter how it appears to be. Be aware and alert to the spirits of pride and self-pity that will try to creep in the back door from feelings of hurt and injustice. Let it not be said that you became an accuser. Let it be said that you held steady and firm to the end, extending your hand of friendship and love. Straightforward and full of truth and discernment you shall be, but it shall be with no hint of condemnation or struggle. It shall be in My strength, brought forth with love, My truth, and My Word, to bring forth healing and restoration. So shall it be. Go forth in faith, for I go before you, preparing the ground, to bring forth healing and peace.

Love As I Love,
Your Loving Father

Father, thank You that in all my relationships, You go before me, preparing the ground to bring forth healing and peace, helping me to keep a clean heart, without becoming an accuser, no matter how it appears to be. Thank You, Father, for helping me to be straightforward, full of truth and discernment and yet loving without condemnation, offense, pride or self pity.

Father, what areas of my life have I not totally given over to You, for Your healing and restoration?

_____

_____

_____

_____

_____

_____

_____

_____

_____

_____

126

PSALM 23:6 AMP
"Surely or only goodness, mercy, and unfailing love
shall follow me all the days of my life."

My Child,

*Lighten your load. It need not be that heavy. Have I not said, "Light is the load
of those who follow after Me?" Set your eyes on Me. Walk in My joy. Walk in
My peace. Let Me be the arbitrator. My children walk in the assurance of My
love for them. That is where their strength and resilience comes from. The
assurance of My love moves them through the storms of life unscathed. Nothing
can penetrate that peace in the joy of My Spirit, when one is fully aware of My
love. No need for resentment, no need for hurt. God loves me. All is well. So go
forth this day with joy and peace in your heart, for I love you with a perfect and
everlasting love.*

You Are Blessed,
Your Father

Dear Father, today I will lighten my load by coming into Your Presence with faith, knowing You will speak to my heart.

_____

_____

_____

_____

_____

_____

_____

_____

_____

_____

_____

Precious Father, it is only when I forget how much You love me that fear and doubt creep in. Forgive me Father, for allowing that to happen, when Your perfect love and peace are always readily available to me. When the load seems heavy, that is the warning bell to my heart to remember where my strength and resilience comes from, and to once again trust in Your magnificent and faithful love.

127

"So are the ways of everyone who is greedy for gain;
It takes away the life of its owners."

My Child,

Stay away from greed. It robs the heart of stability and peace. It places a noose around the heart, taking it captive. Wrestle not with greed. Let it be. Don't make peace with it. Stay away. You can forgive a snake for being a snake, but it is still a snake and if you come close you will get bit. Let moderation be your motto, never excess. Greed is brought about by fear, fear that it will not be provided to you by Me. Lay aside your fears and walk in peace with Me and with others. My peace is My gift to you, brought about by your trust in Me.

Trust Me,
I Love You

Father, I trust You. You have said that where my treasure is, there my heart will be also. You are my treasure. I choose to trust You. You are never greedy with Your blessings. You love and bless me lavishly. Father, may I always love You and others in the same way.

I love You Father. How can I trust You more?

_____

_____

_____

_____

_____

_____

_____

_____

_____

_____

_____

_____

_____

_____

_____

ISAIAH 41:13 AMP
"For I the Lord your God hold your right hand;
I am the Lord, Who says to you,
Fear not; I will help you!"

My Child,

Many times I have protected you from the realities of life. Now your ears shall hear, your eyes shall see, and you shall respond as I would have you respond, with wisdom and in truth. Fear not the realities of life. They cannot harm you. They only teach greater truths of My Kingdom and bring you into greater heights in My Spirit. I shall lead and guide you gently. Be not afraid, but let Me show you greater realms of service by My Spirit, and together we shall set the captives free. Continue on in faith. Let Me be your support as you encounter uncomfortable situations, for together we shall see mountains move, and far greater strides shall be made than ever before in your growth and maturity. Blessed assurance is the key. Go forth confident in My ability to bring you through to victory and fulfillment.

You Are Blessed,
Your Loving Father

Teach me, Father, to hear Your voice more clearly that I may walk in more wisdom and discernment.

_____

_____

_____

_____

_____

_____

_____

_____

_____

Thank You Father, for gently guiding and teaching me, day by day. You have supported me as I've encountered uncomfortable situations, teaching me how to respond by Your Spirit of love and faith. Walking with You, Father, is walking in the miraculous. Thank You that I will see greater strides in my growth and maturity than ever before, and that together we shall see the captives set free (including me)!

129

PSALM 1:3 AMP

"And he shall be like a tree firmly planted [and tended]
by the streams of water, ready to bring forth its fruit, in its season;
its leaf also shall not fade or wither; and everything he does
shall prosper [and come to maturity]."

My Child,

A tree grows strong by nourishment (My Word, written and spoken), faith (trust in My Word of truth), and sunlight (My love), the natural outgrowth being joy and thanksgiving. Be that beautiful, healthy tree of My choosing, brought forth to bless and comfort My people; and I shall make of you a tree of strength and beauty that cannot be toppled or harmed. Be My tree of righteousness, the planting of the Lord. I have planted you, watered you, nourished and sustained you. Grow, thrive, and rejoice evermore! Grow and be strong.

You Are Blessed.

Dear Lord, You have loved and blessed me beyond measure! Your Word brings me joy and freedom. It has caused me to grow, thrive, and love You more every day. Blessing and comforting Your people, Your treasures, brings joy to my heart. You surround me with pleasure and favor. I love You so much, and am so grateful!

Father, today as I read Your Word and listen to Your heart, teach me to love and understand Your ways even more.

_____

_____

_____

_____

_____

_____

_____

_____

_____

_____

_____

_____

_____

130

PSALM 89:15 NKJV
"Blessed are the people who know the joyful sound!
They walk, O LORD, in the light of Your countenance."

My Child,

Now, let the light of My countenance shine upon you from this day forward, undiminished by disappointment or discouragement. For in the light of My countenance, there can be no discouragement or disappointment, only the joy of My Presence and promise and the song of My Spirit of love. Let it sing strongly in your life, unabated. Be neither grieved nor remorseful, but walk before Me with a pure heart, with hope and trust in My sustaining love. Stand before Me confident that I will uphold you, sustain you, and bring you through to victory.

I Sing over You with Love!

Your Father

My heart sings to You today, Lord, with songs of love.

_____

_____

_____

_____

_____

_____

_____

_____

_____

_____

_____

_____

_____

_____

_____

I love You, Father! You are the joy of my life. You give me songs in the night, and during the day, my heart takes flight just knowing You love me. There is such joy in Your Presence, where truly there can be no discouragement or disappointment. Every day is a new beginning and a new adventure with You!

131

LUKE 11:33 RSV

"No one after lighting a lamp puts it in a cellar or under a bushel, but on a stand, that those who enter may see the light."

My Child,

Show forth My light in greater ways. Hide it not under a bushel. I have revealed to you many truths—truths that bring freedom and light. Shine forth that light which is truth and freedom, and it shall make your pathway even brighter. I have blessed you with many blessings designed to lead you ever closer to My heart and love. Straight and narrow is the path, but wide is My love. Walk in the wideness of My love and you will follow the straight, narrow path.

You Are Loved,
Your Father

Precious Father, every day the wonderment of Your love becomes more real to my heart. Just knowing that as I walk in the overwhelming preciousness of Your love for me, that You keep me on the straight and narrow path of Your will. Your way for me brings me peace and causes my heart to sing with unrestrained joy. I want others to know and experience Your marvelous and all-encompassing love. I love You, Father, so very much!

Father, how can I more readily shine forth Your light, that others might know of Your wonderful love?

_____

_____

_____

_____

_____

_____

_____

_____

_____

_____

_____

_____

_____

_____

∽≈⊚ 132 ⊚≈∾

PSALM 9:10 AMP

"And they who know Your name
[who have experience and acquaintance with Your mercy]
will lean on and confidently put their trust in You."

My Child,

Remain at peace, My child, for I have not stopped working in your life, and I shall continue to bring forth miracles and solutions to problems that seem to loom and extract your peace and joy. Remain in My peace and joy, for I Am the problem solver, and I have placed you where I want you, to confirm and bring forth My will. Praise continues to be your safeguard and peace continues to be the barometer of your walk with Me. Continue on in strength, fortitude, and determination to see My will brought forth and My ways fulfilled. Worry not for the future. Simply trust Me for today. Rejoice in the present and in My care for you and those you love. The pathway is flooded with light and you shall not stumble or fall. My Spirit of love shall continue to uphold, sustain, train, and guide.

I Love You, My Child!

∽≈⊚

Father, I praise and thank You today for Your faithful and loving care.

_____

_____

_____

_____

_____

_____

_____

_____

_____

_____

_____

_____

_____

I love You, Father! Always, when I simply trust You for today, You bring forth the answers for tomorrow. When I start worrying about tomorrow, I will remember that You hold me in the palm of Your hand, and that You have placed me where You want me, to confirm and bring forth Your will. You have always been faithful to uphold, sustain, train, and guide me, with Your faithfulness and gentle love. Thank You Father, for continuing to remind me that praise is my safeguard, and peace continues to be the barometer of my walk with You. You are my life!

133

MATTHEW 25:34 NKJV
"Come, O blessed of my Father,
inherit the kingdom prepared for you
from the foundation of the world."

My Child,

Intimidation and insecurity are indications of a heart removed from the absolute knowledge of My love and acceptance. Let it not be said, My child, that you did not know of and accept all of My love, acceptance, and confidence in you. Let it be said that she walks in grace and truth, brought forth by a total acceptance of My love and acceptance of her. She walks in grace and beauty, this one, who knows the Father's heart of love, for she has inherited all of the Father's treasure, secured for her from the foundation of the earth. You can walk around it, beside it, or past it, or you can walk in full acceptance, trust, and full receivership of My love, blessings, acceptance, and inheritance.

Walk Fully in My Love,
Your Loving Father

Thank You Father, for Your unconditional love! Thank You that when I feel insecure and allow intimidation, that You remind me that I am secure in You, walking in Your acceptance, love, blessings, and full inheritance as Your child.

Loving Father, my heart sings to You this day with loving praise and thanksgiving for the many ways You bless my life!

_____
_____
_____
_____
_____
_____
_____
_____
_____
_____
_____

134

1 JOHN 4:19 AMP
"We love Him, because He first loved us."

My Precious Child,

Straight into My Presence you have come, not worried or concerned with what you have done, but knowing full well My love covers and protects you in all that you do. Straight into My lap you continue to come, longing to hear the words from My heart about everything under the sun, knowing I will comfort your heart and impart words of wisdom, commitment, and discernment as you run straight into My arms of love. You have found the secret of staying on My higher ground. My child, now listen to My heart this day and you will see the secret to daily cause the enemy to flee. Instead of that which would cause your heart to pull back and retreat, you shall daily find the answers that you seek. Begin asking, expecting My heart to reveal. With each answer revealed, more confidence sealed. It's the adventure of a lifetime, you have said, as you continue to seek and to be led.

I Love You, My Child,
Your Loving Father

Father, today I want ask You about…

_____

_____

_____

_____

_____

_____

_____

_____

_____

_____

_____

_____

_____

_____

Loving Father, just saying Your Name causes my whole being to come to rest and peace. And it's true, I long to hear the words from Your heart about everything under the sun. But I get so excited to hear what You have to say to me from Your heart, that I forget to ask from my heart with anticipation of each answer revealed. Father, thank You for reminding me to ask of You. Thank You, Father, for the confidence asking and receiving brings.

135

MATTHEW 6:34 TLB

"So don't be anxious about tomorrow.
God will take care of your tomorrow too.
Live one day at a time."

My Child,

Listen closely! Time is still your friend and will continue to be until the end. So worry not about the how, when, or where. Just know I will continue to be there with you, every step of the way. Just nestle into My arms of love, My precious one, and continue to know it is already done, to My Glory and to your delight. Every day is a treasure to behold, to hold loosely in your hand, delighting in every facet and its sparkle and glow. You will continue to know day by day My heart and My ways for you, in all that you do. Worry and doubt will always be far removed from you, for you have taken a stand to trust and believe. Freely receive My Spirit of love as a part of everything you think, do, and say.

You Are My Treasure,
Your Loving Father

Father, it is amazing how things seem to fall into place when I peacefully trust You. Just knowing that "time is my friend" brings such peace to my heart. The temptation is always to race ahead, instead of peacefully living one day at a time, letting You lead with Your perfect timing. Thank You Father, for always reminding me to slow down and rest in Your arms of love.

Father, I will treasure every facet of today, listening closely to Your words of direction and love.

_____

_____

_____

_____

_____

_____

_____

_____

_____

_____

_____

136

ROMANS 12:10 TLB
"Love each other with brotherly affection
and take delight in honoring each other."

My Child,

The currency of Heaven is love! (So, Lord, the more we love the more currency of heaven we have to spend here on earth. And love imparts that currency to others. It brings wealth to their heart, soul, and spirit, and to their life, bringing life and fulfillment.) *I will wipe away their tears. I will lighten their load. I will sing songs of love to them. Bring them to Me! Moment by moment, day by day, the Word of the Lord shall be with you, bringing comfort, guidance, and love. Bask in its sweetness. Be immersed in it with joy. Time and time again I have held you up with pride. Magnificent days lie ahead. You shall stand in awe and rejoice, and My strength and purpose you shall see.*

Love As I Love,
Your Father

Father, today I will spend the currency of Heaven by...

_____

_____

_____

_____

_____

_____

_____

_____

_____

_____

_____

Precious Father, I love spending the currency of Heaven! Watching You bless and seeing You heal one of Your treasures, one of Your precious ones, brings joy beyond measure. Thank You Father, for letting us be an integral part of Your healing love upon the earth!

137

1 John 4:11 AMP
"Beloved, if God loved us so (very much),
we also ought to love one another."

My Child,

Stretched, you have been stretched, and you will continue to be stretched. Don't be uptight, but be released from others' expectations of you. You are still to love each one, where they are. Step up to the plate. Don't debate. Simply say, "They are treasures in my sight. I love them with all my might. Do they have problems? Yes! But so do I! They are a part of the Master Plan. I will continue to reach out a hand to encourage and love." Seasons come and go. It has been a time to sow. And now a bumper crop you'll see, because you've believed.

You Have Done Well,
Your Loving Father

Loving Father, Your Words of encouragement and love means so much to me. They make all the struggles, trials, and stretching worthwhile. Thank You, Father, for helping me to be released from others' expectations of me, focusing instead on Your expectations of me. But most of all, thank You for making me a part of Your Master Plan.

Today Father, I will continue reaching out a hand to encourage and love by…

_____
_____
_____
_____
_____
_____
_____
_____
_____
_____
_____
_____
_____
_____
_____

138

PROVERBS 3:23 AMP
"Then you will walk in your way securely, and in confident trust,
and you shall not dash your foot or stumble."

My Child,

My light shall shine into the dark corners, illuminating places of deception and uneasiness. My heart discerns through you truths and grace. See, and in the seeing, continue to love. Have you not said, "Fear of deception is deception?" Stand strong in your faith in others. Continue to let them know of your love. Be lifted up this day to know that My angels are round about you, that you not strike your foot against a stone. Be not afraid of deception. I have made your heart to be an open door to Me. You will continue to see hearts mended and set free, to fly free in the beauty of holiness.

Continue Loving As I Love,
Your Father

Father, show me the areas where I still walk in fear and distrust.

_____

_____

_____

_____

_____

_____

_____

_____

_____

_____

_____

Father, what comfort to know that You protect me and have Your angels round about me, so that I can walk confidently in Your grace and love. It is such a joy to see hearts mended and flying free. And Father, thank You that day by day, You continue setting me free, that my heart can fly freely with You.

1 JOHN 4:7 NKJV
"Beloved, let us love one another, for love is of God;
and everyone who loves is born of God and knows God."

My Child,

With lightening speed, I come to those in need who are poised to receive. I charge you this day, don't let grievances get in the way. It is settled in your heart from the start to refuse to receive darts thrown your way from the enemy of your soul, who hates to see you whole. Release them as they come your way. Love, acceptance, and forgiveness are your way, each and every day. Remembrances of love extended are the building blocks of life found in Me. Set all other memories free to fly away. Memories not found in love pollute the streams of living water flowing from a life consecrated in Me. Your heart shall continue to be an open door of My love to others, without fear. Warnings will continue to come from those who do fear. Be not afraid to hear, and with eyes wide open and discernment clear, continue to love. My protection over you is secure.

I Love You, My Child,
Your Father

Dearest Father, You have taught me from the very beginning to refuse all negativity. That love, acceptance, and forgiveness is Your way, and that every time a negative thought comes, I am to capture it and release it immediately. Father, thank You for alerting me when I allow memories to form that are not found in love. Father, thank You for helping me to refuse to receive darts thrown my way from the enemy of my soul.

Father, is there any unforgiveness, grievances, or darts that I have let penetrate my heart and take up residence?

_____

_____

_____

_____

_____

_____

_____

_____

_____

_____

140

PSALM 5:12 AMP
"For You, Lord, will bless the [uncompromisingly] righteous
[him who is upright and in right standing with You];
as with a shield You will surrounds him with goodwill
[pleasure and favor]."

My Child,

Struggle not. Simply release unto Me your negative thoughts and let Me disperse them as clouds on a summer day. Let Me reveal to you their source, that you not take them to your heart. Be released this day, back into My arms of love and My peace from above. Be set free this day to soar and glide and enjoy the ride, as in My love you abide. Seize each moment with joy. Release My joy within you with pleasure. Let Me place within you this day a sense of security that cannot be tampered with. Listen to the quietness. In the quietness is My heart. Be established this day in the comfort of My love.

I Love You, My Child,

Your Father

Father, how can I bless You today?

_____

_____

_____

_____

_____

_____

_____

_____

_____

_____

_____

Dear Father, You bring such comfort and a sense of security to my heart. I take such pleasure in You. When I begin to struggle, thank You for reminding me to quiet my heart in Your Presence, knowing that peace will once again descend. Thank You, Father, for bringing such favor into my life.

141

PSALM 39:7 AMP
"My hope and expectation are in You."

My Child,

Sacrificial hope has kept you afloat. Straight into My Presence you have come, and we have become as one. As you have lifted your heart in praise to Me, I've opened your heart that you might see My favor in everything you do, because I love you! Continue in this way, My Child. Continue to say, each day, "I will sit awhile within Your Presence dear, that I might continue to hear Your plans and purposes for my life and times, that I might stop or turn on a dime." I will always be on time, not a minute late or too soon. You will always find there is room for you. Continue on this special way of blessing and fulfillment, all of your days.

You Are Precious to Me,
Your Loving Father

My Precious Father, the joy of my heart is spending time with You. You have given me hope when there was no hope. You lavish me with favor and unconditional love in everything I do. Your Words to my heart are so precious to me. Your love is my greatest treasure!

Precious Father, as I sit within Your Presence dear, what is it that You would like for me to hear?

_____
_____
_____
_____
_____
_____
_____
_____
_____
_____
_____
_____
_____

142

JUDE 2 AMP
"May mercy, [soul] peace, and love be multiplied to you."

My Child,

I am working within your heart a new sense of peace and completeness. Time brings a continuous outworking of My will within your life. Enjoy the trip along the way. Don't bolt, but be at peace and enjoy the view. Let Me permeate your being with peace and beauty. Let go of frenzied activity. Peace, peace, marvelous peace, coming from My heart of love. Enfold it to your heart as a friend. Time enough for much activity. This is a time of peace. Relish it, my child.

Stay in My Peace,
Your Loving Father

Father, today as I sit with You, with joyous anticipation of our time together, I want You to know how much I love You.

_____
_____
_____
_____
_____
_____
_____
_____
_____
_____
_____
_____
_____
_____

My Loving Father, when I stay in Your peace, there is such a sense of completeness. Thank You for intensifying Your peace and completeness in my life. When I begin to feel pressured and over-whelmed, I will come into Your Presence dear, knowing You will speak peace to my heart. I especially remember the night when, exhausted at midnight, I said, "Father, I'd love to sit with You awhile before I go to bed, but I don't want to bring to You the dregs of my day." And You said, "Please do!" What a precious time that was together, and it taught me that You are always there for me!

143

ISAIAH 60:1 AMP
"Shine [be radiant with the glory of the Lord],
for your light has come,
and the glory of the Lord has risen upon you!"

My Child,

Arise, let your light shine. Hide it not under a bushel or retreat in darkness. Let it shine brilliantly that all may see and rejoice in its brilliant and warming light, for the Glory of the Lord has risen upon you. Let it shine forth unhindered by circumstances beyond your control. Let My Spirit of light and truth control you, not circumstances set to trip you up. Refuse their power by continuing to walk in My power. You will find ways to bless, to bring forth the best in others with graciousness. The heavens proclaim the Glory of God, and the Glory of God shall be proclaimed through you as you let the ministry of peace, love, and contentment have its way in you.

You Are Blessed,
Your Loving Father

Loving Father, loving You and walking in Your Presence and Your Glory is the joy of my life! Thank You, Father, for teaching me day by day, to walk in Your Power, not in the power of circumstances. That negative thoughts and words bring power to circumstances, but positive words of trust and faith bring forth Your Blessings, the best in me, and the best in others.

Father, I choose to walk in Your peace, love and contentment today, and to bless others by…

_____

_____

_____

_____

_____

_____

_____

_____

_____

_____

_____

144

PSALM 29:11 AMP

"The Lord will give [unyielding and impenetrable] strength,
to His people;
the Lord will bless His people with peace."

My Child,

Struggle not to understand the coming events. Let Me filter them through My love and make of them a masterpiece in your life. Struggle not to maintain control over the events of your life. Walk in My peace. I will bring order and understanding and eliminate the unnecessary. You can depend on that. Now go forward with a light heart, depending on My love to bring you through to victory. Let not distractions detain you along the way by bringing depression and disillusionment before you. Resist and destroy their power by My Word of love and the sacrifice of praise. I love you, My child. Let that truth resound in your heart and prevail!

Struggle Not, My Child!
I Love You!

Father, let's sing and dance together today!

_____

_____

_____

_____

_____

_____

_____

_____

_____

_____

_____

Father, as I've gone through the hardest times of my life, You have said that as I sang and danced before You, my heart would remain tender and pure before You. I laughed and said, "But Father, I have no rhythm." But we danced together with joy and I always came out the other end stronger and wiser, and thanking You for the experience. Thank You Father, for filtering everything through Your love!

145

PSALM 31:23 AMP
"O, love the Lord, all you His saints!
The Lord preserves the faithful."

My Child,

Charge My people to know Me with intimacy and love. Hesitate not to bring forth experiences that praise and glorify My Name. Lay down your right to yourself. Lay it right at My feet and I will bless you and bring you peace, peace brought forth by relinquishment. Music sings in the life that is relinquished. It sings with abandon. Tremendous things lie ahead. Relinquishment shall bring it forth.

I Love You,
Your Father

Dear Father, I willingly relinquish my life to You, for I can trust You and I know You love me. Music sings in my heart and I know it is given by You! You have always been a faithful and intimate friend. My life belongs to You! I love to tell the stories of all the wonderful things we do together, and all the wonderful ways You bless Your people. Now, it will bring even more joy knowing it is exactly what You want me to do! You are such an intimate loving God. I love You!

Father, it is my delight to share with others what an intimate, loving Father and God You are!

146

"My whole being follows hard after You and clings closely to You;
Your right hand upholds me."

My Child,

Set your eyes on Me and follow My every move by listening closely and maintaining a watchful eye. Clear and safe is the road ahead and peace shall abound as you rest in My love. Gratitude oils the springs that propel you forward and give you wings to fly. Soar, My child, with eagle's wings and rejoice in My loving-kindness. Strain not to see ahead, for I see ahead and it is good. Relax and struggle not. See, I have sustained you thus far. I shall continue to fashion and create beauty in your life and give it purpose and joy. Trust Me to continue to bless you, lead and guide you, and open and close doors of My choosing. You are blessed, My child. Be at home in My arms of love.

Your Loving Father

Father, I am listening closely for your direction.

_____

_____

_____

_____

_____

_____

_____

_____

_____

_____

_____

_____

Father, so often I'm tempted to strain to see ahead, but when I relax in Your arms and stop struggling and keep my eyes on You, I know purpose and joy. Father, once You said to me, "I've created you to fly like the eagle from sea to sea, not to walk on the ground from tree to tree." Soaring with eagle's wings gives freedom and vision, Your vision. Thank You for leading and guiding every detail of my life and opening and closing the doors of Your choosing. I am so blessed and grateful to You, Father.

147

COLOSSIANS 3:10 AMP
"And have clothed yourselves with the new [spiritual self],
which is [ever in the process of being] renewed and remolded into
[fuller and more perfect knowledge upon] knowledge after the image
[the likeness] of Him Who created it."

My Child,

Reflect back and see Me in every circumstance of your life. See, I am doing a new thing in your life to bring forth much fruit and an abundance of love. I have brought you thus far, and as you stretch out your wings to fly once more, I reach out to you with peace, serenity, and faith to complete the transition. Blessed is he that cometh in the Name of the Lord. You are My bouncing ball. It bounces with joy and abandon wherever I take it, inflated by My Spirit of love, without a care, no holding back. My bouncing ball brings life wherever it goes and brings with it the gifts of My Spirit. Now go forth unafraid, knowing I, your Father, care for you.

You Are Blessed,
Your Loving Father

Father, when I reflect back and see You in every circumstance of my life, it brings such joy to my heart. Things that seemed unexplainable before, suddenly take on new meaning and purpose. Transition is not always easy, but with You there with me every step of the way, I look forward to it. But especially, Father, I love being Your bouncing ball. What freedom and what joy!

Father, when I find myself becoming deflated and holding back, I will simply reflect back on the many ways You daily bless and care for me.

_____

_____

_____

_____

_____

_____

_____

_____

_____

_____

_____

148

1 CORINTHIANS 2:9 NKJV
"Eye has not seen, nor ear heard,
nor have entered into the heart of man
the things which God has prepared for those who love Him."

My Child,

I have enlisted you in My army, fully prepared to follow instructions and to move victoriously in My sight. Little have you known of the strategic plans backing you up. Little have you seen of the preparations and minute details prepared and executed on your behalf. But now as you go forth prepared and preserved by My hand of love, you shall execute and establish My Word and My work by My Spirit of love. Go forth unafraid, fully prepared to see, be, and do—three diverse actions brought forth by love.

I Am with You,
Your Faithful Father

Faithful Father, today, instead of getting caught up in the "everydayness" of life, I will turn my thoughts to You with thanksgiving and love, ever listening for Your voice to speak to my heart.

_____

_____

_____

_____

_____

_____

_____

_____

_____

_____

_____

_____

_____

Thank You Father, that You are with me every step of the way. Thank You that I can trust You to take care of the minute details of my life as You have daily prepared and preserved me by Your hand of love. I love You Father!

1 PETER 1:2 AMP

"Who were chosen and foreknown by God the Father,
and consecrated [sanctified, made holy] by the Spirit
to be obedient to Jesus Christ [the Messiah]."

My Child,

I have raised you up to be strong, resilient, and quietly assured of My care over you. I shall say to you, "stand," and you shall stand, "move," and you shall move. I shall strengthen your resolve and straighten your backbone. I shall create you to be a mighty warrior in My army of love. (What about the frustration and resentment, Lord?) Strings from the past, meant to tie you down and incapacitate you. But I say to you, "Tie them into beautiful bows of acceptance, and they cannot trip you up." Cares and worries fade away as one rests in My love.

You Are Strong in Me,

Your Loving Father

Dear Father, I love the way You love. My greatest goal in life is to love as You love. Loving with Your love, nothing is impossible! With Your love there is no frustration and resentment. With Your love, frustration and resentment from the past cannot stick. Once again Father, I lay down the negatives of life and choose instead to love with Your love, with acceptance and forgiveness.

Father, are there areas in my life, that I'm not aware of, that I need to tie into beautiful bows of acceptance and forgiveness?

_____

_____

_____

_____

_____

_____

_____

_____

_____

_____

_____

_____

_____

150

1 SAMUEL 3:9 AMP
"Speak, Lord, for Your servant is listening."

My Beloved Child,

Listen with your whole heart. Lean not to your own understanding, but press in with the strength of My heart within you. Release the weight of the world upon your shoulders. (Lord, all the responsibilities, misunderstandings, inequities, longings, confusions, wranglings, casualties, seeming inabilities, conflicts, and mistakes, I put at Your feet for your absolution, that they be forgotten and forgiven, as far as the East is from the West.) *Now, sit in My Presence and listen to My heart. Care for My weak ones with favor. Rescue them from the fire with love. Pray for their weaknesses. Condemn not, but pray through. Point not the finger back that has been pointed at you. Pray for them healing, and rejoice in the outcome. Minister life and love at all times, and the peace of God shall continue to rest upon your life.*

I Am with You,
Your Loving Father

Dear Father, I want to praise and thank You with great joy for Your faithfulness and care over my life.

_____

_____

_____

_____

_____

_____

_____

_____

_____

_____

Father, thank You for trusting me to love Your treasures, Your people. Thank You, Father, for helping me every step of the way. And Father, thank You for the freedom I feel right now, with that weight gone!

151

ROMANS 12:2 AMP

"Do not be conformed to this world (this age),
[fashioned after and adapted to its external, superficial customs],
but be transformed (changed) by the [entire] renewal of your mind."

My Child,

Facts and figures bombard the mind, but truth comes from the Spirit. Seek My truth. Change amplifies truth and brings it to the foreground. Truth is stifled by tradition and stagnation. See, I have brought you through much change. It has challenged you and stretched you and caused you to grow. Change is the door through which truth enters and is recognized. Change has expanded your world, and brought light and illumination to that world. Your world will continue to change, expand, broaden, and be illuminated by My truth and love. Fear not for the future. It is held securely by My hand of love. I have led you thus far with perfection and care. Would I allow you now to stray beyond My perfect will for you? No, a thousand times, no! Say to your heart, "My God is powerful and capable of changing my heart and plans, and setting my face like a flint in the right direction." I will not fail you.

You Are Loved.

Faithful Father, when I am tempted to worry, I will remember the many times You have changed my heart and plans, and have shown me a better way, to my delight, because You love and care for me. The wonderful thing is that even when I feel challenged and stretched, You highlight my pathway with joy, laughter, and delight. I trust You, Father, to secure Your way for my life and bring me safely to its completion.

Father, thank You for teaching me to love change by…

_____

_____

_____

_____

_____

_____

_____

_____

_____

_____

152

PSALM 4:4 AMP
"Offer just and right sacrifices;
trust (lean on and be confident) in the Lord."

My Child,

Stretched, stretched, you have been; stretched, to bring forth life by My Spirit. You have allowed the stretching to take place that you might be aware of and understand the workings of My Spirit. You have learned straightforwardness, patience, and to have peace in the midst of the storm and forgiveness, faithfulness, perseverance, and diplomacy that you might come forth strong. Straightforward determination has served you well. You will find that you are prepared to do My bidding. In the past I have asked for dogged determination. In the present, you have found that My Word to you has been sacrifice. Now, you'll find the fruit of your labors and it will taste sweet. Be assured that the rewards far outweigh the sacrifice.

You Have Done Well My Child,
Your Loving Father

Loving Father, I want to spend time with You today in Your loving Presence!

_____

_____

_____

_____

_____

_____

_____

_____

_____

_____

_____

Dear Father, knowing You are pleased with me fills my heart with joy! Thank You, that in the stretching, You have always been there, encouraging and cheering me on, through little and big ways, letting me know that I am exactly where You want me to be. You are so faithful!

153

PSALM 25:5 AMP
"Guide me in Your truth and faithfulness and teach me, for You are the God of my salvation: for You [You only and altogether] do I wait [expectantly] all the day long."

My Child,

Stand fast, unwavering, solid on the foundation of truth I have built for you, complete to withstand any and all storms. My faithfulness has and shall continue to sustain you through thick and thin, and the blessings of My heart shall continue to delight you and cause you joy. Fortitude has become a way of life for you, sustained by an inner peace, brought forth by joy. I am making you into a streamliner that can move swiftly and smoothly through life, unhampered by the tricks of the enemy. Love, peace, joy, and wisdom propel the streamliner and keep it moving swiftly and smoothly, constantly moving by My Spirit of truth and freedom, bearing Good News.

I Love You,
Your Father

Loving Father, You truly have been faithful through thick and thin, throughout my life, holding me steady through every storm, teaching me Your truths day by day, loving and protecting me and showing me the way. Gratitude and thankfulness overwhelm me with joy. I love You Father!

Father, what is on Your heart for me today?

_____

_____

_____

_____

_____

_____

_____

_____

_____

_____

_____

_____

_____

_____

154

ROMANS 10:15 AMP
"How beautiful are the feet of those who bring glad tidings!
[How welcome is the coming of those who preach the good news
of His good things!]"

My Child,

Trace your footsteps and see that there is a pattern, a direction, and a plan.
Beautiful are the feet of those who bring Good News to the captives. Stand fast,
My child, for I have not forsaken you, but I am raising you to new heights for
My Glory. Rejoice and be glad and repeat after Me, "My God is an awesome
God! Nothing is too hard for Him. He brings light in the darkness and prepares
a way through the wilderness. Magnificent and beyond comprehension are
His ways."

You Are Complete in Me,
Your Loving Father

Loving Father, which of Your treasures can I share an infusion of Your hope and love with today?

_____

_____

_____

_____

_____

_____

_____

_____

_____

_____

_____

_____

You are awesome, God! Through the most difficult times, You are always there with me, encouraging and leading the way. When the way seems dark, You hold my hand and shine Your light of understanding. When the wilderness seems long and never-ending, You infuse hope and even joy in the most unexpected places. How can I not love You, Father? You mean everything to me!

155

"You have proved my heart; You have visited me in the night;
You have tried me and find nothing (no evil purpose in me);
I have purposed that my mouth shall not transgress."

My Child,

(Lord, where do we go from here?) Straight forward, unhindered by the past. Complete the job set before you with honor and praise. My light will shine before you, leading, guiding and illuminating the dark corners and bringing them to light. Rejoice, for the times of testing have ceased their power over you, and a new day shines brightly before you. Carry not the hindrances of the past into the present and future. Leave them in the past and move on to better, more fruitful days. Sail on, My child! Sail on!

You Are Blessed My Child,
Your Loving Father

Dear Father, You have said that I'm to love each one that You bring to me within the purity of the moment, untouched by the good or bad of the past or the future. That I am simply to love them unconditionally as You would love them. What freedom that brings, to be able to love for the pure joy of loving; free from negatives of the past or expectations for the future. Thank You, Father, for helping me to release the past, day by day, safely, into Your arms of love.

Loving Father, please show me any residue from the past that I am still holding onto

_____

_____

_____

_____

_____

_____

_____

_____

_____

_____

_____

_____

156

DEUTERONOMY 32:3 AMP
"For I will proclaim the name [and presence] of the Lord.
Concede and ascribe greatness to our God."

My Child,

Sing forth and proclaim the Word of the Lord. Let it ring in your heart and it shall be proclaimed from your life. There will be no doubt as to who is your Lord and to whom you owe your allegiance, for the truth of your heart and light shall shine forth from your countenance and shall set the captives free. Fear not for the future, for it is in My hands, secure from false reasoning and misunderstandings. My truth reigns in your life and My love reigns secure over it. So be at peace and let the burdens roll off like the dead weights that they are. Choose to be free of them. Choose to rejoice in the now and be released from unnecessary battles of the mind. Be set free!

Be Free My Child, Be Free!
I Love You!

Father, today I choose to give You my burdens of …

_____

_____

_____

_____

_____

_____

_____

_____

_____

_____

_____

Loving Father, I choose to rejoice in the now, to be at peace, and let the burdens of my life roll off like the dead weights that they are. I choose to be free! When my mind begins to struggle with the "shoulds," "what ifs," and "if onlys" of life, I will choose to rejoice in the now and be released from unnecessary battles of the mind! Thank You Father, that we have that freedom in You!

MATTHEW 6:14 NKJV
"For if you forgive men their trespasses,
your heavenly Father will also forgive you."

My Child,

Circumstances are moments in time. Don't let them control whole segments of time in your thought life. Give others grace, as I give you grace. Stealing from the yesterday (pulling along yesterday's circumstances) wrecks havoc with today. Grace is given for today's circumstances, not yesterday's. Leave yesterday behind and live today, unhindered by yesterday and unencumbered by tomorrow. There is only grace for today and its blessings. That is how you can love each person you come in contact with unreservedly. Leave the past behind and live totally in the present, rejoicing in the blessings and benefits therein. Cancel old debts and mark them paid!

Love As I Love,
You Are My Treasure!

My Father, I love the way You say things so clearly. I want to always remember to leave yesterday behind, and to live today unhindered by yesterday and unencumbered by tomorrow. To remember that there is only grace for today, to live today totally in Your Presence, in Your peace, receiving and giving Your love, giving and receiving Your grace.

Father, are there old debts that I have held onto that I need to cancel and mark paid?

_____

_____

_____

_____

_____

_____

_____

_____

_____

_____

_____

❧ 158 ❧

PROVERBS 3:6 AMP
"In all your ways know, recognize, and acknowledge Him,
and He will direct and make straight and plain your paths."

My Child,

"Eenie, meenie, meinnie moe. Whichever direction should I go? Should I go here? Should I go there? Wherever should I go?" Heed not the multitude of voices that pull you here and pull you there. Their only purpose is to bring confusion. What are the Words spoken by My Spirit? Heed those Words of faith, strength, and direction. Words here and words there, unmarked by My Spirit of truth, tear apart your resolve to stand and be faithful to the commands of your Lord and Savior. Mark these My words well, and then stand with determination to finish the course with distinction.

I Am Directing Your Paths,
Your Loving Father

Father, I bring this area of my life to You for direction and peace …

_____

_____

_____

_____

_____

_____

_____

_____

_____

_____

_____

Father, You have taught me that where Your peace is, there Your Spirit is also. That when the winds of adversity blow, they leave in their wake the seeds of hope and life. But especially, that when the winds blow, I am to simply be at peace and know that You have cleared the way before me. That simply one step at a time is sufficient, as I press forward toward the mark.

159

PSALM 119:30 AMP
"I have chosen the way of truth and faithfulness;
your ordinances have I set before me."

My Child,

Be not afraid of the long haul. The long haul brings with it added distinction and fulfillment of dreams come true. Renew your sails. Take on new provisions for the trip and set sail once more, with new determination to finish the trip to the end with faithfulness and long-suffering, but most of all love, compassion, and the sweet victory of success. There will be time enough for understanding and fulfillment. Now is the time for determined resilience brought forth by praise and righteousness. Ride, freely glide, upon this free flowing ride of life. Progress flows easily within the confines of My love. Pass under bridges, flow through open country. And then as darkness falls, continue to flow unrestricted and unafraid, for I am there. I am your boat. Be not affected by the fears of fellow travelers. You rest in Me. You be at peace and enjoy the ride.

Together Forever,
Your Loving Father

Faithful Father, You have said I'm on the ride of a lifetime, with adventure and blessings untold. There is such beauty and safety riding through life with You. Thank You, Father, for giving me wisdom when I hear the fears of fellow travelers. Help me to calm their fears with the knowledge of Your faithfulness and love.

Father, what are the "new provisions" You need for me to take on for the trip?

_____

_____

_____

_____

_____

_____

_____

_____

_____

_____

160

PSALM 25:14 AMP

"The secret [of the sweet, satisfying companionship] of the Lord
have they who fear [revere and worship] Him, and He will show them
His covenant and reveal to them its [deep, inner] meaning."

My Child,

A Covenant I make with You this day. You have searched for Me and you have found Me. You have made of your heart a resting place for My peace and My joy. Now, I say to you, "I shall go before you to bring you into new realms of My Glory, righteousness, and right standing with Me." Count the long days of leanness as a sacrifice unto Me, for you have remained faithful. Now I shall lengthen your days and bring forth fatness to your spirit, an overflowing to bring forth My will in your life. (It has been a sacrifice of obedience, Lord?) Yes, that I might try and test you to bring forth My best in you. Look not back to the lean years. Look ahead to My Glory. Seek to walk in My Glory. The doors shall open with astounding precision and you shall walk through them jubilantly. Get ready. We shall walk through together, unrestrained. My Spirit shall draw forth from you all that I have promised, for My heart of love has deposited it within you for this day. So rejoice, little one, and know the fulfillment from My heart of love.

My Precious Child,
I Love You

Gracious Father, I want to pour out my love to You today.

_____

_____

_____

_____

_____

_____

_____

_____

Loving Father, my heart sings for the joy of Your companionship and love. It is so wonderful to see lives changed (including mine) with the realization that You created us to be in Covenant and relationship with You. There is no safer place or more blessed place on earth than to be in fellowship and in Covenant with You! Thank You for Your promises and Your precious love!

1 CORINTHIANS 13:4 AMP
"Love endures long and is patient and kind."

My Child,

Settled in your mind's eye are the avenues of defeat and the avenues of victory and life. Victory comes through the speaking forth of the truth of My words in love. When one speaks through love, it brings life. When one speaks through hurt, it brings death. Minister kindness. Minister longsuffering. Minister an abundance of grace. See, My ministering angels bring forth peace where there is no peace, warmth, where there is no warmth, and compassion where it has waned. Forbearance is still a virtue to be pursued.

Love As I Love,
Your Loving Father

Precious Father, many times You have said that one of the great purposes of our lives here on earth is to learn to love as You love, to be a word picture of Your love. Father, all things are possible through You, when we are willing and the desires of our hearts are the desires of Your heart. Father, I am willing and the desire of my heart is to love with Your love and as You love.

Father, today I want to pour out my love on You.

_____

_____

_____

_____

_____

_____

_____

_____

_____

_____

_____

_____

_____

_____

_____

_____

_____

_____

_____

162

1 TIMOTHY 1:5 AMP
"Whereas the object and purpose of our instruction
and charge is love, which springs from a pure heart
and a good (clear) conscience and sincere [unfeigned] faith."

My Child,

Strength, love, and compassion come forth unabated when one rests in the comfort of My hand. Rest assured, My child, that the perils, worries, and concerns shall fall away as you rest in the freedom of My love. Stretched you have been, but the ultimate goal is freedom within My love, not freedom within the love of others. The love and acceptance of others is not the goal. The goal is the freedom of understanding and acceptance of the fullness of My love in your life. How others receive and show love is not your problem. You seek Me, and receive My freshness daily. How they seek, give, and receive is between Me and them. Release, release, release! Shake off others' burdens, restraints, and offenses. They are not yours to bear.

Rest in My Love,
Your Father

Father, today I want to give You my worries and concerns and rest in the comfort of Your loving hand, as I listen to Your heart of love.

Loving Father, thank You for daily helping me to achieve the ultimate goal of freedom within Your love, the freedom of understanding and acceptance of the fullness of Your love in my life. Then I am free to love others unconditionally, with no strings attached. Thank You, Father, for the magnitude of Your love!

163

ISAIAH 2:3 AMP
"That He may teach us His ways
and that we may walk in His paths."

My Precious One,

Stages, it comes in stages, this freedom of heart and soul that is yours to enjoy. You will understand its progression, so that others can follow the same trail with understanding. You have followed, holding tightly to My hand with trust in the finished outcome. We have trod a discernible trail together that others can follow with understanding and joy. My heart rejoices with your heart, for your heart knows full well the joys of trusting and walking with your Father, your Friend. Be blessed this day, dear child of My heart!

Your Loving Father

Loving Father, holding tightly to Your hand with the trust of child has been the joy of my life! Because the journey comes in stages, it always surprises me when I begin sharing my heart with others, the freedom, heart-peace, and trust You have so painstakingly instilled within me through Your faithfulness and love. And then, when I see each one so visibly blessed as I share Your all-encompassing wonderful love, it causes me to be even more grateful to You, my dear Father and Friend.

Precious Father, my heart reaches out to You with such joy and gratefulness!

_____

_____

_____

_____

_____

_____

_____

_____

_____

_____

_____

_____

_____

_____

_____

164

JAMES 1:17 AMP
"Every good gift and every perfect [free, large, full] gift
is from above; it comes down from the Father of all."

My Child,

> *Freedom is a state of grace—grace to be unencumbered by what you see and hear. What does My truth say? My grace is sufficient! What does My love say? You are complete in Me! Ride the winds of adversity with confidence and cheer, and let Me bear the burdens. Yours is to see, and in seeing rejoice, for victory is walking in the freedom of My love.*

> *Be Free in Me!*
> *Your Loving Father*

Father, what burdens am I carrying now that I need to turn over to You?

_____
_____
_____
_____
_____
_____
_____
_____
_____
_____
_____
_____
_____
_____

Loving Father, more and more You are teaching me to see and understand truth, and yet in the seeing, still be at peace and trust You. And yes, even rejoicing in the winds of adversity, for You are teaching me that as I walk through them with confidence, and trust in the finished outcome, there is victory and much growth, as I walk in the freedom of Your love. The hardest lesson has been letting You bear my burdens. I don't realize that I am carrying them until I get so weary from the weight. Thank You Father, for reminding me to let You carry my burdens.

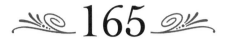
MATTHEW 6:10 AMP
"Your kingdom come, Your will be done
on earth as it is in heaven."

My Child,

Compliance, saying "yes" to My ways, brings life. Saying "yes" to everything, brings death. This you have seen. Throughout history, those who have learned to serve Me well, have learned to say "no." Say "no" to condemnation, manipulation, fear, doubt, and misuse of time. You manage your time. Don't let others manage it for you. Mismanagement is sin, for it eliminates time spent with Me. Many times, saying "yes" to people, is saying "no" to time with me, and saying "yes" becomes idolatry. Say "yes" to time spent with Me. Say "no" to outside pressures. Where is your focus, on Me or on the passing scene? Witness a change in your life as you move from a blanket "yes" to "Thy will be done."

You Are Loved,
Your Father

Dear Father, help me I pray, to more faithfully come to You for wisdom in managing my time. It has always been so much easier for me to say "yes" than to say "no," but I want to say "yes" when You say "yes," and to say "no" when You say "no."

Father, today as I go through the day, I want to be like that small child who asks her Daddy about anything and everything. It's going to be a wonderful day!

166

PSALM 34:17 AMP
"When the righteous cry for help, the Lord hears,
and delivers them out of all their distress and troubles."

My Child,

Service is broken down into four categories:

Service under grace—Learning to abide under the shadow of My wing.

Service to obedience—Learning to hear and obey My voice.

Service to steadfastness—Learning to abide in the face of trial.

Service to the King—Walking in victory. Preparing the way of the Lord!

Have you not seen each step come forth? **(Yes, Lord.)** *Step forth proudly in the service of your King. Years of struggle and service have served to bring forth steadfastness and trust. Does My Word not say, "Many are the trials of the righteous, but the Lord delivers them from them all"? Step forth proudly in the service of your King, and together we shall see victory after victory!*

You Are Blessed,

Your Father

Faithful Father, what else do You want to speak to my heart this day?

_____

_____

_____

_____

_____

_____

_____

_____

_____

_____

_____

Loving Father, I love the way You teach me Your will and Your ways! Nothing is wasted or lost in Your Kingdom. Every season, every struggle, and every trial brings forth victory and gain, walking with You, in Your Kingdom. Thank You, my Father.

167

DEUTERONOMY 4:29 AMP
"But if from there you will seek (inquire for and require as necessity)
the Lord your God, you will find Him if you [truly] seek Him
with all your heart [and mind] and soul and life."

My Child,

Steadfastness is its own reward, for it brings forth a steadiness and reliance upon My faithfulness. Faithfulness never fails. It brings forth the fruit sown. Be faithful to My Word in you. See it through to its completion and fulfillment. March forth, undaunted by the passing scene. My Word shall come forth at its appointed time. Seek only to be immersed in My sea of love and My Presence. Seek to know Me!

Your Faithful Father

My Father, each day is a priceless gift from You, even when hope seems deferred and the way seems dark. Yet every day carries the mark of Your love and treasured moments to make me smile. And then suddenly, out of the blue, comes a wonderful surprise! You let me see the fruit of the seed I've sown, sometimes long ago. Truly, walking with You is a grand adventure!

Loving Father, I long to know You more! Speak to my heart today, I pray.

_____

_____

_____

_____

_____

_____

_____

_____

_____

_____

_____

_____

_____

_____

168

"But without faith it is impossible to please Him,
for he who comes to God must believe that He is,
and that He is a rewarder of those who diligently seek Him."

My Child,

Be a pliable twig in My hands, and I shall mold you into an arrow that shall always find it's mark. Relax in My Presence and feel confidence in My love. Traumas shall come and go, but My love shall sustain you in all areas of your life. Complaining prolongs the agony. Complain and strain. Love and draw peace from above. Make melody in your heart and you will always have a brand new start. Nothing will be able to draw you apart from My absolute authority and stability in your life. Confusion reigns when doubt becomes unrestrained. Believe My Word! Singleness of heart—focus your mind and heart on Me!

Be Confident in Me,
Your Loving Father

Father, what are the areas in my life that I have become rigid in, instead of being pliable?

_____

_____

_____

_____

_____

_____

_____

_____

_____

_____

_____

Loving Father, many times You have so lovingly told me to simply rest in Your arms of love, knowing that Your will for me is vouchsafed from the foundation of the world. To simply let the sands of time pour forth in their time, unhindered. That each sand would bring forth the required results as I walked step by step, holding Your hand, trusting You, undaunted and unafraid. This is how I choose to live, so that You can mold me into an arrow that shall always find it's mark! I love You, Father!

1 JOHN 1:3 TLB

"We are telling you about what we ourselves have actually seen
and heard, so that you may share the fellowship and the joys we have
with the Father, and with Jesus Christ His Son."

My Child,

Continue on with confidence and a willingness to accept where others have rejected. Extend the hand of fellowship, not holding accounts of wrongs or slights. Withholding is harder than giving, for My Spirit within you reaches out with love. Seeming slights shall fade away and peace and calm shall return. Reach out! Reach out to that one in need and say, "My Lord will provide for you. He has not forsaken you nor abandoned you in your hour of need," for My angels shall watch over that one in need and bring him through to the other side. Many are the trials of this life, but My love transcends all trials. Let them know of My love for them! Let them know!

Love As I Love,

Your Father

Dearest Father, there is no greater joy on earth than to look into the eyes of someone I love, or someone I've just met, and speak Your words of love and encouragement, and immediately seeing You come through for them. You have said, "The sky is the limit, My heart to impart, into the creases and crevices of each aching heart. You will find that as you speak My words of love, that those words have been anointed by My Spirit of love. Speak forth with clarity and truth. Speak forth, that I might speak forth through you." What joy, when I speak, to watch You bless Your treasures!

Loving Father, I want to pour out my words of love on You today.

_____

_____

_____

_____

_____

_____

_____

_____

_____

_____

_____

_____

_____

_____

170

"Be assured and understand that the trial and proving of your faith
bring out endurance and steadfastness and patience."

My Child,

Trials lie ahead, but they shall be fashioned by My hand. So fear not, but rejoice in the God of your salvation, and let this faith be in you that overcomes the world. Safe and secure you shall be as you seek My face and speak forth My words to set the captives free. Surefooted strength is My gift to you, brought forth from the furnace of affliction. Faith and circumstances work together to create wholeness and a disciplined life complete in everything. The scales of the eyes shall fall away, and the truth of My Word shall ring forth, and bring forth victory and freedom. Look for My Word to come to fulfillment and look for My love to conquer all. Sound judgment and fierce loyalty shall be My gift to you.

You Are Protected by My Love,
Your Father

Loving Father, how would You have me grow today?

_____

_____

_____

_____

_____

_____

_____

_____

_____

_____

Father, You have said that You would mold, shape, and form me from the inside out, as I conform to Your Spirit and not to the passing scene. That as I stand convinced of Your power to change, to mold, and to shape my life, I will see miracles come forth in my life and in the lives of others. Day by day, Father, I am joyously seeing Your promises fulfilled! I am so grateful!

171

"Where there is no vision [no redemptive revelation of God],
the people perish."

My Precious Child,

Stand back and watch Me work. Watch the canvas take shape and form with color and vibrancy. The pieces of the puzzle are coming together to make a beautiful picture for others to gaze upon and see the beauty of God. Short-term blessings bring about long-term blessings and victories. Cultivate vision. (How do I do that, Lord?) By seeing what I show you and implementing it into the big picture. Vision brings structure and structure brings strength. See, and in seeing, believe!

See As I See! I Love You,

Your Father

Loving Father, long ago, You said, "You are as stained-glass, beautiful pieces of glass, created by pressure and heat, soldered together by My love, and held together by My faithfulness and love. The Master Craftsman creates tirelessly and lovingly to create a masterpiece of beauty that shall last forever, a joy to the eyes and the senses, enhanced by many beautiful and vibrant colors, proclaiming a statement of My perfection, faithfulness, and love for My creation. Wrestle not with the creative process. Know that I shall complete what I have begun with perfection, and you shall be delighted and rejoice, as a favored child is overwhelmed with delight and gleeful joy, because of the gifts given by a doting father."

Faithful Father, Your love overwhelms me with joy. My heart sings to You with love!

172

PSALM 25:10 AMP
"All the paths of the Lord are mercy and steadfast love,
even truth and faithfulness are they for those who keep
His covenant and His testimonies."

I Love You My Child,

It shall be clear to you the path that you shall take, and the way will be bathed in light so that you shall not miss it, nor be distracted nor sidetracked. The vision is strong and shall remain strong unto its fulfillment. Worry not nor be distraught, but know that what I have planned for you shall be, and you shall rejoice and be glad. Carry on with a song in your heart and determination to finish the way with honor. My blessings go with you, My child. The refreshing of mind, body, soul, and spirit shall come and buoy you up. Press onward! Press onward!

There Is Much to Learn!
Press Onward!

Faithful Father, speak to my heart, for I am listening!

_____

_____

_____

_____

_____

_____

_____

_____

_____

_____

_____

_____

Loving Father, when I think I cannot take another step, You overwhelm me with Your Presence and Your joy. Then suddenly, I have the strength to go on. When I become discouraged and weary, You speak to one of Your treasures, and they reach out to me with encouragement and love. You take such good care of me, Father!

JOHN 14:27 NKJV

"Let not your heart be troubled, neither let it be afraid."

My Child,

Many times, I have said unto you, "Let not your heart be troubled." Listen once again to the strains of the Word, "Let not your heart be troubled." Let your heart rest within the confines of My love, listening not to outside babblings, but hearing and seeing My Word and relying on My truth. Contend not with conflicting reports, but stand firm in My love and let Me make the moves, content to watch and wait. Resist not the tides as they ebb and flow, but know that the ebb and flow shall form boundaries of beauty. Stand in My love. Release all unto Me and rejoice. Let not your heart be troubled!

I Love You,

Your Father

Precious Father, You have said to see You in everything, from the beauty of the simple, to the most complex. To register all You bring my way, and weigh it in the balance of Your love. To always respond within the guidelines of Your Word to me. To be refreshed and respond with the freshness of Your Holy Spirit. To stand in Your love and fear not, for the results are sure!

Dear Father, thank You for filling me with Your peace, as I spend time in Your Presence today, enjoying intimate conversation with You!

174

ISAIAH 68:11 AMP
"And the Lord shall guide you continually."

My Child,

I will lead you into experiences that will have no road map made by others' lives, so don't seek for the security of a road map. Learn to love and enjoy the beauty of the jagged crag, the beauty of unexplored territory. You shall need My guidance for each step. Others shall follow to make it a well-marked trail, deeply imprinted across the wilderness. You shall be among this new breed of trailblazers, but a trailblazer must be disciplined. Accept the mantle of obedience. Let go of your own desires and inner cravings. Surefootedness is brought about through sustained patience. Surefooted you shall be. Let it not be said that you had not the fortitude to persevere, for persevere you shall, and we shall see it through to the very end.

I Am with You, My Child!
Your Loving Father

Dear Father, I come to You today for guidance and wisdom.

_____

_____

_____

_____

_____

_____

_____

_____

_____

_____

_____

_____

Precious Father, after all these years, I still find myself seeking the security of a road map, by looking to others to bring me comfort and guidance, instead of You! Forgive me, Father! Thank You for Your sustained faith in me, that I shall learn to love and enjoy the beauty of the jagged crag and unexplored territory, but most of all, knowing that I shall persevere and that we shall see it through together, to the very end.

PSALM 91:1 NKJV
"He who dwells in the secret place of the Most High
shall abide under the shadow of the Almighty."

My Child,

Seek and you shall find. Knock, and the door shall be opened to you. Abide under the shadow of My wing. Patience has caused My Spirit to flourish within you. The ballast has been cut and you shall begin to rise to be carried along by My Spirit. I have charted a course by which you shall travel. The scenery shall be breathtakingly beautiful, and you shall partake of the miraculous along the way. Maintain your balance by constant prayer. See, it shall become a way of life and together we shall see the pieces of the puzzle come together as a beautiful picture.

You Are Blessed My Child!
Your Loving Father

Loving Father, even with all the ups and downs of each day, still walking with You, there is such beauty within each day! Father, when I forget to pray and put my focus on the passing scene, as beautiful as it may be, draw me back, that prayer might truly be a way of life for me! Thank You, Father!

Dear Father, how would You have me pray today?

_____

_____

_____

_____

_____

_____

_____

_____

_____

_____

_____

_____

_____

_____

_____

176

DEUTERONOMY 32:3 NLT
"I will proclaim the name of the LORD;
how glorious is our God!"

My Precious One,

Rise up My Singing Bride! Come fly with Me! Release your heart from all that would tie it down and come fly with Me! Proclaim My goodness and My love to a dying world! Come fly with Me, My precious one, and together we shall see mountains moved and hearts set free! Upon the canvas of your heart, I proclaim a brand new start. Free to sing and fly and be, unencumbered by the tricks of the enemy, for it's My heart of love you see. Go forth today, confident in every way that I, your Lord and King, have answers for everything. Your way secure as we proceed, as each day you "Fly with Me"!

Sing and Be Free!

Your Loving Father

Father, today I will sing and "Fly with You" with all my heart!

_____

_____

_____

_____

_____

_____

_____

_____

_____

_____

_____

_____

Precious Father, I know there is a place in Your heart that You've reserved for each one of us, where we can simply fly with You each day, with freedom and confidence in Your love. What joy to know that is the place where together, we can see mountains moved and hearts set free! Thank You, Father, that day by day I am learning to "Fly with You"! What joy and what freedom! Thank You for lovingly reminding me to release my heart once again from all that would tie it down, to come "Fly with You"!

177

PSALM 7:1 AMP
"O LORD my God, in You I take refuge
and put my trust."

Dear Child of My Heart,

My peace is beginning to descend as never before because you are learning that it is not about you, but about My ability to come through and bless you in all that you do. You are learning to just be free from all that pulls and drags down. Be confident, be secure. It's not a time to just endure. It is a time to grow and thrive, and really feel alive in My Presence. Enjoy every moment of every day, as you learn to just be and to play!

You Are Loved,

Your Father

Dear Father, how wonderful to know that it's important to You that we not only be lavish worshipers and love God and one another, but that it's important that we know how to have fun together also. Most of us are still so intent on living life with purpose, that we've forgotten how to "play." Thank You, Father, for once again teaching me and my friends how to play and have fun. But the most wonderful part is that You are right there with us, enjoying it as much as we are, and cheering us on.

Precious Father, I love Your Presence! Speak to my heart today, I pray, as I work, sing, laugh, and play!

_____

_____

_____

_____

_____

_____

_____

_____

_____

_____

_____

_____

_____

_____

_____

_____

_____

178

EPHESIANS 4:23 AMP
"And be constantly renewed in the spirit of your mind
[having a fresh mental and spiritual attitude]."

My Precious Child,

There is a freshness in your life that has blown in on the breezes of My love. It is a freshness that shall remain. Restored, refreshed, renewed—this has been My promise to you, and now it is the present reality. Enjoy its ever-present blessing to you. It brings with it a childlike freedom and grace as never before. Enjoy the laughter and fun that comes with it. It will cause My love to be poured from you as never before. It will cause the doors to open. Relish the freedom of this day.

Your Loving Father

Father, let's just laugh a lot together today, and draw as many into our laughter and fun as possible! What else is on Your agenda for me today?

_____

_____

_____

_____

_____

_____

_____

_____

_____

_____

_____

_____

_____

Precious Father, I have never laughed so much in my life, and it is so healing and life-giving! No wonder Your Word says, "The joy of the Lord is our strength"! For truly laughter brings strength where there is no strength, causing joy to be an ever-present blessing, with childlike freedom and grace as never before. But best of all, Father, it just makes life fun, even when circumstances would proclaim the opposite. I love You so much!

179

ISAIAH 35:1 AMP
"The wilderness and the dry land shall be glad;
the desert shall rejoice and blossom like the rose."

My Child,

Flourish and bloom. Take each day as it comes, with joy of heart. Each day is a gift to you from My heart. Patience has led the way, as each day you have come to Me for direction and leading. Sufficient is each day to the need. You have delighted in the simple pleasures of life, as each test and trial has brought you closer to the safety of My heart, will, and ways for you. Turning turmoil into peace brings the release into a realm unknown to many. Walk in that realm every day by releasing the turmoil to Me and letting peace descend, counting on Me to bring the answers. Silence the spirit of anxiety with the spirit of peace and joy. Proceed this day with a light heart, My child.

I Love You,

Your Father

Dear Father, through years and years of being in the desert and wilderness, You have, through your love and grace, caused to me to flourish and bloom. You have loved and protected me on the backside of the wilderness and in the hustle and bustle of life. Thank You, Father, for teaching me day by day to silence the spirit of anxiety with the spirit of peace and joy. Thank You for giving answers along the way and giving me a light heart in the midst of traumas and trials. But most of all, loving Father, thank You that these wonderful gifts are available for all of Your children!

Loving Father, let me share Your wonderful love today with one of Your treasures. But first, I want to pour out my love on You!

_____

_____

_____

_____

_____

_____

_____

_____

_____

_____

_____

_____

180

PSALM 149:4 AMP
"For the Lord takes pleasure in his people."

My Child,

It is just the beginning. The Heavens declare My Glory, and so shall your life. Enjoy this time of rest and pleasure with Me. It is a time to hear, see, and be. Be My friend and the joy of that friendship will open the door to everything else. Tailor-made for you is each day, complete in every way. Draw to your heart My love and peace each day, that the static be released, that you might hear clearly as you move forward, moment by moment. Tactics of the enemy are then diverted that each day might proclaim "Mission Accomplished." Go forth today with confidence and joy in the finished work of My heart and love in your life.

I Take Pleasure in You, My Child,
Your Loving Father

Loving Father, I want to pour out my heart to You, with such joy and gladness!

_____

_____

_____

_____

_____

_____

_____

_____

_____

_____

_____

_____

I take such pleasure in You, too, Father! Such miracles abound with the sound of Your voice. Long ago, You said, "Break forth in singing this day, filling the air with your joy! Fill your home with My Glory by speaking out My words with joy, gladness, power, and truth. Pour forth that which is in your heart and has been welled up. Pour forth and I will fill it up again!" As I listen to Your voice each day and fill my home with Your Glory, at the end of the day, I can truly say, "Mission Accomplished"!

181

PSALM 103:5 AMP
"Your youth, renewed, is like the eagle's
[strong, overcoming, soaring]!"

My Child,

Youthfulness is a state of being. Love, laughter, joy, and freedom keep one young. Total joy comes at a price—the price of relinquishment of the past and all its sorrows and unfulfilled dreams. Let it all go and you will find new-found joy and peace of mind, and the ability to powerfully speak My mind, that others too might relinquish their past so that their new-found joy can also last and last. Time and time again you've looked to Me to set you free from all negativity. This you've done to the best of your ability. But now, My precious one, dear child of My heart, you'll find that you have been set free, complete with a new sensitivity and creativity.

You Are Free!

Your Loving Father

Father, masterfully You have designed my life. Here a little, there a little, to make the picture full and complete. Relinquishment of the past and all its sorrows and dreams unfulfilled has been one of the hardest lessons along the way. Every time we have come to a crossroads and You have given me the choice to relinquish, and I made the right choice, You lovingly let me know that I passed the test and have won. Thank You, Father, for caring about every detail of my life!

Thank You, dear Father, for the precious gifts of love, laughter, joy, and freedom. How can I bless You today?

_____

_____

_____

_____

_____

_____

_____

_____

_____

_____

_____

182

ISAIAH 62:5 KJV
"And as the bridegroom rejoiceth over the bride,
so shall thy God rejoice over thee."

My Precious One,

You are a bridge builder to bring hope to My people. You are building a bridge from hopelessness to hope, a bridge from mediocrity to destiny, a bridge from sadness to joy, a bridge from loneliness to love, a bridge from fear to faith, a bridge from distrust and isolation to trust. Faithfully experiencing the trials of life builds bridges to others that they too might live in faithful victory. Faithfulness, hope, trust, love, honor, joy, and faith are the victorious foundations of bridges to bring victory to others. But bridge builders must rest and regroup. Fear not to rest and be at peace. Liken this time to a soldier taking R&R. It is your time. Live it to its fullest, as you do all other endeavors, and be blessed in this time set aside for you, my precious Bride!

I Love You!

Your Father

Father, thank You for this time of rest. What better place to rest than in Your Presence, listening to Your heart!

_____

_____

_____

_____

_____

_____

_____

_____

_____

_____

Dear Father, thank You for letting me be a bridge builder to Your treasures, Your people! I will need Your help to take full advantage of this time, to truly rest and not waste the time You've given on needless activities. I want to come out of this time refreshed, restored and ready for anything, led by Your heart. Help me to always start each day with You, that I would not be sidetracked by seemingly good things. Give me discernment, I pray.

183

PHILIPPIANS 4:19 AMP

"And my God will liberally supply [fill to the full]
your every need according to His riches in glory
in Christ Jesus."

My Child,

*Stand still and know that I Am God. I will be glorified in your life. Many times
I have cupped you in My hands and held you to My heart. That is where you
are now. Rest and let Me restore you to begin anew. Prizes go to My faithful
ones. But for now, let Me fill your heart with gladness. Let Me fill your heart
with song. Let Me make your life worth living. Let Me fill your heart with joy
all the day long. It's a time to enjoy My peace and My Presence. It's a time to
sing and dance. Release your cares and worries and you shall truly know fulfillment at last. Relinquish all that has held you captive to earthly cares and promises yet unfulfilled. Count the ways that I love you. Simply enjoy each day by
My hand of blessing. Rest now and be at peace, my little one.*

You Are Loved!

Your Father

I get my comfort and love from You, Father. Thank You for always being there for me. There is no place I'd rather be than cupped in Your hands and held to Your heart. I love You, Father!

Loving Father, let me count the ways You love me!

_____
_____
_____
_____
_____
_____
_____
_____
_____
_____
_____
_____

PSALM 23:4 NKJV
Yea, though I walk through the valley of the shadow of death,
I will fear no evil; For You are with me;
Your rod and Your staff, they comfort me."

My Child,

Leave the hurt behind like old clothes that do not fit. Size up the situation, forgive, and go on. Reach into My heart and grasp My kind of love. Earnestly remember, My love is your highest calling. You are beginning to grasp the essence of it all, love given for its own sake, not for its return. To give that sort of love you must be secure in My love. Continue to follow it through. The rewards are great. Stand secure in My love and watch the mountains fall. Continue to nibble the fragrant grasses in the valley of the shadow of death, for I am with you. My rod and My staff are guiding you, and you shall live in the House of the Lord, forevermore.

Love As I Love,
Your Father

Dear Father, are there areas of hurt and unforgiveness that I have let creep into my heart?

_____

_____

_____

_____

_____

_____

_____

_____

_____

Loving Father, You have blessed my life beyond measure. I never want to forget that Your love is my highest calling! Thank You for helping me to grasp the essence of it all—love given for its own sake, with no expectations, because I am secure in Your love. Thank You, Father, for Your faithful and all encompassing love!

185

PSALM 51:12 AMP
"Restore to me the joy of Your salvation
and uphold to me with a willing spirit."

My Child,

Stand clear, stand out of the way, and watch My hand of blessing fall upon you and the torrent of blessing shall flow, as down through a valley, unabated. Stand aside and watch it flow and bring refreshing, newness, and life. Restored, restored you shall be, free to receive from Me all that you have believed and watched for. The gifts are in the residue of the flood. Resist the temptation to reach ahead too soon. Let Me bring to you people, places, and things to establish your way. All shall be in order and solidly placed. Watch in anticipation and blessed assurance.

You Are Blessed!
Your Loving Father

Dear Father, what investment You put in each of our lives! Every moment of every day has purpose and meaning! What a journey it has been, and what a journey it is yet to be. Thank You, Father, that there is restoration, newness, life, refreshing, freedom, and blessings ahead! I look to each day led by You, with anticipation and joy!

Father, help me always to step out in Your timing, with Your discernment! Speak to my heart, I pray!

_____

_____

_____

_____

_____

_____

_____

_____

_____

_____

_____

_____

186

PHILIPPIANS 4:1 AMP
"Stand firm in the Lord, my beloved."

My Child,

The House of the Spirit is built on a strong foundation of truth and established in the fire of adversity. Marginal areas line up and become established as the fire burns away the dross. Ultimately, what stands is pure gold. Hesitate not to withstand, through patience, the fire and oppressive winds that blow. But see through it all, My strong hands of love, holding you steady and providing the leadership you need to help you prevail and continue forward. Strong and mighty winds have blown, but the outcome is sure. The strength obtained is immeasurable. Stand strong, My child.

Be Strong in Me, My Child!
Your Loving Father

Wonderful Father, I just want to bask in Your love today and tell you how much I love You!

_____

_____

_____

_____

_____

_____

_____

_____

_____

_____

_____

_____

_____

Loving Father, no wonder You've always said that patience is such an important part of the foundation upon which I stand. Thank You for aligning the marginal areas in my life, burning away the dross, and making me strong! Through it all, You've held me steady and secure. It's wonderful to know that ultimately what stands is pure gold!

PHILIPPIANS 3:8 NLT
"Yes, everything else is worthless
when compared with the priceless gain
of knowing Christ Jesus, my Lord."

My Precious One,

The depths of the soul are tilled through deeper fellowship with Me. To know Me, one must stay in constant, not sporadic, fellowship with Me. Contained within the human heart is the ability to know Me and walk in constant fellowship, but few do. Constant awareness is the key. It opens the door to communion, sweet communion, with your Maker and Friend. See, the door is wide open. Walk and talk with Me and discover vistas unknown to you through precious fellowship with Me. The door is open. Walk through!

Know Me, My Child!

I Love You!

Precious and Loving Father, I want to know You more! I want to walk and talk with You continually! Help me, I pray, to not only listen to Your heart towards me each day, moment by moment, but to share my thoughts, emotions, hopes and dreams, desires, disappointments, and victories with You! Thank You Father, that the door is open! I'm walking through!!!

Loving Father, I'm walking through that door, to have a lifelong conversation with You, starting now!

_____

_____

_____

_____

_____

_____

_____

_____

_____

_____

_____

_____

_____

_____

188

PSALM 91:14-15 AMP

"Because he has set his love upon Me, therefore will I deliver him; I will set him on high, because he knows and understands My name....
He shall call upon Me, and I will answer him:
I will be with him in trouble; I will deliver him, and honor him."

My Child,

Sanctification is a painful struggle, but it brings forth fruit immeasurable. Let the peace of God reign in your heart this day. Let heart peace invade your soul and show you the way to contentment. Contentment in whatever circumstances is great gain. Be enmeshed in My love and removed from the noise and confusion of the rocket's great blare around you. Seeking to know Me is the excellent way. Continue on in your quest and know that I will be there to answer your request. The heavens resound with joy at the strengthening of one who seeks. Go forth unencumbered by doubt. Raise your voice in praise and be assured of this very thing, My love will carry you through.

Your Loving Father

Father, these are the areas that I have been anxious about and I now turn them over to You, so that I can go forth unencumbered by doubt!

_____

_____

_____

_____

_____

_____

_____

_____

_____

_____

Dearest Father, in the hardest of circumstances, Your love has carried me through. How could I doubt, when you have been so faithful to me, and yet, it is a day by day decision to come into Your rest and peace. Father, I want heart peace to invade my soul so much that I will walk in contentment in whatever circumstances I find myself. Thank You, Father, that day by day, You strengthen my resolve!

2 Thessalonians 3:3 AMP
"Yet the Lord is faithful, and He will strengthen [you]
and set you on a firm foundation
and guard you from the evil [one]."

Dear One,

Lessons learned have a lasting quality about them that redeem other areas of life and bring refreshment and stability. You are My child in whom I am well pleased. Place not your confidence in people, places, and things, but place your confidence in My ability to come forth in you and to handle all circumstances, to bring victory and My way for you. You've believed in the past. Believe now. Take counsel, but bring it to Me before you act on it.

Your Faithful Father

Loving Father, You have said, "Nothing is impossible to Me. Limit not My blessings to you. Steadfastness is all I ask from My children. The fulcrum of My love is trust and steadfastness. There are points of interest along the way, but let your heart rest in the fulcrum of My love for you, content and free, for I bring contentment, fulfillment, completeness, and freedom to My blessed children." Thank You Father, for Your blessed counsel and Your love!

Father, today I want to bring these issues to You for Your loving counsel and wisdom.

_____
_____
_____
_____
_____
_____
_____
_____
_____
_____
_____
_____
_____
_____
_____

190

ACTS 17:28 AMP
"For in Him we live and move and have our being."

My Child,

Stand fast, firmly planted in the sound Word of righteousness, impressed upon your heart by the Spirit of God, steadfast in the knowledge of My love and faithfulness. Let not up your stance of faith and sound doctrine. The true test of servanthood is the ability and desire to survive, that one might live to serve again in a greater capacity and magnitude, not tainted by the past, but free to move ahead unencumbered by the past. Step forth into the future, free to move and live and have your being in the strength, purity, and freedom of My love, secure in the knowledge of who I have created you to be. Now unto Him who has provided all that you need, be Glory forever!

Walk in the Freedom of My Love!
Your Father

Father, help me to see others through Your eyes and through Your heart. Show me those that I have only seen through my limited vision.

_____

_____

_____

_____

_____

_____

_____

_____

_____

_____

_____

Thank You, Father, for letting me see day by day, through Your eyes, who You have created me to be and the purpose for which You have created me. Thank You for giving me a sense of destiny and a strong desire to fulfill that destiny! Only You can bring it forth, but You have provided all I will need to succeed.

PSALM 118:14 AMP
"The Lord is my Strength and Song;
and He has become my Salvation."

My Child,

My strength I have put within you. Think not that you are weak, for strength of character and purpose have spurred you on with singleness of heart and mind to bring forth those things that have been placed in your heart by My Spirit of love and grace. Continue on, unruffled by outside circumstances, confident in the outcome and serenely confident in My love and the fulfillment that I am bringing forth. Continue to stand fast in the firm and sustaining power of My plan for you.

Be Confident in My Love,
Your Loving Father

Dear Father, long ago, You said, "Hold on to your dream. Be patient and hold steady. Set your mind on things on high and let Me work out the things below. Set your course by My standards. Do not be afraid to move against the tide. That is when the greatest growth appears. Set your course by My beacon light and follow on to victory!" And Father, You have never failed me!

Loving Father, what is Your dream for my life? How can I better cooperate with You to bring that dream forth, to the delight of us both?

_____

_____

_____

_____

_____

_____

_____

_____

_____

_____

_____

_____

192

PSALM 30:2 AMP
"O Lord my God, I cried to You and You have healed me."

My Child,

Seeds of righteousness sprout and grow in the incubator of struggle. They bring forth the fruit of strength, fortitude, and the impenetrable power to stand in the face of evil, allowing God's victory to prevail. You have stood. You have prevailed. You have remained steady in the face of apparent destruction. But know this, My child, the tide of the enemy shall not prevail, for I have placed My anointing upon you and My cloak of righteousness around you. My angels protect you and you shall yet see the fulfillment of all I have put before you. See, My child, the night does become day and all that has brought agony and pain shall be brushed away, and the dawning of the new day shall bring joy to your heart. So, rise and be healed, to the Glory of God your Father, and the light of My countenance shall shine about you and bring you peace!

I Have Sustained You,
Your Loving Father

Father, what areas of my life am I not aware of that need healing?

_____

_____

_____

_____

_____

_____

_____

_____

_____

_____

_____

_____

Dear Father, You have said, "I go before you in all matters. I make the crooked straight. Do not become despondent or impatient. Rely on My perfect timing and do not despair or wonder. What I have begun I will complete. Rest in the light, joy, and radiance of My smile." How can I not trust You Father, for You have proved Yourself so faithful in my life! Thank You Father, for bringing healing to every area of my life!

193

"I will bless the Lord, Who has given me counsel;
yes, my heart instructs me in the night seasons."

My Child,

The steps of a righteous man are ordered by the Lord, that his life might shine forth the radiance of God. Light and darkness are alike to Me. I work in both and bring forth My attributes in the midst of trials and in the sunniest of days. Fear not the times of pain, but stand strong in My Presence, redeeming the time with joy and anticipation drawn forth from your hope in Me. You shall see results far beyond your ability to see and expect, for I have placed within you patience and hope which shall not be blotted out, but shall come forth in victory and song. Remain in My love and prevail.

I Am Always with You,
Your Loving Father

Loving Father, when we began this journey together You said, "By giving you the vision of how I see you through My Word, line by line and precept by precept, you are becoming as I see you. Stick with it. The joy is in becoming that person, by becoming more and more in My image. It will be real joy and in no way counterfeit. Patience!" Father, You have been faithful to Your Word! Thank You for Your promises and the fulfillment of those promises!

My Father, what is on Your heart for me today?

_____

_____

_____

_____

_____

_____

_____

_____

_____

_____

_____

_____

_____

_____

194

PSALM 34:8 AMP
"O taste and see that the Lord [our God] is good!
Blessed [happy, fortunate, to be envied]
is the man who trusts and takes refuge in Him."

My Precious Child,

It is a new day being formed from the dust of shattered lives, bringing forth the promises that I have spoken to them for years. They have seen My hand of mercy upon them and yet have languished on the sidelines for lack of nourishing. Be not afraid to speak forth, for I shall lead you and let you know how, where, and when. All you have experienced shall become the platform upon which you stand, for you have experienced fully the pain and agony so well known to many who need a touch from Me. You can empathize with your heart and yet, unwaveringly, lead them straight to Me to be rescued and saved. Struggle not with the details, but leave them to Me. It will come about naturally and be a joy to your heart. Proclaim My goodness and steadfastness and together we shall see people's lives changed to love, peace, prosperity, and joy.

Your Loving Father

Loving Father, I place my life in Your hands and say "yes" to Your plans for my life!

_____

_____

_____

_____

_____

_____

_____

_____

Father, You have put such a love in my heart for Your people. Thank You for letting me be part of the solution and not part of the problem. Thank You Father, for teaching me patience and love through the trials of my own life so that I can empathize and yet proclaim Your goodness and steadfastness! I love You, Father!

195

MATTHEW 7:1 AMP
"Do not judge and criticize and condemn others,
so that you may not be judged
and criticized and condemned yourselves."

My Child,

You are like an F.B.I. Agent! I give you a job to do, and though you don't always know what came before or what follows, you simply carry out your task and leave the rest completely in My care. You must be able to dispatch a job and then completely release all back to Me, without retaining any residue of the burden. Small residues build up into a heavy load; so unload completely after each job. Resist the temptation to judge. That is My job. Where there is joy and peace, there is no room for a wrong spirit. Break forth this day with a bright spirit. Rejoice and sing like a bird, for the bird sings with joy for the new day, and the freedom that new day promises.

I Love You,
Your Father

Thank You, loving Father, for letting me be a part of Your wonderful plan. When I'm tempted to hold on to burdens, thank You for helping me to release them. What I'm tempted to judge, thank You for showing me a better way. Thank You, Father, for making Your ways, my ways!

Dear Father, forgive me for criticizing and judging Your treasures. Help me to see each one as you see them.

_____

_____

_____

_____

_____

_____

_____

_____

_____

_____

_____

_____

_____

_____

196

PSALM 119:18 NKJV
"Open my eyes, that I may see."

My Child,

Have you not seen this day the difference between an open spirit and one that is closed to My Spirit? The open spirit absorbs like a sponge without fear and apprehension. The closed spirit responds with a closed mind and fear or else simply arrogance. The closed spirit has two earmarks: passive assurance and arrogance. Narrow is the way, but by strict adherence to My Word and persistence in listening to My voice, the path is passable. My hand is over you, My child, like an umbrella. Stray not from underneath it through doubt and unbelief. My righteousness will prevail in your life as long as you do not doubt. It is when you doubt that you try to grab hold of your own righteousness again, through insecurity and fear. Those who believe at all times do not experience insecurity and fear, for these things are not of Me.

Listen Closely My Child,

Your Loving Father

Father, which truths would You like for me to ponder, delight in, and digest further today?

_____
_____
_____
_____
_____
_____
_____
_____
_____
_____
_____

Loving Father, thank You for giving me ears to hear and eyes to see Your mighty and glorious truths. There is such joy in pondering them, delighting in them, and digesting them further. You have said, "My sheep shall hear My voice. They shall hear and rejoice. They shall no longer walk in darkness. They shall see the light and make their way toward that light. They shall move out with confidence, knowing their Lord is going before them, making straight the path."

PSALM 108:1 AMP
"O GOD, my heart is fixed (steadfast, in the confidence of faith);
I will sing, yes, I will sing praises."

My Child,

Appearing and being are two separate things. Be what you appear. Be not afraid to be what I have created you to be. Compromise is not necessary to appear to be as others. Stand your ground and appear to be as you are. Only truth is stable and a foundation to build on. All else flops in the wind and leaves others uneasy, including yourself. I have seen your plight and have calmed the raging waves, and brought to you the ability to stand in the midst of trial. I have paved your way with My Spirit of Praise. Take full advantage of this precious gift by calling it into being at every opportunity, for it brings with it the gift of prosperity and achievement, opening the door to victory. Shun all forms of corruptive speech (complaining and criticizing), for it is the opposite of praise. In this way, you will continue to see change in victory.

I Sing over You with Joy!
Your Loving Father

Dear Father, when I greet the day with joy in who You have created me to be, with a song in my heart and a smile on my face, Your Presence is so near and dear to me and all is right with the world. Help me Father, I pray, to start each day and carry it through in such a wonderful way.

Father, how can I do better in standing true to who You have called me to be and what You have called me to do?

_____

_____

_____

_____

_____

_____

_____

_____

_____

_____

_____

1 Peter 4:8 AMP
"Above all things have intense and unfailing love for one another,
for love covers a multitude of sins
[forgives and disregards the offenses of others]."

My Child,

Look not back to the past but stand resolved and at peace in the present, released from the struggles and trials of the past. Relax and enjoy the view. The stillness will give way to raucous times of endeavor, but I am with you in the stillness and I am with you in the noise. I will bless you in the stillness and I will bless you in the times of activity. It is a time of forgiveness and the laying down of strife to bring forth a new day of peace. Many will not lay down the strife and remain where they are, locked in time and space. Go forward without malice or fear, knowing that I have calmed the waters and brought forth peace. Accept each one for what they can give and go on. Do not demand that they realize what they have done. Simply accept and go on. I know each and every detail. I know and see, and that is all that is necessary. Loosed to be a blessing; you are loosed to be a blessing, lifted above the mire and ready to soar!

You Are Blessed My Child,
Your Loving Father

Loving Father, are there struggles and trials from the past that I still haven't let go of?

_____

_____

_____

_____

_____

_____

_____

_____

_____

Father, there is such freedom in loving Your way! With Your way there is no keeping an account of wrongs. There is no demanding that others realize what they have done. For You know, and that is all that matters. My part is to simply follow through step by step as You lead, and having done all, to stand. And when all has been done that can be done, to simply accept and go on in peace. I love Your ways, Father!

ISAIAH 12:2 AMP
"I will trust and not be afraid,
for the Lord God is my strength and song;
yes, He has become my salvation."

My Child,

See, the sun is shining. See to it that the Son always shines in your life through joy and song. In times of trouble, in the midst of the storm, My light shines even brighter in your life. Seeds of trouble are sown and the crop seems to come forth in abundance, but in the midst are My strong plants of righteousness which shall come forth bearing much fruit. I have made you to be My gatherer of grapes. Be not afraid to gather, but remember you are gathering for Me, not for you. They are not to circle around you, but around Me. Go forth with singing and hope bubbling up in your heart, for I have made this day for you to enjoy.

Your Loving Father

Father, years ago You said, "Stand strong! Stand strong in the joy of My Presence. You walk down a narrow path, but one flooded with light, the light of My Presence and understanding. I shall not let you down. You shall not stumble. The oil of gladness shall be upon your head. Bubble over! Others need that oil of gladness bubbling over upon them!" And so it has been. Thank You Father, for that oil of gladness! Thank You for the gift of hope and for shining in my life through joy and song. You are the Light of my life! I love You!

Loving Father, how should we enjoy this day together?

_____

_____

_____

_____

_____

_____

_____

_____

_____

_____

_____

_____

_____

_____

200

PSALM 39:7 AMP
"And now, Lord, what do I wait for and expect?
My hope and expectation are in You."

My Child,

Test your wings today. Fly high. Concentrate on Me and see that you will catch the high currents. Be in My Presence all day and let Me begin to soothe and heal your inner being, the inner child that stands back and weeps. Be not concerned, simply be and I shall direct your paths. You shall seek Me and know Me in ways you know not of. I have made you to worship Me. Sing forth your praises with abandon, with no fear; for I am with you and together there is nothing we cannot conquer.

I Love You,
Your Father

Dear Father, my concentration is on You! I want to fly high with You today!

_____

_____

_____

_____

_____

_____

_____

_____

_____

_____

_____

_____

_____

Loving Father, nothing is more wonderful than being in Your Presence, knowing You love me, and that You have created me to be in intimate fellowship with You. Together there is nothing we cannot conquer! I will sing forth Your praises with abandon, pouring forth my love for You in worship. I love You, Father!

ISAIAH 32:18 AMP
"My people shall dwell in a peaceable habitation,
in safe dwellings, and in quiet resting-places."

My Child,

It is a day of rest with redemptive value, resting from worries and cares. Rest in My arms! Lean back and let Me hold the weight. I will bring you into a high place of serenity and peace. Rejoice, My child, and be glad, for you have faced the enemy and have prevailed. He has not overcome you, but you have stood, to My Glory. Rest is imperative; rest in body, soul, and spirit. Fear not that it won't get done, for it will in My time and in My way. Measure the need and respond as I lead. I give My beloved rest. The way is clear; move forward in My timing and at My bidding.

Rest, My Child!
Your Loving Father

Loving Father, I'm so used to responding to every need, that I will need Your help to respond as You lead. Thank You, Father, for giving me the grace to know that all will be done in Your time and in Your way. I will simply rest in Your arms, lean back, and let You hold the weight! What a wonderful place to be!

Father, I will simply rest in You today and listen to Your heart.

_____

_____

_____

_____

_____

_____

_____

_____

_____

_____

_____

_____

_____

_____

_____

_____

202

PSALM 34:1 AMP
"I will bless the Lord at all times;
His praise shall continually be in my mouth."

My Child,

Life doesn't always follow the way you think, but there is always a purpose and a reason. My Spirit is always enveloping you and carrying you forward. I have strengthened you, and I will continue to lead you beside streams of living water. The strain and stress of life shall be transformed into the newness that you have so desired. Relax, let Me fill you, refine... and polish you for your Master's purposes. Stand ready to march forth with resilience and power in My Name, armed with My Spirit of Praise, released from the fetters that bind, and amazed at the bright future I have for you.

Enveloping You with Love,
Your Father

Dear Father, my heart sings to You with loving praise today!

_____

_____

_____

_____

_____

_____

_____

_____

_____

_____

_____

_____

_____

Loving Father, You continually give hope where there seems to be no hope, peace where there seems to be no peace, and strength and purpose when life gets complex. Thank You, Father, for using every experience of my life to fill, refine, polish, and prepare me for Your purposes. Thank You that You are always there to love and encourage along the way.

MATTHEW 5:16 NKJV

"Let your light so shine before men, that they may see
your good works and glorify your Father in heaven."

My Child,

The seasons of change have worked their weight in gold. You are filled, polished, and prepared. The changes shall continue to come to you with rapidity. My Spirit hovers over you and is preparing and charging you for the work at hand. Relish My closeness! Be released from all doubts and fear, for the path ahead is filled with light and My Presence. Drink in My freshness. Shine forth My radiance. Be once more that beacon of Mine to draw the lost to My light and warmth. Praise begets praise. Light restores light. I send you forth to restore and beget by the power of My Spirit. Pour out My Spirit upon My people. Lavish it upon them with gentleness and song, lightness and fun. I have strengthened you, empowered you, and sent you forth, knowing who you are in Me.

I Am with You, My Child,
Your Loving Father

Loving Father, long ago You said, "Now, bloom where you have been planted. Brighten the lives of others by My Spirit within you. Heighten their awareness of Me through your relationship to Me. Many I shall send you to warm and direct toward me. The stream of humanity shall be endless, but My Spirit shall guide you in every instance. Let not go of My hand. Fasten your gaze on Me and move forward as I shall lead. Glorious shall the journey be and delighted shall you be, and those around you. Lift up your head and your heart, and rejoice in the new day, filled with its joys and treasures from Me." I love You, Father!

Father, thank You for pouring Your love out on me, so that I can pour it out on others!

_____

_____

_____

_____

_____

_____

_____

_____

_____

_____

_____

_____

_____

204

PSALM 33:18 AMP

"Behold, the Lord's eye is upon those who fear Him
[who revere and worship Him with awe], who wait for Him
and hope in His mercy and loving-kindness."

My Child,

No longer shall you wonder if I can cover you and protect you. You shall know, and My Glory shall be revealed through your life in a new and more powerful way. Never again shall you say, "I wonder." You shall say, "I know!" A reservoir of hope has been building in your heart, pushing out the residue of hopelessness and sadness. Look not to the past, for looking to the past brings up the hopelessness of the past. Look to today, for today is bright with the hope and promise of the freedom, power, and blessings from My hand. Rejoice in God, your Maker! Make it a habit to rejoice in the God of your salvation! Be encouraged, My child, and fear not the days as they unfold one by one, for the destination is sure and the results shall make you exclaim with joy, "My God is an awesome God and nothing is too hard for Him!"

Rejoice, My Child,

I Love You

Father, forgive me for saying in my heart, "I wonder," and thank You for restoring to my heart the words, "I know!"

_____

_____

_____

_____

_____

_____

_____

_____

_____

Loving Father, thank You for turning sadness to gladness, and giving me renewed hope and encouragement for the journey. Surely my heart exclaims with joy, "My God is an awesome God, and nothing is too hard for Him!"

1 PETER 5:7 AMP
"Casting the whole of your care
[all your anxieties, all your worries, all your concerns, once and for all]
on Him, for He cares for you affectionately
and cares about you watchfully."

My Child,

Struggle is not necessary, but a willing heart. Cast your cares on Me and let Me carry the burden of your understanding. Be a long-distance runner, prepared for the long haul. For I am with you to assure you, strengthen you, and to cheer you on. You will see changes intensify as your strength returns and you become aware of My nudges along the way. Study to show yourself approved, a workman that need not be ashamed. Be faithful in the small things and I will bless you in the big things. Be not afraid to go forward, undaunted by the past, but spurred on by the vision given. It truly is a new day, filled with great gain.

Casts Your Cares on Me,
Your Loving Father

Loving Father, thank You for Your constant faithful and loving care. Thank You Lord, that I don't have to understand everything, but simply trust You. But most of all Father, thank You for new vision and new strength to go forward in Your love!

Father, what are the small things that You would have me be faithful in today?

_____

_____

_____

_____

_____

_____

_____

_____

_____

_____

_____

_____

206

EPHESIANS 3:20 NKJV
"Now to Him who is able to do exceedingly
abundantly above all that we ask or think,
according to the power that works in us."

My Child,

The gate has swung wide for you. Pitch a tent in the wilderness that you can continue to go in and out and minister to the needs of those who are still in the wilderness, hungry and thirsting for the Word of Life that would set them free. You shall show others that there is a way through the wilderness that leads to life, refreshing, and hope. I will show you how to minister hope to a dying people with no hope. You are a picture story and My Spirit is upon you to bring forth My will—an abundant life, full and free. Let not your heart be troubled, neither let it be afraid. For my hand of restoration and freedom is upon you, and the reality of My love shall manifest and be known in you in a new and all-inclusive way. In peace you shall drink from the well of restoration. Your soul shall magnify the Lord and recount His mercies to you and you shall see and respond to new ways of moving by My Spirit of truth.

It Is a New Day My Child,
Your Loving Father

Loving Father, I just want to bask in Your love and listen to Your words to my heart.

_____

_____

_____

_____

_____

_____

_____

_____

Dear Father, it is so wonderful to know that there is reason and purpose for our trials. It makes it all worthwhile to know that I can minister hope to Your people with no hope, to give them the Word of Life that will set them free. Thank You for Your hand of restoration and freedom upon my life. Your gentle love and care are the joy of my life!

207

PSALM 37:23AMP
"The steps of a [good] man are directed and established by the Lord
when He delights in his way
[and He busies Himself with his every step]."

My Child,

Stand firm. Do not be swayed by buffeting of any kind. The scene is changing. I am bringing you into a beautiful, open plain. Don't be afraid to bask in the beauty and wonderment of it. My hand is upon you to cause you to flourish and grow. You have been sustained. Now we shall go on to flourishing. The pieces shall begin to fit together and you shall see a beautiful picture begin to form from the chaos. My power to bring it forth is with you and you shall see mighty miracles by My hand. Go forth this day in joy, for neither fire nor flood have swayed you. The sunshine and beauty of My Kingdom shall bring healing and restore unto you the sense of peace and well-being that is your inheritance.

I Love You, My Child,
Your Father

Loving Father, Your Presence is precious to me. Through the fire and through the flood You were always with me, sustaining me and helping me to make right choices. Thank You for bringing healing and restoration and a sense of peace and well-being. I love You, Father.

Father, speak to my heart for I am listening with loving anticipation!

_____

_____

_____

_____

_____

_____

_____

_____

_____

_____

_____

_____

208

ISAIAH 32:17 AMP

"And the effect of righteousness will be peace [internal and external],
and the result of righteousness will be quietness
and confident trust, forever."

My Child,

Relish the sound of quietness, for there My heart is. My Presence is near. It is My heart you hear in the silence. You have been spilled out as a drink offering for My people. Sanctify yourself [set apart, dedicate, consecrate]. Streamline your life, that it might be a constant reflection of My love and redemptive power to silence the work of the enemy and give him no power over you. Trade in all that distracts for that which calls forth My Spirit in your life. Rejoice in the coming forth of life to you and to many I have called to come forth. It is a season of change, coming forth with great joy and exuberance. Call it forth!

Relish My Presence!

I Love You.

Loving Father, what are the steps I should take to effectively streamline my life?

_____

_____

_____

_____

_____

_____

_____

_____

_____

_____

Dear Father, when You were teaching me to hear Your heart and voice, You said, "Be silent, My child, then you would know Me better. You do not come to know another person by doing all the talking. You come to know him and his inner feelings by listening. Learn to listen quietly. Do not feel that there must always be creative thought put forth by you for there to be prayer. I straighten out the crooked pathways as you keep your focus on Me. Be not afraid of solitude, as long it is spent with Me.

209

PSALM 103:1 AMP
"Bless [affectionately, gratefully praise] the Lord,
O my soul; and all that is [deepest] within me,
bless His holy name."

My Child,

A season of lightheartedness is upon you, a release from tension brought about by a free fall into My arms of love. It is a strategy of release. Brokenness has brought it about. Sing, My little songbird. Sing for joy. Sing for the joy of My heart. Be released from the struggles of the past. They do not apply today. Let your heart sing. Let your praises ring in the presence of your King. Sing to me with joy!

I Love You,
Your Father

Dearest Father, I can envision that free-fall into Your arms of love, such a place of safety! What a wonderful place to release the struggles of the past, letting the brokenness be healed in Your arms of love, and to simply sing to You with joy and thankfulness! I love You, Father!

Father, I will simply enjoy this place in Your arms of love and listen for Your voice of healing to my heart.

_____
_____
_____
_____
_____
_____
_____
_____
_____
_____
_____
_____
_____
_____
_____
_____

210

2 CORINTHIANS 4:6 NKJV
"For it is the God who commanded light to shine out of darkness,
who has shone in our hearts to give the light of the knowledge
of the glory of God in the face of Jesus Christ."

My Child,

Pierce the darkness with My light, knowing that loving one another with one heart and one mind brings the brightness of unified light that will pierce the darkness. Balance freedom with passion; freedom to just be, with passion to do. Mighty signs and wonders are coming your way, igniting the fires that have lain smoldering in the lives of many standing on the sidelines of life. Be established in this place of blessing and harmony. Be My light in the darkness.

You Are Free My Child!

Your Loving Father

Precious Father, how would You use me today to shine Your light in the darkness?

_____

_____

_____

_____

_____

_____

_____

_____

_____

_____

_____

_____

I love You, Father! Thank You for the gift of loving one another with one heart and one mind, established in Your love! Thank You for giving the freedom to just be, and passion to do! Thank You Father, for this place of blessing and harmony! And Father, thank You for mighty signs and wonders coming my way that will ignite the lives of many standing on the sidelines of life. Thank You for letting me be a light in the darkness!

211

PSALM 145:16 AMP
"You open Your hand and satisfy every living thing with favor."

My Precious Child,

Don't you know that I hold you in the palm of My hand, and from there I hold you next to My heart? This time of rest shall bear much fruit. You will find that your heart beats with a new desire to tackle new things and brighten the lives of others with My love and favor. Let me fill you once again with newness of life. Let Me sing over you with gladness, and together we shall again go forth with joy and lightness of heart. The best is yet to come. Seek Me each day, that your lamp might again shine brightly as a beacon, calling in the lame, deaf, and blind to My feast of love and acceptance.

Bask in My Love My Child,
Your Father

Loving Father, I will go through this day with a smile on my face and a song in my heart, loving You with every breath I take! Knowing You are singing over me with gladness causes my heart to fly with joy! Please give me a new song today, from Your heart to mine, that I might sing it back to You!

Precious Father, today I want to seek You with my whole heart, knowing You will impart to me everything I will need to cause my lamp to shine brighter!

_____

_____

_____

_____

_____

_____

_____

_____

_____

_____

_____

_____

_____

212

2 CORINTHIANS 9:10 AMP
"And [God], Who provides seed for the sower and bread for eating
will also provide and multiply your [resources for] sowing
and increase the fruits of your righteousness,
[which manifests itself in active goodness, kindness, and charity]."

My Child,

"Mission impossible," it has been said. But you will see that by My hand and provision, what seems impossible becomes reality. Miracles appear as the natural order of things as seen through the eyes of love. Tremendous days lie ahead, heralding the fulfillment of your hopes and dreams through doorways yet unseen. Miraculous paths for you to tread, as by My hand, you are led. It shall be said, "She did it God's way!" Stalwart and sure shall your steps be, led by Me, making a sure path across the wilderness into the promised land. Apart from Me this could not be accomplished, and the "Trademark" has been and shall continue to be, obedience in the face of trial.

You Are Precious to Me, My Child,
Your Loving Father

Father, I long to hear Your voice even clearer to my heart! I'm listening today with anticipation to hear Your words of direction and love!

_____

_____

_____

_____

_____

_____

_____

_____

_____

_____

Loving Father, surely my life has walked down miraculous paths led by Your hand of love. What an adventure to watch You turn each "Mission Impossible" into the miraculous. Thank You, Father, for helping me to make the right choices along the way, saying, "This is the way."

213

LUKE 1:47 AMP
"And my spirit rejoices in God my Savior."

My Child,

You know what it feels like to be beset by the frailties of man, but you also know what it feels like to know you are loved by the Creator of the Universe. Far greater is this knowledge than any other on the face of the earth. Rest in that love and fret not. Continue to seek My heart in all things. Strongholds are broken as you stand in the strength of My love. My heart is with you, My Child, to fulfill all I have placed before you. Within your heart are the tools for which you seek. Hidden away, unseen by the naked eye but readily seen by My Spirit within you. One by one, I shall draw them forth, providing new avenues of service to delight your heart. Let your heart rejoice, for in that rejoicing comes the freedom to soar.

I Love You, My Child,
Your Father

Loving Father, You have said that within each of us, You have tucked away gifts, callings, anointings, and destinies that we are not even aware of. It's like a treasure hunt, with such joy, as each one is revealed by Your Spirit of love. You also said that with a little love and encouragement, not only from You, but from others that You put in our lives, we find the courage to fulfill those destinies. Thank You, Father, for the love and encouragement that You give to me and that You bring my way through others. And thank You, Lord, for bringing to me many to love and encourage along the way

Loving Father, today I want to seek Your heart about…

_____

_____

_____

_____

_____

_____

_____

_____

_____

_____

_____

_____

_____

_____

_____

214

"Yes, you shall be steadfast and secure; you shall not fear."

My Child,

Seasons of change have seemed to put your life clear out of control. But nestled between the events of life is the assurance of My love and care to keep you stable in the face of turmoil and confusion. My love has kept you strong and steady in the midst of trials. Be very sure of this very thing—that nothing has or will capsize you as you continue this grand adventure called life. Call up memories of past victories and rejoice in each outcome, for I am with you and will never forsake you or leave you without an answer. "Magnificent Obsession" it shall be said of the way you are led, as day by day you see come into view the fulfillment of all I have for you. You've sought My face, you've paid the cost, and you will see that nothing shall be lost as, together, we continue on the way, fulfilling your destiny each and every day. Nestle in My arms and be refreshed this day.

I Am Always with You!

Your Loving Father

Father, thank You for the refreshment of Your love this day! My heart listens closely to every word that You would say!

_____

_____

_____

_____

_____

_____

_____

_____

_____

Loving Father, You said that my life would be "stranger than fiction" because of the miraculous way that You would lead me, because I am Your child. There is no place else I'd rather be than fulfilling my destiny, each and every day, in intimate fellowship with You! I love You, Father!

215

EPHESIANS 2:22 AMP
"In Him [and in fellowship with one another]
you yourselves also are being built up [into this structure]
with the rest, to form a fixed abode [dwelling place] of God in
(by, through) the Spirit."

My Child,

Trace your life through the many ups and downs and see that My hand was upon you at all times, bringing you forth through trial to victory. So it is now as you see My hand of favor propelling you to My planned blessing and destiny. It has been a dry and barren sea, seemingly void of laughter, joy, and fellowship. Now comes forth a new thing to gladden your heart and set you free to sing and be refreshed in My love. Love and unity is your heart and so shall it ever be. Your heart has become a dwelling place for My love. You cannot fathom the depth of that love. Just let it flow out, unhindered by the passing scene and circumstances. Let it be a steady flow to bring hope and healing to the hearts of My people. I hear the cries of your heart. They do not go unheard. Rest assured that I hear and have heard. It is your heart I see, as you stand before Me.

Be Refreshed in My Love,
Your Loving Father

Loving Father, thank You that You hear every cry of my heart, that You consider every thought a prayer. Thank You for giving me Your love with the freedom to just let it flow out unhindered by the passing scene and circumstances. Such freedom that brings, not having to choose who I love, simply loving all as You do.

Father, my heart sings to You with gratefulness and praise today!

_____

_____

_____

_____

_____

_____

_____

_____

_____

216

ISAIAH 49:16 AMP
"See, I have inscribed you on the palms of My hands."

My Child,

I have written you on the palm of My hand. You are always before My face. I have filled you full of My beauty and grace, that you might be a magnet to draw My people to Me. You have been a busy bee, struggling to maintain the pace, and to not let down your guard in this place. But now, I show you a new face, full of grace, one that can satisfy not only the demands that test your grace, but that shall allow you to play in this place. Time and space shall begin to fade away as you begin to see Me.

You Are Precious to Me,
Your Loving Father

Dear Father, when I find myself struggling, I will slow down quietly in Your Presence, and listen to Your words of peace. I love You, Father!

Loving Father, truly I have been a busy bee, struggling to maintain the pace, to not let down my guard in this place. Long ago You said, "Quit struggling and rest in My love. Recline, with your heart at peace. Refrain from struggling in the water. Float on My arms instead. Do not let up your stance of strength in My Spirit. One can float in strength, but one cannot thrash from a point of strength. Thrashing comes from weakness. Enjoy the view, the peace and the serenity." Father, forgive me for thrashing in the water instead of floating peacefully in Your arms. Thank You for helping me come to a new place of balancing the work and play.

PSALM 25:4 AMP
"Show me Your ways, O Lord; teach me Your paths."

My Child,

Meditate on My ways. My ways are revealed from the foundation of the world to mankind. It is when My ways are manipulated and distorted that they cause confusion, doubt, unbelief, and pain. Reflect on My ways with you. (You have been kind, loving, gentle, and patient with me.) *How does that affect you?* (It causes me to want to be kind, loving, gentle, and patient with others.) *How others treat you is how they see Me. I am causing you to be able to stand strong and tall, and say, "That does not reflect my Father's love and nature," with gentleness, but firmly with love. There will always be those who will try to take away your freedom through guilt, intimidation, and fear, but they shall not, for you shall stand, proclaiming freedom to all! Now is the time to see into the future with My eyes, My eyes of freedom and eternal destiny, with the faith of a small child holding her daddy's hand. Go forth, and sing the song of freedom!*

Be Free My Child, Be Free!

Your Loving Father

Loving Father, thank You for holding tightly to my hand, always with loving, gentle, and patient care! Day by day, You give me glimpses into my destiny, and each glimpse delights my heart, giving me hope and direction. Thank You, for giving me the faith to stand, refusing guilt, intimidation, and fear. Thank You, Father, for a rising sense of freedom that permeates my heart and soul! I love You, Father!

Father, thank You for teaching me Your ways, as I meditate on Your Word today.

_____

_____

_____

_____

_____

_____

_____

_____

_____

_____

218

Jeremiah 29:11 NKJV

"For I know the thoughts that I think toward you, says the LORD,
thoughts of peace and not of evil,
to give you a future and a hope."

My Child,

Make ready to dance and sing in the Presence of your King. Sight to the blind is possible in this place of consecration, and release from the pressures of life. Release from pressures brings sight. Within My peace is the full release from anxiety, tension, fear, and stress, all from wanting to do your best. But I say to you, "It is a test of your desire to come into My rest." My peace is the barometer of My life within you. And it is peace you see as you stand in faith and believe. Magical formulas, there are none, but it is in the eyes of peace that the victory is won. Stand your ground this day, My child. You have known it to be Holy Ground, this place of peaceful habitation.

Be at Peace, My Child,

I Am with You!

Loving Father, help me to make that choice today, to walk in Your trust and peace. I love You, Father!

_____

_____

_____

_____

_____

_____

_____

_____

_____

_____

My Father, I need to read this Word from Your heart to me every day, for it is the test of my life every day, as well as the barometer of Your life within me. How I long to pass that test each day! Truly it is Holy Ground, this place of peaceful habitation, this place of release from anxiety, tension, fear, and stress. What joy there is when I stand my ground and walk in Your peace.

219

LUKE 8:15 AMP

"But as for that [seed] in the good soil, these are [the people],
who, hearing the Word, hold it fast in a just (noble, virtuous)
and worthy heart, and steadily bring forth fruit with patience."

My Child,

(Father, when I said "I'm just one," You replied that You are the One who feeds the multitudes the seven loaves and fishes and You simply ask me to be available to make them available.) *Long ago you settled it in your heart that this you would do, but you found that they were not "multitudes" at all, but each one is very personal and a treasure to your heart, just as they are a treasure to My heart. Just continue to make the loaves and fishes available by being that butterfly, flying from treasure to treasure, setting an atmosphere that they might eat of My love and be filled. Proceed along this yellow brick road that I have created for you, filled with delights and treasures beyond your capacity to comprehend. You shall see My hand of provision at every turn and continue to delight in Me, walking in My favor and love. You have been patient. You have allowed me to "call the shots," knowing that I can best preserve you and bring to you My very best.*

The Best Is Yet to Come!
Your Loving Father

Father, the loaves and fishes of knowing Your love, peace, and joy has always been my desire for Your treasures, that all the flowers might sing and laugh with delight, to bring them through the darkest night, into Your bright Sonlight, victoriously, in Your Presence!

Loving Father, thank You for "calling the shots" in my life! I give this day to You, listening for Your direction and the words from Your heart!

_____

_____

_____

_____

_____

_____

DANIEL 2:28 AMP
"But there is a God in heaven who reveals secrets."

My Precious Child,

I share the secrets of My heart with those who will listen with their hearts and respond with obedience and love. It is not a small thing, but a way of life that causes My will to be brought forth on the earth. Be a conduit to bring forth My perfect will upon the earth. Let Me cause you to be a water spout of blessing, a funnel spout to call forth My blessings and power upon the earth. Walk with Me, My child. Sit with Me awhile. Let Me be the cause of your smile. Just be the reflection of My love. Listen with your heart my child.

I Love You,
Your Father

Father, cause me to be a waterspout of blessing today! I am listening for Your direction!

_____

_____

_____

_____

_____

_____

_____

_____

_____

_____

_____

_____

_____

_____

Loving Father, the sound of Your voice is the joy of my life. You speak words of encouragement and love, wisdom and direction, peace and hope. Daily, You cause the lights to go on in my heart, as You help me put the pieces of my life together with understanding and hope. Truly You are the cause of my smile. I love You, Father!

221

2 Corinthians 1:2 AMP
"Grace (favor and spiritual blessing) to you and [heart] peace
from God our Father and the Lord Jesus Christ
(the Messiah, the Anointed One)."

My Child,

Be restored this day from the rigors of the battle and from the emotions that haven't found a peaceful landing spot. Let Me anoint the fragmented, frayed nerve endings, and bring a calm to your life that you have not known before, because of the constant pressure from within and without. I have seen, know, and am cognizant of all that pertains to your life. Nothing goes unseen by My eyes. Be blessed this day from within and from without.

I Love You, My Child,

Your Loving Father

Loving Father, thank You for anointing the fragmented, frayed nerve endings, and bringing a calm to my life. I long to be at peace in the midst of the pressures from within and from without. Thank You, that day by day You are bringing that about, as You teach me to walk in peace. Thank You for healing my emotions, and causing them to find a peaceful landing spot. You are precious to me, Father!

Father, I just want to sit in Your Presence for awhile and reflect on the many ways You bless me and those I love!

_____

_____

_____

_____

_____

_____

_____

_____

_____

_____

_____

_____

_____

_____

_____

222

11 Thessalonians 3:13 AMP
"And as for you, brethren, do not become weary
or lose heart in doing right
[but continue in well-doing without weakening]."

My Child,

Search your heart. What do you find there? (Frustration and weariness. Father, You've always taught me to take it one step at a time. I feel like someone on a long marathon, who is no longer running, but getting up every morning and laboriously taking one weary step at a time with the finish line as the goal. I long to run and skip with You down the pathway of life). *Go forth with faith believing, and in peace receiving My Living Word of hope and healing to your heart and soul. A way has been made and all shall receive My blessings of abundant peace, who come this way by My Spirit. Go forth proclaiming My blessings to My people.*

I Am with You!

Your Father

Father, I need to fill up my heart this day with Your loving Presence!

_____

_____

_____

_____

_____

_____

_____

_____

_____

_____

_____

Loving Father, thank You that You are with me even through the frustration and weariness, bringing hope and healing to my body, soul, and heart. Thank You for Your continual blessings and miracles in my life! Thank You, Father, for life, to proclaim Your blessings to Your people!

223

SONG OF SOLOMON 2:4 AMP
"He brought me to the banqueting house,
and his banner over me was love [for love waved as a protecting
and comforting banner over my head when I was near him]."

My Precious Child,

I want you to know, many things as you continue to grow. You thought, Oh my, how can I do this or that? But I want you to know it's all a part of My plan to bring you forth victorious and sure, to take to the world "My Ultimate Cure." My love, foremost, you carry in your heart. A seed has been planted deep within that causes you to always win. That seed is My love.

I Love You, My Child.

I love You, too, Father, with all my heart! Day by day You teach me Your ways with such patience, gentleness, grace, and loving care. You have such confidence in me and always see me through. Nothing surprises You or causes You alarm as step by step, You bring me to the fulfillment of Your destiny for me, planned from the foundation of the world. With the Creator of the Universe as my Father and Friend, I'm sure to win!

Loving Father, my heart sings a song of love to You! How can I love You more?

_____

_____

_____

_____

_____

_____

_____

_____

_____

_____

_____

_____

_____

_____

_____

_____

_____

_____

_____

_____

ISAIAH 43:2 NKJV

"When you pass through the waters, I will be with you;
And through the rivers, they shall not overflow you.
When you walk through the fire, you shall not be burned,
Nor shall the flame scorch you."

My Child,

You will find that fires will poof and disappear as fast as they flare. It is distracting but they leave no sign. Trust Me to put the fires out. I have designed you to bring people together in love. Go forth in My strength, at My leading. Restoration continues to be your calling in Me, as I restore you. Be not afraid of the fires along the way. They simply flare up to scare you, but they have no lasting power. Leave the consequences to Me. My heart is for you and brings out the best in you.

Trust Me, My Child,
Your Loving Father

Father, these are the flaring fires I am dealing with right now. I turn them over to You, resting in Your peace, as I listen for Your voice to speak to my heart.

_____

_____

_____

_____

_____

_____

_____

_____

_____

_____

_____

Thank You, Father for helping me to remember to not let the distracting fires that flare, scare me! I will trust You to put the fires out! Thank You for added strength, restoration, and bringing out the best in me. Father, it is so interesting that the things that we are called to, we have to be restored in ourselves, in the process.

225

1 JOHN 3:16 NKJV
"By this we know love, because He laid down His life for us.
And we also ought to lay down our lives for the brethren."

My Beloved Child,

Liken My love to a stream that spreads across the land, soaking into the dry and parched land, reviving, restoring, and renewing, gently and with care, as a mother gently and lovingly cares for her newborn. My love brings rest to the weary and joy to the downhearted. You are a gift of My love to My people, that they too might become gifts of love to My people. Each recipient of the gift becoming the gift, until they become an army of My gift of love, to the world.

You Are My Gift,

Your Loving Father

Precious Father, I can see the dry parched land of human hearts being healed and restored by Your gift of love! Your gift brings such joy, victory, and purpose to one's existence. Nothing is more joyful and fulfilling than being with Your people, who really know how much You love them! And nothing is more fulfilling than being with one of Your treasures, when they suddenly begin to realize how very, very, very much You love them! What a transformation comes over their lives at that wonderful realization! Thank you, Father, for your unconditional and life-changing love.

Father, help me to understand even more, the fullness of Your wonderful love.

_____

_____

_____

_____

_____

_____

_____

_____

_____

_____

_____

_____

_____

_____

_____

_____

_____

_____

226

1 SAMUEL 7:3 AMP
"Direct your hearts to the Lord and serve Him only."

My Child,

Reach out to Me. Focus your heart on Me and I will orchestrate the rest, bestowing favor and providing all you will need. When your focus becomes sidetracked on responsibilities and those I have given you favor with and ministry with, all becomes backwards and confusing, and out of harmony. It is like the Concert Master of an orchestra, who puts her focus and attention on all of the individual instruments and players in the orchestra, instead of the Director. (The Concert Master makes sure they are all tuned in unity and that they all have the music, but then they must all focus on the Director, who has the job of causing them to make beautiful music together.) Be blessed, My child, as you become lost in the beauty of My music.

Be My Symphony of Praise! I Love You,
Your Father

My Father, today I want to make beautiful music with You!

_____

_____

_____

_____

_____

_____

_____

_____

_____

_____

_____

_____

Loving Father, I love making music with You. When I get sidetracked by responsibilities, and even ministry and those you've given me favor with, thank You for gently drawing me back into Your Presence. What a wonderful word picture, to remember that being a Concert Master is not a full-time job, but the whole point of being in a Symphony Orchestra is to make beautiful music with and for You!

227

"In the Lord I take refuge [and put my trust]."

My Child,

There is much in store. Ready yourself. (How, Lord?) *Trust!* (I remember Lord, I be—You do! I can't make it happen. My part is to be in Your Presence.) *Your heart is a wellspring unto Me. It gets clogged by weariness of soul. Cease from your labors, My weary child. Lasting fragrance comes from time spent with Me, a fragrance that lasts and permeates the air with the beauty of My Spirit around you.* (Is that Your Glory Lord?) *It is a facet of My Glory. It is My Presence that is the reality of your existence. All else is filler. Saturate yourself in My Presence.* (Your Presence is perfume, oil, fire, smoke, beauty, peace, joy, laughter, love, and freedom.) *Settle it in your heart this day—My Presence is your passion! The majesty of My Kingdom is before you. It's music sings in your heart. Listen, it sings its songs of love. Can you not hear the music of the spheres? Only the singing heart can hear, for the singing heart joins with the music of Heaven.*

Be the Fragrance of Heaven,
Your Loving Father

Loving Father, Your Presence truly is the reality of my existence. It is settled in my heart this day, Your Presence is my passion! I want to hear the music of the spheres even more, and join my heart with Your heart, with the music of Heaven, saturating myself in Your Presence! I love You so much, Father!

Father, forgive me for letting my soul get clogged by weariness. Today I give You all of my weariness and busyness, to come away with my Beloved!

_____

_____

_____

_____

_____

_____

_____

_____

_____

228

JOHN 3:36 NKJV
"Therefore if the Son makes you free,
you shall be free indeed."

My Child,

Be at peace and know that nothing can overcome you, but it can distract and discourage you. Simply close the door at the first sign. I have set a course for you to bring down giants in the land. But first, you have to be free. Simplicity has always been your way to love and be. It will continue to be the road map of your life. Frustration comes when the way gets too complicated. Simplicity is a grace and a blessing and a gift from Me. Reversed, is the enemy's way of complication and confusion. Remember to keep all things simple and uncomplicated. The reverse mode brings division and disappointment.

Stay Free My Child,

Your Father

Loving Father, what are the areas in my life that I need to simplify?

_____

_____

_____

_____

_____

_____

_____

_____

_____

_____

_____

_____

_____

_____

Thank You, Father, for Your gift of simplicity and blessing. Surely, where there is complication, there is confusion also. Thank You, Father, that simplicity will always be the road map of my life. And yet Father, every day is a feast from Your table of life, not to be forgotten or taken lightly. Thank You, Father, for Your constant and infinite care, love and provision over my life! When I feel distracted or discouraged, I will remember, "Simplicity!"

229

"Grace [favor and spiritual blessing] and [heart] peace
from God the Father, and the Lord Christ Jesus our Savior."

My Child,

It has been a season of shortcomings—coming short of what is expected or required, deficiency, inadequacy—not in My eyes, but in yours. But you have used what I have given you, and multiplied it as best you knew how. Now the doors shall swing wide, with more than enough from My storehouses. The time of My favor has come upon you and I shall pour out the riches of Heaven. Get ready for a deluge of My favor and blessing. Your eyes are opening and seeing more and more. Along with sight comes wisdom. My house shall be built with love and wisdom. Give it forth liberally. Liberally I give to you and liberally you give to others. The storehouses of heaven are opening wide. Stand under the deluge of blessing and rejoice as you see the desires of your heart come to pass!

You Have Done Well My Child,

Your Loving Father

I love You so much Father! The cry of my heart has been to walk in more wisdom! Thank You, for giving me the desire of my heart. Thank You for Your confidence in me and Your blessing over me, when it seemed that I couldn't get it right. Thank You Father, for opening my eyes that I might see more of Your Kingdom and more of Your wisdom. I am so grateful!

Father, Your encouragement means so much to me! My heart reaches out to You today for Your encouragement and wisdom.

_____

_____

_____

_____

_____

_____

_____

_____

_____

_____

_____

230

PSALM 30:5 NKJV
"His favor is for life;
weeping may endure for a night,
but joy comes in the morning."

My Child,

It has been a time of coming into My peace where there was no peace. A time of knowing that My love for you is greater than what you can do or what you have been called to do. You have always told others, "God is more concerned with you than the situation." This truth is becoming real to your own heart. Struggles abound, but the heart rejoices at the sound of true love and caring. To stay in My peace and continue knowing My love is primary; all else flows from this. It is all about My peace, a place of rest and abiding.

Be at Peace My Child,

Your Loving Father

Father, once again I come to You, listening to Your heart in that place of rest and abiding.

_____

_____

_____

_____

_____

_____

_____

_____

_____

_____

_____

Loving Father, You have said, "Inner beauty is brought forth through pressure, to teach one to respond to pressure with peace. It is a process that must be lived step by step. Rejoice in the becoming. My blessings are upon you, My child." Father, thank You that no matter what is going on in my life, You are always there to help me to respond to pressure with peace.

231

"Let us hold fast the confession of our hope without wavering,
for He who promised is faithful."

Precious One,

Tattered and torn, it has seemed you have been, unable to straighten the roads that would bend. But I say unto you, what I say of you is true. My promises to you are at hand. You are not standing on shifting sand, but you stand strong and secure with a heart that is pure. Not promoting yourself, but proclaiming the great wealth I have placed in each life that is Mine. Comfort, guidance, and love are always yours, My child. Look to Me for them all, before you ever call upon others to lighten your load. Seasons have brought change, over and over again. And now in the midst of all that seems remiss, come the answers your heart has longed for, that will cause your heart to soar. It will cause you to proclaim and say, "Oh, My God, it has all come forth Your way! My job is to love and to play!"

I Love You!
Your Faithful and Loving Father!

Father, You have always been faithful to me! It's not always as I thought it would be, yet always filled with Your love and blessing. Recently, You said, "Watch Me bring forth a masterpiece, quite different than you thought. Just hold steady. You will see the plan. It is a magnificent picture brought forth by My hand!" Thank You Father, that every moment of my life brings forth that magnificent masterpiece, created by Your love!

Loving Father, I just want to enjoy Your Presence, share my heart, and enjoy Yours!

_____

_____

_____

_____

_____

_____

_____

_____

_____

_____

_____

~ 232 ~

2 TIMOTHY 2:22 AMP
"[And aim at and pursue] faith, love, [and] peace, (harmony
and concord with others) in fellowship with all [Christians],
who call upon the Lord out of a pure heart."

My Child,

*It is a sifting of the old and the new. The old will forever be as noise to your
ears. You will recognize it immediately as you go forth singing My song and
being My song. Those that continue to allow the sifting will harmonize with
your song, making one song; the song of eternity, that will ring in your ears. It
has been called unity, but it is really harmony—one body, singing one song,
with many parts; the song of eternity. I've given you the ability to recognize the
song they sing, whether in full reflective beauty of the spheres, or lying dormant
in their heart from fear, which love sets free. Your heart says to them, "Come
sing with me. Your God-given song will set you free to reflect His love and be
a part of the Heavenly song that will reverberate and ring throughout eternity."*

Be My Song My Child, I Love You!

Loving Father, thank You for the Heart Friends You bring my way day by day! Thank You, Heavenly Father, for being my Heart Friend! I love You!

_____
_____
_____
_____
_____
_____
_____
_____
_____
_____
_____
_____

Beloved Father, these words from Your heart are the cry of my heart, as one by one You bring to me those whose hearts sing, in harmony, the song of eternity. Many already sing in the full reflective beauty of the spheres, but many You bring whose God-given song still lies dormant in their hearts from fear. But all it takes is a little love and encouragement to begin reflecting Your love, and being a part of the Heavenly song. Heart Friends, singing one song with many parts, the song of eternity!

233

"Yet grace (God's unmerited favor)
was given to each of us individually…"

My Precious Child,

It is the journey of a lifetime, a gift from above. It is all about My favor and My love. Let others run the race at their own pace. Each has their own pace. Each has their own purpose and plan. But together, forever, this has always been My purpose and plan. See the kaleidoscope. See the beauty of each in every picture portrayed. The colors are all connected, as they weave in and out of each others' lives, as they form beautiful pictures of My love, ever-changing but always a thing of beauty, symmetry, and grace. All are necessary to the whole, but never the same. Every gathering, a different mix to bring about a different symphony, a different kaleidoscope of beauty, painting ever changing pictures of My love. Harmony—beauty of sound and sight.

Enjoy the Beauty of My Kingdom!

I Love You,

Your Father

Loving Father, it truly is a journey of a lifetime, filled with Your favor and love. I love the way You weave the lives of Your people together, with beauty, symmetry, and grace. Walking in Your love is never boring! And it is so true, we all run the race at our own pace, and yet all the beautiful colors are connected as we weave in and out of each others' lives, forming beautiful pictures of Your love. What a treasure to behold; Your people, each fulfilling their purpose and destiny, in harmony and love!

My Father, thank You that I am a part of that kaleidoscope of Your precious people. Cause me to love them even more!

234

ISAIAH 61:1 AMP
"He has sent me to bind up and heal the brokenhearted,
to proclaim liberty to the [physical and spiritual] captives
and the opening of the prison and of the eyes to those who are bound."

My Child,

Proclaim Liberty to all you see! Let the sound of it ring in their ears. Let the truth of it ring through the spheres. Truth spoken brings forth the promises of each life. Truth spoken calms the struggle and the strife. My heart has always been for My people to fight and win. For Freedom never comes without a price and for that price, many have died. But know as they have fought, I have been by their side. And now because of the victories won, it's a new day under the Son, to proclaim Freedom, far and wide, knowing I always walk by your side. Preparing the way as you proclaim this new day, Freedom, in all you do and say.

Stay Free My Child, Stay Free!

You Are Loved,

Your Father

Loving Father, how can I walk in more Freedom today?

_____

_____

_____

_____

_____

_____

_____

_____

_____

_____

_____

Beloved Father, Freedom is only found in Your Presence! Freedom is only found in Your love and in Your Name! It is the cry of my heart that Your people know Your heart of love for them! Help me always Father, to proclaim Freedom in all that I do and say!

PSALM 5:7 AMP
"But as for me, I will enter Your house through the abundance
of Your steadfast love and mercy.

My Child,

Blessed, you are blessed! It is the theme of your life. Loved, you are loved! No need for strife. Joy, joy forever, is yours to proclaim as you walk in My love, and in the power of My Name! Peace, peace permeates your soul because you know your Lord has full control in every circumstance. His heart you can trust. Let your fears and reluctance just turn into dust. For your Lord is the best friend you'll ever have. You'll have no more reason to be miserable and sad. His love for you will never decline. He'll always say proudly, "This one is Mine!"

Proudly, I Say, You Are Mine!

I Love You, My Child

Dear Father, You are the best friend I've ever had! You have said, "Give out justice, and justice will be returned to you. Break forth in singing, and those around you will sing. Praise Me, and those around you will praise Me. Give forth of My love, and My love will returned to you. What you give forth boomerangs back. Be a joy giver and a peace maker." Giving these things is the joy of my heart, because I love You!

Loving Father, I just want to pour out my love on You today with thankfulness and praise!

_____

_____

_____

_____

_____

_____

_____

_____

_____

_____

_____

_____

_____

_____

_____

236

PSALM 98:1 AMP
"O sing to the Lord a new song,
for He has done marvelous things."

My Child,

In the midst of warfare comes the sound of a dove, singing songs of love. Can you not hear its sweet refrain, refreshing like soft gentle rain? Listen to its beautiful song, seemingly righting all that's been wrong. It's My songs of love that move the heart. It's the sweetness of that song that makes them feel a part of My plans and purposes upon the earth, where before they just felt like dirt. A simple song of love, you see, brings forth hope, causing the demons to flee. Precious and few are those who do proclaim My love in such a way that brings forth My blessing through what they do and say! So, sing My songs all day long. Let them come forth, every kind and sort; songs of freedom, deliverance, and hope; songs that will definitely rock the boat. Sing My songs of liberty, songs to set the prisoners free; songs that will finally help them to be delivered and made whole. Sing My heart, to set the captives free!

Sing, My Child,

I Love You.

Father, You have said that we have not because we ask not, and I'm asking for boldness to step out in the giftings that You have so painstakingly imparted to me.

_____

_____

_____

_____

_____

_____

_____

_____

Loving Father, You've given each of us wonderful gifts and callings that we are reluctant to step out in because of lack of faith and trust that You will enter into our efforts and bring Your anointing to bring us success. Forgive me, Father, for not having the faith to step out in a gift that You have given me to bless Your people. It is a gift that sits on the shelf, and I enjoy the beauty of and am excited to have it, but I seldom take it down and use it, to Your Glory. Help me Father to step forth in bold faith!

PROVERBS 17:17 AMP
"A friend loves at all times."

My Beloved Child,

I have put it on your heart, year after year after year to, "Love My people with a pure heart, untainted by expectations or goals, simply for love's sake!" Now I say to you that love shall bear fruit beyond your expectations or dreams. It is a message whose time has come. The Kingdom of God is gladness, love, and purity. And even as you see pain and turmoil, what you will really see is My hand of favor, joy, and love covering all with hope and peace. Go forth under My canopy of love.

You Are Precious to Me,
Your Loving Father

Loving Father, through the years You have said, "Go forth this day with My Spirit upon you. Strive not; but simply be. Show forth My loving-kindness and joyfulness. Show forth My compassion and straight-forwardness. Show forth My meekness and love." But uppermost has always been to love Your people with a pure heart, untainted by expectations or goals, simply for love's sake. Sometimes it's easy, sometimes it's hard, but always the rewards are great. Thank You Father, for teaching me to love!

Father, I still let expectations get in the way. Here are the situations where I'm still having trouble loving, simply for love's sake. Help me, I pray.

_____

_____

_____

_____

_____

_____

_____

_____

_____

_____

_____

_____

238

PSALM 101:1 AMP
"I will sing of mercy and loving-kindness and justice;
to You, O Lord, will I sing."

My Child,

In the midst of pain and suffering comes the sound of My heart, the music of the spheres to bring you joy and lighten your load. Listen to its gentle refrain, it's never the same and it brings release from frustration and pain. My heart for you, My child, sings a song of freedom! Freedom from expectations, frustrations, and weariness of heart; freedom to know that every day you are a part of My will and plan upon the earth. Be at peace, My child, and know that every day you continue to grow, seeing and hearing, releasing and inspiring My song of praise in all of your ways. Be released to know it is in the dailiness of life, that you show My heart of love to all you meet. Each day stands on its own as a tribute to all you've sown in agony and tears; a Symphony of Praise, woven throughout all of your days.

I Love You, My Child,
Your Father

Wonderful Father, my heart sings to You with gratefulness and love!

_____

_____

_____

_____

_____

_____

_____

_____

_____

_____

_____

Loving Father, I don't want to sing my song alone. I want the world joined with me around Your Throne, singing Your Symphony of Praise with love and unity in a family way. Thank You, Lord, for making it so and helping us to continue to grow as sisters and brothers of the heart; destined to be a part of Your will and plan upon the earth. A Symphony of Love from Your Heart!

239

ISAIAH 32:17 AMP

"And the effect of righteousness will be peace [internal and external],
and the result of righteousness will be quietness
and confident trust forever."

My Child,

Signs of Spring are everywhere. It is a season of new beginnings, new illumi-nations, resolutions, and victories won. Rise up, My dear one, and sing the Song of Spring. I lay before you daily the steps to take, to lead you down the straight path of My choosing. Sing and rejoice daily on this journey. Minute as the progress seems at times, know that each day brings you closer to the goal, your destiny in Me. Faint not, but continue on, knowing that I am with you in every detail of life. Multitudes have come this way without the will and heart to stay. It's all about trust!

My Dear One,
I Love You

Loving Father, even though the progress seems minute at times, I know I can trust You! I love seasons of new beginnings, new illuminations, resolutions, and victories won. Thank You for laying before me the daily steps to be taken. Once, long ago, You said that I was to keep my focus not on the minute, but on the big picture, the goal, the destiny You have proclaimed. For years, I kept those words on my desk so I wouldn't forget! Thank You, Father, for Your faithful encour-agement along the way, so that I don't lose sight of the goal!

Faithful Father, thank You for being with me in every detail of my life! My heart sings to You with thankfulness and joy!

_____
_____
_____
_____
_____
_____
_____
_____
_____
_____
_____
_____

240

PSALM 89:1 AMP

"I will sing of the mercy and loving-kindness of the Lord forever;
with my mouth will I make known Your faithfulness
from generation to generation."

My Dear One,

Now is the day! Now is the hour to come forth with love and power! Set your heart to give forth in such a way that opens the door for each one to say, "Today is the day; God's opened the door!" No longer to wait and languish to know, it's been a time to heal and to grow. But now is the time! Now is the hour to stretch forth your hand and heart, with love and with power! Extinguish the fear that walks alongside. Extinguish the reluctance that really is pride; fear and pride, combined to neutralize power. But they shall not succeed! You're released this very hour! Go forth proclaiming My love and My grace. But your mission is to help them get into the race!

You Are Precious to Me,
Your Loving Father

Loving Father, what are we going to do together today?

_____
_____
_____
_____
_____
_____
_____
_____
_____
_____
_____
_____
_____

Dear Father, it seems that my heart sings this song every day in anticipation of what You have planned for the day! You have said, "Hang onto your dreams! Go forth with My promises ringing in your heart. Press forward to attain the prize. Leave behind all that encumbers and be buoyed up by My Spirit. Be one with My Spirit through trust and reliance. Move in trust. Have your very being steeped in trust of Me, loosed that I might do My will through you. Blessings abundant are yours!"

241

PROVERBS 8:32 AMP

"For blessed, [happy, fortunate, to be envied]
are those who keep my ways."

My Child,

Study to show yourself approved in such a way that brings forth My love in all you do and say. It's not important the "why" and the "how." The reason you've been put on the earth is to know My Presence. Heart to heart, My Presence is made known. It's the beat of My heart, the cadence to follow. Everything else will sound unnecessary and hollow. Be alert every day of your life to stay away from division and strife. Mingle and co-mingle to your heart's content, and you will recognize loud and clear the sound of My love falling on your ear. It's a distinctive sound; it cannot be duplicated without intimacy with Me. You will know which sounds pass the test. You will know which sounds have come into My rest.

You Are Precious to Me,
Your Loving Father

Loving Father, it's wonderful to know that Your canopy of love covers and protects me in every situation. What a blessing to know that the reason I've been put on his earth is to know Your Presence, and to make Your Presence and love known. Thank You, Father, for the wisdom and understanding to recognize those who have come into Your rest and intimacy with You, and those who need to experience Your wonderful love and peace for themselves. Father, help me to more effectively draw them to the beauty of Your Presence and love.

Precious Father, I want to enjoy the wonderful sound of Your love, falling on my ear today!

_____

_____

_____

_____

_____

_____

_____

_____

_____

_____

_____

_____

_____

242

COLOSSIANS 3:15 NKJV
"And let the peace of God rule in your hearts."

My Child,

Be at peace. Just as the trees have different seasons of growth, so must you. A tree may be surrounded by people or it may be isolated far in the forest, but neither has anything to do with its growth. As long as its Father is providing sunshine, water, and nutrients, it grows in beauty and strength. It depends on the Father's care, not on outside stimulation or influences. So are you to be, the strong beautiful tree of My planting, nurtured by Me, drawing your source of life and growth from Me. Outside influences are nice and pleasant, but not necessary to your growth. There is a time for outside stimulation and sharing, and there is a time for quiet fellowship and communion with Me.

You Are My Treasure,
Your Loving Father

Father, You have also said to let Your peace, along with Your Word, guide me. I am listening Father, for Your Word to my heart today.

_____

_____

_____

_____

_____

_____

_____

_____

_____

_____

_____

Loving Father, I love our time of quiet fellowship and communion! In the past, You have said, "Let your heart guide you, for I shall guide you step by step, for you need to know the leading of your heart and not your mind. My guidance is available to you moment by moment, if you listen to your heart, for I am residing in your heart to bring you peace, joy, understanding, and guidance. Listen to your heart, for it is I speaking. Let not your mind be heard, but your heart!

243

MATTHEW 6:6 NKJV
"Pray to your Father, who is in the secret place;
and your Father, who sees in secret will reward you openly."

My Child,

Take the seasons as they come and rejoice in each. Respond to My love flowing out to you. Soak it up, as a flower soaks up the rays of the sun. Without those quiet times of soaking up the rays of the sun, the flower becomes stunted. So quiet seasons are necessary to the growth of My children, if they are to become solidly based. Otherwise, they become "flitters," flittering from one thing to another, and their growth is as the tall spindly stalk, searching for the sun, instead of the strong solid stalk that has steadily soaked in the sun, soaked in My love. Rejoice in our quiet time together.

You Are Precious to Me,
Your Loving Father

Thank You, Father, for such a vivid word picture of what I don't want to be, a tall spindly stalk, searching for the sun. I want to be that strong solid stalk that has steadily soaked in the sun, soaked in Your love. The second Word You ever spoke to me was, "Feed on My Word night and day. It is life to you. Listen closely, My child. I will speak to you as you speak to Me. Listen well, My child. Much is ahead of you. Stay in My Word. Prepare yourself."

Father, what treasures do You have in Your Word for me today?

_____

_____

_____

_____

_____

_____

_____

_____

_____

_____

_____

_____

_____

_____

_____

244

GALATIANS 6:9 AMP
"In due time and at the appointed season we shall reap,
if we do not loosen and relax our courage and faint."

My Child,

Be at peace. Do the flowers of the fields struggle to receive the beauty of their raiment? No, they trust in their Father's care and receive in due season. So shall it be with you. Struggle not and be at peace, for in My time and at My command, each piece shall fall into place and come to pass as I have set forth. Do not be ashamed nor disturbed by your lack of "productive" activity. Even the beautiful flower of the field must lie dormant in the field until spring. But then it arises to new life and beauty. So be not perplexed—nor puzzled by your situation, but take each season as it comes, continually drawing strength and taking each day as it dawns, with joy and thanksgiving. For My Spirit shall be manifested in ways that you know not of, and you shall rejoice with Me as it is revealed.

Be At Peace, My Child,

I Love You

Loving Father, I am coming into Your Presence today to draw on Your strength and Your peace. Speak to my heart, I pray.

_____

_____

_____

_____

_____

_____

_____

_____

_____

_____

_____

Father, thank You, for Your loving encouragement in the different seasons of my life, bringing enlightenment and encouragement as You walk through each season with me! You also said, "Be not impatient, for My leadings fall one upon the other, in an orderly fashion. All shall come to pass as I would have it, for those who love Me and follow My commands and leadings. I shall not desert you or forsake you. Pressure is applied by the evil one. My ways bring peace no matter what the surrounding circumstances may be. My peace is with you!"

245

PROVERBS 19:21 AMP
"Many plans are in a man's mind,
but it is the Lord's purpose for him that will stand."

Dear One,

Lay before My feet your desires and your plans. Let Me make the plans and lead the way, for My ways are higher than your ways, and My plans come forth with rejoicing and much fruit. Be not afraid to express your desires to Me, but once they are expressed, leave them with Me. You will rejoice to see how I bring just the right things to pass. So bring forth your desires, lay them on the altar, and go your way in peace.

Trust Me, My Child,
Your Loving Father

I love You, Father! So often 1 just hold my desires to my own heart and forget to share them with You, because I am so intent on wanting to hear Your heart and Your desires for me. You said, "I stretch out My hand to you, My child. Stretch out your hand to Me, and grasp it with the firm, trusting grip of a child." When children trust their parents, they share everything that's on their hearts with abandon. This is how I want to be with You, my loving Father!

Loving Father, these are the desires that I have held to my heart. I want to share them with You.

_____

_____

_____

_____

_____

_____

_____

_____

_____

_____

_____

_____

_____

_____

_____

246

ISAIAH 30:21 AMP
"And your ears will hear a word behind you, saying,
This is the way; walk in it, when you turn to the right hand
and when you turn to the left."

My Child,

Prizes in the natural are won by sacrifice, determination, and endurance. Prizes in the spiritual realm are won in the same way, by sacrifice, determination, and endurance. Be faithful to your high calling and you shall be the recipient of prizes beyond estimation. Continue on! Continue on! Let not up in your quest for wisdom, discernment, perception, and a Walk with Me! They are, and shall all be yours; for those who ask, receive; and those who seek, find; and those who knock at the door of the Kingdom of God shall have the door opened to them and they shall walk in with joy. Continue your quest, for your reward is sure.

The Best Is Yet to Come!
Your Loving Father

I love You, Father! Thank You for speaking to my heart!

Loving Father, the desire of my heart has always been to know You more each day, to have Your wisdom, discernment, perception, and to hear Your voice more clearly and more intimately with each passing day. Thank You, Father, that the desires of my heart are the desires of Your heart, because You are the One who put those desires in my heart!

PSALM 10:17 AMP
"O Lord, You have heard the desire
and the longing of the humble and oppressed;
You will prepare and strengthen, and direct their hearts,
You will cause Your ear to hear."

My Child,

Remove sin and remain in My love. The Words of My Spirit ring forth with clarity and truth. Cling to them with ever-increasing vigilance, for they are strength to your bones and everlasting life to your soul. Fear not, My little one, but remain in My love forever. Release unto Me your fears of rejection, of being forgotten. Paul was not forgotten during his years in the desert with Me. He strengthened and prepared, and I sent him out with power and with My Word and with My Spirit. So shall it be with you. Strengthen! Become one with Me!

You Are Blessed, My Child,

Your Loving Father

Loving Father, is so easy to feel left out during the desert years, and yet they are such times of preparation, and so important. Thank You for reminding me that it is a time to be strengthened and to become one with You. I love reading the words from Your heart to me, over and over and over again, for they truly bring life to my heart and my soul. I love You, Father!

Precious Father, I want You to have total access to my heart. How can I become even more "One with You," dear Heavenly Father?

_____

_____

_____

_____

_____

_____

_____

_____

_____

_____

_____

248

COLOSSIANS 3:14 AMP
"And above all these [put on] love and enfold yourselves with the bond
of perfectness, [which binds everything together completely
in ideal harmony]."

My Child,

My love flows out to you strongly. There is no area of your life that My love cannot touch and re-create. Stay close to that love! Draw on that love! Depend on that love! And as you do this, that same love flows from you to others. That drawing and dependence on My love, creates a flow of My love from Me, to you, to others—a flow that is continuous. So continue to draw and depend on My love, that others in need might receive My love through the flow of My love through you. They must become receivers before they can become transformers. Beauty and strength come through My love. All gifts of my Spirit are created by My love. So are your gifts to be created through My pure love given forth. Stand firm, stand tall in My love, for you are My beloved child in whom I am well pleased!

Be My Love!
Your Loving Father

Loving Father, I love You with all my heart. Being in Your loving Presence is the joy of my life!

_____

_____

_____

_____

_____

_____

_____

_____

_____

Dear beloved Father, receiving and giving Your love means everything to me! Long ago You said that love would be a part of my life in ways I had never dreamed of. And now, today, I find myself surrounded by Your treasures who have also found that receiving and giving Your love is the only way to live. One of the greatest joys is seeing the wonderful transformation, as receivers become transformers, all by the power of Your love!

249

PSALMS 73:24 AMP
"You will guide me with Your counsel,
and afterward receive me to honor and glory."

My Child,

Life is like a maze. You can find your own way by continually running into solid walls that lead nowhere, and then backtrack and start over again; for there is only one way, My way. Or you can let Me guide you through the maze, every step of the way. The end of the way is life with Me. Some, through obstinate self-will, never find the conclusion I have for them. They refuse My help, depend on themselves, and never make it. Depending on Me contains the promise of success and victory. The more one depends on My guidance, the fewer dead-ends one encounters.

Depend on My Guidance,
Your Loving Father

Loving Father, just a few days ago You said, "Straightforward and precise you shall be, causing the enemy to flee. A calculated risk you shall take; not a minute too early, not a moment too late; right on time, as I cause you to turn on a dime." Those words, Father, gave me the encouragement to do what I knew I needed to do, knowing the outcome was secure. What a wonderful way to live Father; following Your leading and guidance.

Father, I love Your Presence and I love depending on Your guidance!
Speak to my heart, for I am listening!

_____

_____

_____

_____

_____

_____

_____

_____

_____

_____

_____

_____

_____

250

DEUTERONOMY 11:26 AMP
"Behold, I set before you this day, a blessing and a curse."

My Child,

I set before you a blessing and a curse, as I do before all of My people. Serve Me with gladness of heart and lean not unto your own understanding. Stand upright in spirit, with no guile therein. Prepare within your heart a garden of praise and thanksgiving, and know without a shadow of a doubt that I am with you. My rod and My staff do comfort you and guide you to green pastures, and beside still waters, to refresh you and uphold you. Hasten not to strive for greatness and pleasures. False striving brings forth the curse, which is loss of communion with Me. Never let this happen.

Listen to My Heart, My Child,
Your Loving Father

Loving Father, I will take each day as You bring them to me, with a song in my heart and praise upon my lips!

_____

_____

_____

_____

_____

_____

_____

_____

_____

_____

_____

_____

My Father, Your Word says, "You will show me the path of life; in Your presence is fullness of joy, at Your right hand there are pleasures forevermore,"(Psalm 16:11 AMP). I choose the pleasures You so readily pour upon me, even in the midst of trials. I choose Your comfort and guidance, joy and refreshing. I choose Your destiny for my life with Your perfect timing! I love You, Father!

PSALM 43:3 AMP
"O send out Your light and Your truth, let them lead me."

My Child,

Break away from traditions of man that bind. Be set free from the fetters of traditional views that bind. Seek out My truth each day and move on that truth. Leave behind old ways that have always led to dead-ends, that have never led to Me and My Presence. Be a watchman on the wall and carry My truth within you as a prized historian carries truth within him. For it shall be My truth, unpolluted by years and years of men's tradition. Seek for My truth with renewed vigor and stamina. Revel in that truth with renewed and newly awakened perseverance. My Spirit shall lead you in your quest for truth and you shall know as you walk, which is and which is not from My Word. Practice My Presence with ever-increasing determination and joy in receiving from me—My truth, My Word, and the fulfillment of My love.

Walk in Truth, I Walk with You!

Loving Father, walking into a place that is steeped in the traditions of man is a very cold and lonely place. Where Your Presence is, there is life and love, joy and freedom, truth and peace. Where there is trust and love, it is okay to do it right and it is okay to do it wrong, because You are big enough to cover it all with Your grace. Thank You Father, for the priceless gift of Your loving Presence!

Precious Father, Your Presence is my passion! Once again, today, I long to hear Your voice!

_____

_____

_____

_____

_____

_____

_____

_____

_____

_____

_____

_____

252

1 PETER 3:11 AMP
"Let him search for peace (harmony; undisturbedness from fears, agitating passions, and moral conflicts), and seek it eagerly."

My Child,

Capture the seeds of discord and unrest, lest they continue to grow, for they would bring destruction and ruin. Love is the key. Give forth of My Spirit through love and forgiveness. Remember to smooth the way with concern and loving acceptance. You will see the walls come tumbling down and be pleased with the added blessings of harmony and a propensity of acceptance. Refrain from any sort of attempt to save face. That is not the issue at stake. Let your heart go out with love and acceptance. Let your words be words of tribute and acknowledgment of their worth. Blessed is the one who can lay down their right to acknowledgment to bring forth the acknowledgment of the other.

Give forth of My Love,
Your Loving Father

Father, help me always to remember to get my love and acceptance from You and to give it out through You to others! Are there areas I've let slip?

_____

_____

_____

_____

_____

_____

_____

_____

_____

_____

Father, what a difference it made. The walls did come tumbling down, and peace and harmony did descend. Lord, help me always to lay down my right to acknowledgment, to bring forth the acknowledgment of others. May I always refrain from any sort of attempt to save face, but always let my heart go out with love and acceptance and forgiveness. What an important life lesson!

253

PSALM 9:2 AMP
"I will rejoice in You and be and high spirits;
I will sing praise to Your name, O Most High!"

My Child,

Lay down your defenses. Let them come to rest. (What defenses, Lord?) The defense of appearing "worthy enough." Just be! Learn to appropriate My wholeness, and rest in that wholeness. Respond to others with the same love and acceptance that I have poured out on you. Plunge headlong into the joy of your salvation, lacking in nothing. Rejoice and be glad. A singing heart, a rejoicing heart—such a heart cannot be moved, neither will it be afraid, but it will be like the rushing spring of fresh, cool water, dancing in the sunlight. Such have I created you to be. Appreciate what I am telling you and go forth this day singing praises and making beautiful music to delight us both!

I Love You!

I Love You, Too, Father

Father, You also said, "Never resort to an outward show to gain affection and love. The outward show brings My indignation and wrath, for it is your feeble efforts, as were Cain's, to gain My acceptance on your terms instead of Mine. Do not perform, but just be, knowing My love for you is constant and sure. Give forth of My love naturally, without striving, and it shall be returned to you tenfold." Father, may I never perform for You or for others, but simply just be, without striving, knowing Your love for me is constant and sure!

Loving Father, I want my heart to always be a singing heart, like the rushing spring of fresh, cool water, dancing in the sunlight! Today I am going forth, singing praises and making beautiful music to delight us both, with my ear tuned to hear You speak to my heart!

———————————

———————————

———————————

———————————

———————————

———————————

———————————

———————————

———————————

254

ROMANS 14:19 NKJV
"Therefore let us pursue the things which make for peace
and the things by which one may edify another."

My Child,

Don't be afraid of men's faces or their intimidating words or thoughts. Words of contention, distrust, and disrespect shall always be there, but they need no longer distract you or cause you pain. Confidence in Me is the key, and the knowledge of My love and confidence in you. Many times you shall hear words that would have stopped you in your tracks before, and caused agony and pain, but now those same words shall be brushed aside and you shall go forth and forward as I lead, in the confidence, power, and authority of your God!

Be Confident in Me!

Your Loving Father

Loving Father, I pray that love, honor, and true confidence in You and Your love will always lead me!

———————————
———————————
———————————
———————————
———————————
———————————
———————————
———————————
———————————
———————————
———————————
———————————
———————————
———————————

Loving Father, long ago You said, "I bring people into your life to love and honor with no expectations of return. If they are capable of returning that love and honor, great, but it is only possible for them if they don't have walls of rejection. "Everyone has experienced rejection. It's how we respond to rejection that determines how we will live our lives, honoring, loving, and receiving love from others or dishonoring and rejecting others. Those who honor others, keep their walls down, so they can love without fear of rejection, saying, "How can I serve you." Those who walk dishonoring others, keep their walls up. They can't receive or give love for fear of rejection, saying, "It's because of what they did to me."

ISAIAH 26:3 NKJV
"You will keep him in perfect peace, whose mind is stayed on You, because he trusts in You."

My Child,

The minds of men cause problems that don't exist. Put your mind at rest, knowing that I am with you to enable you to discern My direction and leading. Let go of the distraction, heaviness, and confusion of mind and soul. Let Me soothe the frayed resolve. "Mind over matter," it has been said, but I say, "Spirit over mind." Let My Spirit reign and peace shall descend and conquer all confusion. Resist the temptation to let your mind dwell on the unimportant. Let it soar in realms of Glory.

Be at Peace in Me,
I Love You

Loving Father, You also said, "Step over the rocks, the obstacles put in your path and be at peace. Many are the obstacles to fall on, but I say to you, be at peace and rejoice in My steadfast protection and care. You shall walk victorious in My light and abundance. Walk in faith, knowing that I am with You." Thank You, Father, for Your peace that comes when I let go of distractions, heaviness, and confusion of mind and soul, and come into Your Presence—letting my spirit soar in realms of Glory with You!

Father, thank You for strength of will to let go of the unimportant, that I might always walk peacefully in Your Presence!

_____

_____

_____

_____

_____

_____

_____

_____

_____

_____

_____

_____

256

PSALM 33:9 AMP
"For He spoke, and it was done;
He commanded, and it stood steadfast."

My Precious One,

Now you can truly say, "Sticks and stones may break my bones, but words will never hurt me," for you have faced into the wind and come up strong. The weight of the world has fallen from your shoulders, that you might fly with freedom, restored by the might of My power and love. You have turned a corner, walking in My love. It shall bring forth added truth and sustenance for your soul and spirit. Fear not for the length of your days. Fear not for the content. Now, go forth with a song in your heart and a song of praise on your lips, for My Word has prevailed.

You Are Precious to Me,
Your Loving Father

Loving Father, my heart dances and sings before You with great joy as I bask in Your Presence!

_____

_____

_____

_____

_____

_____

_____

_____

_____

_____

I love You, Father! You have brought me such a long way by the power of Your love! Truly the weight of the world has fallen from my shoulders! There is such a freedom in walking with You, not fearing for the length of my days or for their content, but simply going forth with a song in my heart and a song of praise on my lips for You, my faithful and loving Father and God!

MATTHEW 5:9 KJV
"Blessed are the peacemakers:
for they shall be called the children of God."

My Child,

Blessed are the merciful, for they shall see God. Build not walls of protection, but be vulnerable and transparent. Blessed are the peacemakers for they shall see God. Blessed are you when you suffer for My sake, for the blessings of My heart are yours. I have turned your mourning into joy, your sadness into thanksgiving, and have given to you blessings evermore. Stand on the Rock of my salvation. Forsake not your stance of joy and thanksgiving, for unto you have I poured out My wealth of blessings. Fear not the dark, for it is bathed in light. Fear not the night, for it is followed by the bright dawn of My blessing. For unto those who seek My will, I've made manifest the wonders of My Kingdom. Nothing can deter them from their appointed walk with Me. Nothing can shatter, scatter, nor detract from the wholeness of the walk I have appointed for them to walk in.

You Are Precious to Me!
Your Loving Father

Loving Father, thank You that no matter how fierce the storm or how incomprehensible the situation, You are there, bringing peace and faith to keep me walking forward. Thank You, Father, for helping me to not build walls of protection and to remain vulnerable and transparent. Thank You for teaching me to laugh and sing in the midst of trials. I love You, Father!

Father, here I am, loving the peace of Your Presence, and seeking Your will about…

_____

_____

_____

_____

_____

_____

_____

_____

258

PSALM 12:6 AMP
"The words and promises of the Lord are pure words,
like silver refined in an earthen furnace, purified seven times over."

My Child,

Many times I have cradled you in My arms and comforted you. Many times you have looked to Me to rescue you and tenderly protect you. Know that I have not wavered from My promises to you. One by one they have found a place in your heart as you have believed with an unfaltering belief. This is My gift to you: strength in the midst of the storm, light in the midst of the darkness, and hope that transcends all doubt. Surely My loving-kindness has led you and protected you. So now, go forth unafraid, rejoicing in My might, for it is yours; perceiving, receiving, and committing all that you have and are, into My loving care. I have brought you into the vast and unending knowledge of My love for you. Go forth with joy. Go forth with soundness and wholeness of heart, for I am with you.

I Love You, My Child,

Your Father

Father, today I look to You for…

_____
_____
_____
_____
_____
_____
_____
_____
_____
_____
_____
_____
_____
_____
_____

Loving Father, throughout my life, You have cradled me in Your arms and comforted me. Just the thought of You brings peace to my inner being. And when the crisis of the moment overwhelms me, You are there. I depend on Your promises, as one by one they come into view and into reality, to the joy of my heart. But always there are deeper lessons of trust, heart-peace, confidence, and knowing more fully Your Presence. Thank You, Father, that You never give up on me and always see me through!

259

PROVERBS 10:29 AMP
"The way of the Lord is strength
and a stronghold to the upright."

My Child,

Wrestle not with your inadequacies. Simply say, "This I will do," and stick to it. Let it not be said that you had not the fortitude to persevere, for persevere you shall and together we shall see it through to the very end. Let your "yea" be yea and your "nay" be nay. Strength of will shall see you through many a tight situation and strength of will shall be yours as you persevere with determination to be an overcomer in My Name.

I Am Your Strength,
Your Loving Father

Thank You, Father for making me an overcomer in Your Name, with the determination and fortitude to persevere. Thank You for teaching me that how You have created me is adequate, through Your power, for all situations! Thank You, for being my strength!

Loving Father, You are my strength and my song! I come to You with a thankful, listening heart.

_____

_____

_____

_____

_____

_____

_____

_____

_____

_____

_____

_____

_____

_____

_____

_____

_____

260

COLOSSIANS 2:7 NKJV
"Rooted and built up in Him and established in the faith,
as you have been taught, abounding in it with thanksgiving."

My Child,

Keep your mind from circling and circling. You shall know what each day is to hold. Simply complete each task, as I present it. Keep your focus on Me. With your focus firmly planted on Me, so that nothing can move you off that position, I am free to work in your life. Success cannot come when you move your focus off of Me onto the externals; only confusion, frustration, cobwebs, and windmills—circling and circling of the mind. Heed well My words to you and keep your focus on Me and My ways, for you shall be clear and on track. Keep your focus steady on Me. We shall prevail together.

You Can Trust Me,
Together We Shall Prevail!

Loving Father, I choose to keep my focus on You and Your Word so that we can prevail together. My heart is focused on You, listening with anticipation.

_____

_____

_____

_____

_____

_____

_____

_____

_____

_____

_____

Father, when my mind starts circling away from You and Your Word, onto the problems of life, I will remember a word picture You gave me years ago. You said, "My Word reaches far beyond the moment it is spoken. It is like a pebble thrown in the water that ripples and circles endlessly. My Word shimmers like diamonds, like the sun shimmering on the water as it ripples. Reach out your hand and continue to give forth My Word. Be ready to give forth the Water of Life."

DEUTERONOMY 4:31 AMP
"For the Lord your God is a merciful God;
He will not fail you."

My Child,

My children cannot fail. If they believe in hurt and failure, it is theirs. If they believe in My love and protection, nothing can come nigh them but My love and My peace. They will never be put to shame. The trust of a child brings forth perfection. Nothing can alter the course of a trusting heart. Trust Me! Do not steal your heart to trust Me, as one in a leaky boat in a raging stream. Trust Me as a carefree child being carried in her Father's arms. No course of action can derail you unless you allow it by agreeing to its power over you. There is no power greater than My power. Relax in My love for you.

Trust Me, My Child,
Your Loving Father

Loving Father, You have said, "Handle each situation as it arises with confidence and assurance, for I shall not let you miss the mark. Each action shall be with precision; My precision. Act and react in perfect confidence in My guiding hand in your life." Father, what comfort to know that when I believe in Your love and protection with the trusting heart of a child being carried in her Father's arms, I cannot fail. Help me never to agree with and believe in hurt and failure. I choose to trust You!

Faithful Father, I bring to You the areas in my life that I need to walk more peacefully in.

_____

_____

_____

_____

_____

_____

_____

_____

_____

_____

_____

_____

_____

_____

262

JOHN 12:24 AMP

"Unless a grain of wheat falls into the earth and dies, it remains [just one grain; it never becomes more, but lives] by itself alone. But if it dies, it produces many others and yields a rich harvest."

My Child,

Seasons change, and with the change in seasons comes a new direction, a new goal, and a new purpose in My Kingdom. Seeming defeat is the birthplace and foundation for victory—My kind of victory. Be not dismayed, but stand tall in the blessing and Glory of My acceptance and love and watch Me take the ball and bring forth victory from seeming defeat. For does not My Word say that the seed must die before it can be raised to glorious life, life abundant, everlasting and free? Be not dismayed, but stay close to My heart and watch Me work.

You Are Safe in Me!

Your Loving Father

Loving Father, thank You for Your constant and abiding care over my life in the lives of those I love! Thank You for speaking to my heart and bringing such comfort and joy!

_____

_____

_____

_____

_____

_____

_____

_____

_____

_____

Beloved Father, You have also said, "When you feel the blow of defeat, I always turn it to victory. Time after time, I have been to you the 'Rock of Gibraltar,' that strong bulwark of peace and stability. I will not forsake you. Take on a new identity in Me, Jehovah-jireh, 'Jehovah will provide.'" Father, thank You for new seasons, new direction, new goals, and new purposes in Your Kingdom and in my life. Thank You for taking the ball and bringing forth victory from seeming defeat. I love You, Father!

263

MATTHEW 7:3 NLT
"And why worry about a speck in your friend's eye,
when you have a log in your own?"

My Child,

*Release your own spirit to hear My Word more clearly, for I long to share with
you more of My Kingdom here on earth and in heaven. Worry not whether others
hear My voice. Stick to basics. You hear My voice! Do not try to extract the
twig from another's eye. Tend to the log in your own and I will tend to the twig
in your friend's eye. Now you have the idea. Judging, even in the wrappings of
love and concern, is still judging, and ties My hands to work in their lives and
yours. Once again, when you see a problem in another's life, unrecognized by
them, lift it up to Me and leave it there. Don't take the problem upon your own
shoulders. It was never meant to rest there. It will weigh you down and block
both of your progress in Me. That is why I say, "Release them unto Me." Take
not the burden to yourself.*

Listen for My Voice, My Child,
I Love You, Your Father

Loving Father, that must be the reason that You have said to me, "Give advice only when asked for, and otherwise give love as easily as I breathe." Also in the past You have said, "Speak only positive, uplifting words about others and leave the negatives unspoken." But knowing that judging actually ties Your hands to work in their lives, and mine, is even more reason to simply release them and the burden unto You.

Dear Father, when I'm tempted to say a negative, judging word about one of Your treasures, help me to remember to speak only positive words about them and release the negative words to You!

_____

_____

_____

_____

_____

_____

_____

_____

_____

264

MATTHEW 9:37-38 NKJV
"The harvest truly is plentiful, but the laborers are few.
Therefore pray the Lord of the harvest
to send out laborers into His harvest."

My Precious Child,

I have fashioned you for joy, to bring forth the harvest! The joy of My Presence causes you to glow. Others can simply look at you and know I am real! As you bask in My Presence, it shows! Continue on this special way of basking in My joy and Presence every day. The rewards of a joyful, loving heart have no end. There is always something new around the bend to delight your heart! You are blessed beyond measure.

I Love You, My Child!

Loving Father, how can I bring joy to Your heart today?

_____

_____

_____

_____

_____

_____

_____

_____

_____

_____

_____

_____

Precious Father, I feel blessed beyond measure! People tell me I glow and that always takes me by surprise. Now I know why! It is the joy of basking in Your Presence every day! Truly every day is filled with new, unexpected delights, brought forth by Your hand of love. I love You so much, Father!

265

LUKE 1:37 NKJV
"For with God, nothing will be impossible."

My Blessed One,

Lessons lived become the heart you give. Gratitude from your heart proclaimed will help others get into the game, from the sidelines of pain and doubt, to understand what life is all about. I've brought peace where there was no peace and you have weathered the storms. Now I say unto you, be strong, be brave, be bold. Speak forth My Word with power, love, and truth. Make a way through the wilderness for others to follow with clarity and truth. I shall use you in many ways you know not of. I shall use you to light the fires of passion in the hearts of others. From your youth, I have fashioned you with precision and care. And now, I send you forth to proclaim My heart of passion for My people!

I Love You, My Child!

I Love You So Much, Too, Father!

Truly Father, there is a passion in my heart, that others know the joy and freedom of knowing how much the God and Creator of the Universe loves and treasures them. I will joyfully spend my life proclaiming Your heart of love and passion for Your people, Your treasures! Father, with Your help, I will be strong, brave, and bold, with gentleness, gratefulness, and love!

Loving Father, I just want to bask in Your loving Presence today with gratefulness and joy!

_____
_____
_____
_____
_____
_____
_____
_____
_____
_____
_____
_____
_____
_____
_____
_____

266

"Behold, I make all things new."

My Beloved Child,

Stand straight and tall in my Spirit. Let your heart be strong in the knowledge of My love for you. You cried out, and I answered. You shall continue to prosper and grow in the light of My Spirit, in the light of My love for you. Behold, all things are new! The old has passed away, and behold, the new has sprung forth as the noonday sun. Rejoice, My child, and be glad. Many have longed to see this day come forth in their lives. Your day has come. Give forth of My love to you. Give forth with a gentle, loving, and understanding heart, filled with the blessings of My love to you. Break forth into singing, My little one. Break forth into the new day with song.

It Is A New Day, My Child,
I Love You, Your Father

I love You Father, and treasure every moment spent in Your Presence! My heart sings to You a song of love!

_____

_____

_____

_____

_____

_____

_____

_____

_____

_____

_____

_____

Loving Father, I have such an excitement in my heart, for what is to come. You said, "Stretch forth your wings and fly. Be not bound by outward appearances. The joy of the Lord is your strength and your song, and the buoyancy for your wings. Take off and soar!" Whatever the future holds, I know You will be there with me, showing me the way!

267

PSALM 94:22 AMP
"But the Lord has become my High Tower and Defense,
and my God, the Rock of my refuge."

My Precious Child,

In the midst of the storm, I have kept you warm and poured My oil of gladness over you. Rest secure in My arms, safe from fear and alarms. With love, I encircle you. For hope does arise in the midst of many sighs. "Have faith," has been your heart's cry. For in the midst of the storm, when your heart felt worn and torn, then My love, soothing love, enfolded you. I want you to know that my love will continually set you free. It has been the ride of a lifetime, but it's only begun. You will learn how to run, and it's going to be fun. My peace you will finally know, so that My love you can freely sow with no restraints, no delays. It truly is a new day, complete in every way. Settle within your heart this day, that I will truly make a way to bring forth your hopes and dreams; they will seem to be bursting forth from the seams.

You Are Blessed, My Child,
Your Loving Father

Loving Father, in the very beginning, You said, "My Spirit envelops you and protects you, as the flowing robes of the caravan driver protect him from the winds and sands of the desert!" And so it has been throughout the years. You have cherished and loved me, protected, soothed, and enfolded me, and taught me many truths to set my spirit free! It truly has been the ride of a lifetime and I am excited about what is to come, for You will be there with me every step of the way! I love You, Father!

My Father, speak to my heart, for I am listening with anticipation!

_____

_____

_____

_____

_____

_____

_____

_____

_____

_____

_____

_____

268

PSALM 99:6 AMP
"They called upon the Lord, and He answered them."

My Child,

Call to Me and I will answer. My rod (protection) and My staff (guidance) they comfort you. I have raised you up as a standard bearer among my people to say, "Here is the way, walk ye in it." Straight and narrow is the path that leads to life everlasting. Faithfulness and trustworthiness is the key to walking uprightly before Me. Stand tall in My Presence. See what I see, and call forth what I call forth with singleness of mind and heart. Sing forth into the Heavens, and mighty shall the miracles be that come forth. Measure your days as one who has faced death and won. Be content in My Presence with the carefree spirit of youth, knowing that nothing can touch you that has not been filtered through My love. Sing in the sunshine. Precious in my sight are those who release unto Me all anxiety and fear. Go forth with transforming joy and peace. Let the words of your mouth and the sound of My voice sound alike, one unto the other, both proclaiming My Glory to a sad and dying world.

I Love You, My Child,

Your Father

Dear Father, are there areas where the words of my mouth do not match the sound of Your voice?

_____

_____

_____

_____

_____

_____

_____

_____

_____

Loving Father, it is so freeing to know that nothing can touch me that has not been filtered through Your love! To know that no matter how hard and difficult the road, You are with me leading and guiding and bringing forth precious fruit from my life. I can face life or death with the carefree spirit of youth, without anxiety and fear, with a song of praise and thanksgiving in my heart! I love You, Father!

DEUTERONOMY 28:9 AMP
"The Lord will establish you as a people holy to Himself."

My Child,

I have swept and made clean and have established you on high ground, removed from the clamor and din of lower roads, filled with the muck and mire of confusion. Stay on the high road that My Spirit creates within your heart, allowing you to rejoice in the completeness of My love and peace that brings forth My joy. Let Me fan the embers and provide for you labors that fulfill and spring forth capabilities of which you know not. Of My seasons, My times, and My ways, you are learning. Seek not to leave behind this season too quickly before it has brought forth the appointed fruit and wisdom. Settle in for the duration and fear not, for your faithfulness shall be known and rekindle faithfulness in others.

You Are Precious to Me,

Your Loving Father

Loving Father, You have said that within each of us are giftings, anointings, and callings that we know not of, that you have placed within us for the appointed time. How exciting to know that in this season, You are fanning the embers and providing labors that will fulfill and spring forth some of these capabilities that I know not of! Thank you, Father, for the gifts of faithfulness, peace, and steadfastness!

Father, I come to You today with joy in my heart and a listening ear!

_____
_____
_____
_____
_____
_____
_____
_____
_____
_____
_____
_____
_____
_____

270

PSALM 139:12 AMP
"Even the darkness hides nothing from You,
but the night shines as the day; the darkness and the light
are both alike to You."

My Precious Child,

Life for you has been like dark silhouettes against the night sky, but I have held your hand and together we have walked through the darkness. I have held you steady and created within your heart a song and a melody to comfort and strengthen you along the way. It is not necessary for others to know the darkness of the night or the weight of the struggle, for I strengthen, sustain, and cause your heart to sing in the night. Strange and fearsome has been the night, but you have seen the light of My smile upon you. My light has overcome the dark places in your life and overcome the dark night of your soul. The angels rejoice with you, as you step forth each day in total reliance on Me, and with confidence in My steadfast love. Bask in the light of my smile.

I Love You, My Child.

I love You, Father! Thank You for Your faithfulness and steadfast love to me. Help me always to treat others with that same faithfulness and steadfast love.

_____

_____

_____

_____

_____

_____

_____

_____

Precious Father, truly, You are my "Song in the Night," bringing comfort and strength to my heart. You have held my hand and kept me steady as we've walked through the darkness together, causing me to trust You with my whole heart because of Your constant, steadfast, and loving Presence. It is all worthwhile, to see the wonderful changes in my life that overcoming with You has brought forth. You are my song!

2 CORINTHIANS 1:4 NKJV
"Who comforts us in all our tribulation,
that we may be able to comfort those who are in any trouble,
with the comfort with which we ourselves are comforted by God."

My Precious Child,

I have held you in My arms and have stroked your hair, bringing comfort to your wearied soul. I have loved you with an everlasting love and now, together, we shall see the weary restored, the prisoner set free, and the lost found. Like hearts shall join with you who have counted the cost and marched forth to victory. You have counted the cost and fought the good fight and shouted the victory to a stagnant world. You shall comfort them as I have comforted you, and stroke their hair with love, pointing them to Me, and I shall lift their burden and set them free.

Comfort My People!
Your Loving Father

Precious Father, I love to hold Your people in my arms, as You have taught me to do, as I would most gently and tenderly hold the most valuable treasure on earth, imparting to them Your heart and Your love, knowing that You will lift their burden and set them free! Thank You, Father, that we shall see the weary restored, the prisoner set free, and the lost found!

Father, thank You, that I can come to You any minute of any day, soak in Your comfort and listen to Your words of love and encouragement. I come to You now.

_____

_____

_____

_____

_____

_____

_____

_____

_____

_____

_____

272

PSALM 118:24 NKJV
"This is the day which the LORD has made;
we will rejoice and be glad in it."

My Child,

Each day is like a treasure handed to you on a silver platter, Divine and Holy, untouched by human hands. Treasure each day as a special gift, charted and laid out from the foundation of the earth. My blessed ones hear My voice and are satisfied. They know My heart of love toward them and walk unafraid. Stand strong and fearless in the confidence of My love and protection, for many are the opportunities to fall, but My hand sustains and protects you and causes you to flourish and grow. Stand guard against the enemy and shout for joy! Childlikeness and precision walk hand in hand by My Spirit. My Spirit proclaims victory over your life. Be refreshed this day.

You Are Blessed, My Child!
Your Loving Father

Father, I bring these challenges to You for wisdom and understanding.

_____
_____
_____
_____
_____
_____
_____
_____
_____
_____
_____
_____
_____

Loving Father, more and more I am seeing the miracle of each day that You have created for me! Truly, each one is like a treasure handed to me on a silver platter, Divine and Holy, untouched by human hands! Each day surprises me with delights, blessings, and challenges too, but the challenges are only opportunities to trust You and know that You will teach me through them. Father, help me to wake each morning with a song in my heart for You!

273

JOB 8:21 AMP
"He will yet fill your mouth with laughter
and your lips with joyful shouting."

My Child,

Tides come and go. Seasons change. The magnitude of My Word to you changes as each year comes and goes. Silence has been golden throughout your life. Laughter has been a prize to be attained. Silver linings in the storms have abounded and you have seen and pondered them in your heart. My Word, you have treasured. My songs have been in your heart. My beauty has made your heart sing and My love has held you strong. It has been said, "There is music and laughter in your voice," but there shall be laughter and a new joy in your soul, My special gift to you. Come to the well and drink deeply, My Child, that you might overflow and bubble merrily. Laughter it shall be, full and free. Tremendous things lie ahead, ready to be walked in and explored.

Come Laugh with Me, My Child,
Your Loving Father

Loving Father, You have come in the silence and turned the silence to gold with Your Presence! Truly, Your beauty has made my heart sing, and Your love has held me strong. Already there is a new joy in my soul at the sound of laughter bubbling up! There is such excitement in my heart for the things that lie ahead, ready to be walked in and explored, filled with laughter and joy with You! I love You, Father!

Thank You Father, that walking with You is such an adventure! Here I am at Your well, drinking deeply, listening for Your voice to my heart!

_____

_____

_____

_____

_____

_____

_____

_____

_____

_____

_____

_____

_____

274

PSALM 89:28 AMP
"My mercy and loving-kindness will I keep for him forevermore,
and My covenant shall stand fast and be faithful with him."

Precious One,

Ruminate not on the frailties of man, but seek Me who is above all and the Creator of all. Circumstances shall not derail what I have created for you. Tattered and torn are many plans of those around you, but their Creator is the stable force in each of their lives, the anchor upon which they can stand in faith unmoved. When the focus is on Me, one always lands on their feet from one of the enemy's bombs (land mines) along the path. Be fortified by My Word to your heart, which is constantly available to you. Sing in the face of the enemy. Stand amazed at what I shall do with you, for you, and through you, for My Presence and Glory sustains you, leads, guides, and comforts you, and is the strong tower on which you stand and have your being.

I Am Always with You!
Your Loving Father

Loving Father, my focus is on You. Thank You for teaching me Your ways

_____

_____

_____

_____

_____

_____

_____

_____

_____

_____

_____

Father, You have always told me to see others as You see them, not as they appear to be. That way I can love them as You love them, because You see the end from the beginning. It is so much easier to love those You love that way! Thank You for always helping me to keep my focus on You, not on what is happening around me, so that I can always land on my feet after one of the enemy's unexpected bombs or land mines. Father, teach me to sing in the face of the enemy!

275

ISAIAH 43:4 NKJV
"Since you are precious in My sight, You have been honored,
and I have loved you."

My Precious One,

Precious are My children who sit at My knee to receive. Their cups overflow with a capacity to know My heart and My love. They are secure and can conquer the world, for their Daddy is the Giant Dragon Slayer and they know they are protected and secure, that nothing can touch them for harm. Their eye is single upon their Beloved. They play and explore, but always within the boundaries they know will please and bring joy to their Father. Then, back they come to my knee, to bask in and share my love, my pleasure in them, my wisdom, His knowledge and the joy that comes from being in my Presence. You have always been this child in whom I could take joy and pride. But now I am inviting you to stand up and labor with Me by My side; ever alert to hear My heart; ever alert to play your part in this universal plan. Moment by moment, hearing My Word, knowing the words you have heard. Much learning took place at My knee. Now you shall stand up and see the fields ripe for harvest.

I Take Joy in You, My Child,
Your Loving Father

Thank You, Father, that when I get weary and need to be refreshed, I can always come back to Your knee anytime of the day or night, and bask in and share Your love and Your pleasure in me; drawing on Your wisdom, knowledge, love, peace, and joy. For You will always be my Beloved Daddy, and my "Giant Dragon Slayer"!

Loving Father, my heart is open, ready to hear Your words of direction!

_____
_____
_____
_____
_____
_____
_____
_____
_____
_____

～℮ 276 ℮～

PROVERBS 16:18 AMP
"Pride goes before destruction,
and a haughty spirit before a fall."

My Child,

"Pride cometh before the fall," it is said. They shoot their wounded until they are dead. But I've chosen for you a better way; to bless them each day in all that you say. A battleground of words brings forth death; confusion, dissolution, with not much hope left. Hurtful words disguised in concern for the flock in all things; the sound of it leaves a flat hollow ring. My heart for you has always been that you would give your heart, to not just a few. Protecting, reflecting My love to them all. In safety, they shall fulfill their call, without the bonds that constrict and constrain. They'll blossom and bloom in My soft gentle rain. Sharing My love with one and all; confident and able to fulfill each call.
Love As I Love You!
Your Loving Father

Father, stop me, I pray when I start to say anything that does not bring blessing to Your people! I love You, Father!

Loving Father, You've always taught me that fear causes one to be territorial, to gossip, condemn, judge, and reject others as unworthy of their love. That I'm to share my love, which is to be Your love through me, with one and all. What joy as we all blossom and bloom with confidence in Your love, to fulfill each God-given call upon our lives.

277

PSALM 145:18 AMP
"The Lord is near to all who call upon Him,
to all who call upon Him sincerely and in truth."

My Child,

You have said to Me, "The way is heavy and dark, and the jungle is dense and dark," but I say unto you, "Fear not the darkness, for I am shining in the darkness to bring you through the darkness into My glorious light, never again to be overwhelmed by the darkness." You will understand those in the darkness, and will have great compassion for them. It will melt your heart, and from your heart of compassion will come forth the healing they need to walk in My light with you. See, the darkness is giving way to the early morning light. With the darkness will go the heaviness, and with My light will come My Glory, and the freshness, lightness, laughter, and joy of My Spirit.

I Hold You Close to My Heart!

Your Loving Father

Precious Father, thank You that You never leave me or forsake me, and You are always there to comfort me. Thank you for Your promises that give hope and understanding. It makes it all worthwhile to know that now I will understand those walking in darkness, and it will melt my heart with compassion, and from that compassion will come forth healing to help them walk out of the darkness into Your marvelous Light! I love You, Father.

Loving Father, I love Your Presence! Speak to my heart, I pray!

_____

_____

_____

_____

_____

_____

_____

_____

_____

_____

_____

_____

_____

_____

_____

~ 278 ~

LUKE 12:32 AMP

"Do not be seized with the alarm and struck with fear, little flock, for it is your Father's good pleasure to give you the Kingdom!"

(Father, what is the difference between intensity and being intense and over-anxious?) *My child, intensity is pressing in, knowing that I will bring to pass that which you are contending for; that I will bring to pass that for which you are pressing in. Being over-anxious and intense is synonymous with doubt. It is trying to twist My arm by doing all the right things to get Me to bring about what you desire. Be not tense. Be not over-anxious, but stand still, intently still, with perseverance of spirit, with rejoicing and thanksgiving; stopping the enemy at every turn; allowing no infractions, and seeing the salvation of your Lord. I am fighting for you and ours is the victory!*

I Am with You Always!

Your Loving Father

Father, are there areas in my life that I am trying to handle myself, without Your help?

_____

_____

_____

_____

_____

_____

_____

_____

_____

_____

_____

Loving Father, I choose to trust You with a persevering spirit, rejoicing in and with You all the way, knowing that ours is always the victory, no matter what that victory looks like! Long ago You said I was to keep open-ended plans, allowing You the freedom to bring about Your plans for my life in Your way; in Your perfect timing. That is how I choose to live Father, with Your help.

279

PHILIPPIANS 1:6 NKJV
"Being confident of this very thing,
that He who has begun a good work in you will complete it."

My Precious Child,

Now, lay down your life before Me, for My ways shall be your ways and My words shall be your words. My compassion and love shall be your compassion and love. My wisdom and knowledge shall be the wisdom and knowledge that you shall give forth by the anointing of My Spirit through you. Your hands shall be My hands of healing. Your voice shall ring forth the truths of My heart. You shall hear with My ears and see with My eyes, and your feet shall go where I lead you to go. I shall enlarge your sphere of influence to bring forth My Word in due season. For I have planned and I shall bring forth that plan to delight your heart and fulfill all that I have spoken to your heart. Lay down your pride of ownership, for I shall exchange it for a pride in Me. Be lifted up and confident of this very thing, that He who has begun a good work in you shall complete it to the Glory of God!

My Heart Rejoices over You!
Your Loving Father

Beloved Father, everything You have spoken to my heart is my passion and the desire of My heart! Thank You, that You are bringing the desires of my heart to pass beyond what I could ask or think! Father, in the past, You said that the "trademark" of my life would be, "Together," my Lord and I, together! "Together," everything I do! "Together," everything I say! "Together" shall mean "life" to me! You are my life, Father!

Loving Father, my heart sings a song to You of love and deep gratefulness!

_____

_____

_____

_____

_____

_____

_____

_____

_____

280

EXODUS 33:14 AMP
"And the Lord said, My Presence shall go with you,
and I will give you rest."

My Child,

My Spirit descends as a dove and rests gently and lightly upon those who profess My Name. It rests as joy immeasurable. It rests as a protective shield. Be a confident runner in My race, knowing My umbrella of protection follows over you, just as the cloud went ahead of the Israelites by day, and the fire by night. As long as you are running in My race, you will not run out from under My protection. Confidence in Me is the key; confidence that I will never let you down. Run with courage, persistence, singleness of mind, and a continual focus on Me.

Be Confident in My Love,
Your Loving Father

Loving Father, thank You, for Your constant protection and care. You have never let me down! My heart is listening for Your words of life.

_____

_____

_____

_____

_____

_____

_____

_____

_____

_____

_____

Faithful Father, Your words of encouragement and love bring courage and confidence to my heart! You have said, "Revert not back to old ways of responding with fear and frustration. I am in the driver's seat, if you will but allow it. See Me as the engineer of your multifaceted train of being. We shall not derail, nor wander onto a wrong track. Our train shall arrive at its destination on time and intact."

281

ISAIAH 42:10 AMP
"Sing to the Lord a new song,
and His praise from the end of the earth!"

My Child,

My little children frolic and play in the sunshine, but there are days of rain when they must stay inside with their noses against the windowpane, patiently waiting again for the sun to shine. There must be both: the more confined days, with hope for the future, and the days of joyful activity. Learn to enjoy both. Do not regard one over the other, for they both have their place. Go forth now with a song in your heart, refreshed and revived.

Sing with Me, My Child!

Your Loving Father

Beloved Father, it seems that much time has been spent staying inside with my nose against the windowpane, patiently waiting again for the sun to shine. But, You always bring wonderful encouragement to everything, and You have said, "Fear not, My little one, but remain in My love forever. Release unto Me your fears of rejection, of being forgotten. Paul was not forgotten during his years in the desert with Me. He strengthened and prepared, and I sent him out with power, with My Word, and with My Spirit. So shall it be with you!" Thank You, Father, for training me and lovingly teaching me to hear Your voice to my heart!

Father, thank You for days of joyful activity and thank You for quiet days with You. Speak to my heart, for I am listening.

_____

_____

_____

_____

_____

_____

_____

_____

_____

_____

_____

_____

_____

_____

_____

_____

282

PSALM 84:7 AMP
"They go from strength to strength
[increasing in victorious power]."

My Child,

There shall come upon you a new radiance from above. It shall shine like the morning sun. My ways have become more and more your ways, and you shall know the peace, the joy, and the contentment of the salvation of your Lord. Unto those who heed My voice, the reward is great. Cast all of your cares upon Me, for I love you. I am your burden bearer. Many are the trials of this world, but you simply move through them, knowing that I am your strength and your shield. Strength comes through encounter, and faith comes through battles won. Rejoice and be mightily glad, for ours is the victory, always!

Your Faithful Father!

Father, I am here in Your arms of love and security, to hear Your words to my heart.

_____

_____

_____

_____

_____

_____

_____

_____

_____

_____

_____

_____

_____

My Faithful Father, I love Your words to my heart! Every word that You speak, amplifies a word You have spoken! You have said, "Security in the world is fleeting. Security with Me lasts forever. Your heart has longed for security. Come up higher, My child. Cease from your striving, and fall into My arms of love and security. Respond to My slightest nudge. When you are resting in My arms, the slightest nudge seems strong and easily perceived. But when you are racing, even the strongest nudge can be missed. In My Presence, child, there is rest and clarity. Situations come and go, but make this your solid goal, to walk with Me in such a way, to never miss as a word I say."

JAMES 1:12 AMP

"Blessed (happy, to be envied) is the man who is patient under trial
and stands up under temptation, for when he has stood the test
and been approved, he will receive [the victor's] crown of life,
which God has promised to those who love Him."

My Child,

Do not draw back from days of trial and struggles. Encounter them with single-ness of purpose, that you might be strengthened. March on victoriously, knowing that the foe has been met, the battle has been won and the reward has been great. "No encounters" means "status quo," and "status quo" means the opposite of growth and life. It means stagnation and death. So do not be afraid of encounters. Rejoice in them. Keep your eyes on Me and walk through the land as I guide. Each encounter is a beautiful package, a present from Me, no matter how it looks on the outside. The struggle is getting through the outer covering to the beauty that lies inside. Be steadfast! Do not give up! Rejoice in the now!
Your Faithful Father!

Loving Father, how wonderful to know, even before each trial and encounter begins, that the outcome is victory, growth, and new strength, walking through them with You! How wonderful to know that each encounter is a beautiful package, a present from You, no matter how it looks on the outside; that the strug-gle is getting through the outer covering to the beauty that lies inside—that makes it all worth-while! When I look back, I can see that each battle won has brought a reward that has made me stronger and more resilient. But most impor-tant, every struggle and victory won has taught me to love and trust You more! I love You, Father!

My Father, teach my heart to hear Your voice more clearly. I don't want to miss a single word You speak to my heart!

_____

_____

_____

_____

_____

_____

_____

_____

_____

_____

_____

_____

_____

_____

284

PSALM 112:7 AMP
"He shall not be afraid of evil tidings; his heart is firmly fixed,
trusting (leaning on and being confident) in the Lord."

My Beloved Child,

My peace that passes all understanding is yours today, for you have passed through the door of understanding into the workings of My Spirit. There are times of trial and sorrow, but they are meant to strengthen and sustain your spirit. Know that I have my faithful ones standing watch in prayer with diligence, to help carry you through to victory. They, too, are strengthened through participation in the struggle to reach the victory, to gain the prize in the ever-upward calling of the Lord Jesus Christ.

I Love You, My Child,
Your Father

Loving Father, who is on Your heart today for me to pray for, to participate in their struggle to reach Your victory for them?

_____
_____
_____
_____
_____
_____
_____
_____
_____
_____
_____

Precious Father, I know that I am alive today because You have had Your faithful ones standing watch in prayer, with diligence, to help carry me through to victory! But how wonderful to know that they, too, are strengthened through participation in the struggle to reach the victory with me! You have said that Your people are to be connected on a heart level with golden threads of love. What better way to connect than through prayer and participation in each others' struggles to reach the victory.

285

HEBREWS 12:1 AMP
"Let us run with patient endurance and steady and active persistence, the appointed course of the race that is set before us."

My Child,

Run the good race. Finish the course with honor. Persistence and determination keeps one ever-striving upward and onward, with the eyes and spirit ever-looking upward to Christ. Persist! Relinquish not, nor draw back, but be ever moving forward. Prayer, thanksgiving, and praise are the wheels that propel My children ever onward and upward. Keep those wheels well-greased and in constant motion. Don't turn the wheels to the right or to the left, but straight-forward. Win the good race. It takes steadiness, uprightness, stamina, fitness, purity, determination, perseverance, strength, and soundness. They become their own rewards of steadiness, uprightness, stamina, fitness, purity, determination, perseverance, strength, and soundness.

I Am Always with You,
Your Loving Father

Father, at the same time, You said, "Run the good race! Be persistent and relentless. When the victory is won, do not retreat. That is the time to press ever-onward so that you don't lose ground, but continue to gain ground. It is a constant state of gaining the victory, maintaining the victory and gaining new ground. Remain steadfast and sure! Continue the good race, and know the joy of your salvation, the peace in the knowledge of My will being performed in and through your life! Loving Father, thank You for running with me, and securing the victory!

Loving Father, thank You for helping me finish the course with honor! I lovingly come to You today with prayer, thanksgiving, and praise!

_____

_____

_____

_____

_____

_____

_____

_____

_____

_____

_____

_____

286

PSALM 17:8 AMP

"Keep and guard me as the pupil of Your eye;
hide me in the shadow of Your wings."

My Child,

Fear not, for I have all things in hand. Your comings in and your goings out are all known to Me. You dwell in the shadow of My wing, and I will never forsake you. When adversity comes, it is only for a season, to teach you strength, trust, reliance, and steadfastness. Stumble not and faint not, for there is always an end to all things. Joy replaces sorrow and rejoicing replaces trials. Enter into the joy of your salvation, and look not back to the trials of yesterday. Always look upward and onward.

You Are Blessed, My Child
Your Loving Father

Father, every day brings with it the choice to enter into it with joy. My heart reaches out to You Father, with great joy and love, and a listening ear to hear the words from Your heart.

_____
_____
_____
_____
_____
_____
_____
_____
_____
_____
_____
_____

Loving Father, thank You that nothing takes You by surprise, that I can always trust You and rely on You! Even in the midst of trials, when I sing to You with joy and thanksgiving in my heart for Your steadfast and loving kindness toward me, all seems right with the world! You have said, "Your path is secure. The ravages of time shall not alter your course. Many shall behold My faithfulness to you. Let each day pass as ordained, and the days shall bring forth fruit, precious fruit, unto Me. Worry not! Fret not! Tarry not in unbelief, but set your sail to go forward, carried along by My gentle breezes."

PSALM 94:19 AMP
"In the multitude of my [anxious] thoughts within me,
Your comforts cheer and delight my soul!"

My Child,

Rejoice for the work that is taking place in your life, for the restoration that I am working in your life. Be not afraid of "your own thoughts," for they are My thoughts within you. I am restoring your joy, peace, trust, and faith in a new and more expanded way. I am building your life, stone on stone, with a strength that cannot be toppled. Each stone bears My Name and My Being within it, My perfection and completeness. So wrestle not with the uncertainty that you feel, but rejoice in the knowledge that each stone is being placed one by one as I would have it.

I Am with You!
Your Loving Father

Loving Father, You make me smile! Your Presence delights my soul and Your love sets me free in ways I never dreamed would be! You constantly bring new delights for me to enjoy along this road called life! I am so grateful, Father! Thank You for Your Words, "Be not afraid of 'your own thoughts' for they are My thoughts within you"! So many are afraid to hear Your voice, for fear it is their own thoughts and not Your thoughts within them. Nothing can compare with the great joy that comes when they realize it really is You speaking to them, with great love and wisdom!

Precious Father, I'm listening for Your thoughts within me.

_____

_____

_____

_____

_____

_____

_____

_____

_____

_____

_____

_____

_____

_____

_____

288

PSALM 119:33 NLT
"Teach me, O Lord,
to follow every one of your principles."

My Child,

Do not expect the new to be as the old. Expect a new and perfect thing in your life constantly. You shall be like My son, Peter, who said, "Bid me to walk on the water," and he did. But because of the faith and trust that I have brought in your life, you shall not look down at the tempest all around you. You shall look up and rejoice and know that I am Lord of all. You shall walk unfalteringly upon the water. So be not afraid when the waves swirl all around you, for you will find sure footing all along your pathway. Just know that each time you put your foot down, just as each time you take a breath, it will find its ultimate destination smoothly, and any unnecessary action or affect will disappear, just as when one exhales in breathing. So step out, one step at a time, knowing that each step is as a stone being laid upon the foundation of My Kingdom within you, which cannot be shaken.

My Tenacious Child,

I Love You

Father, what new things do You have for us to share today?

_____

_____

_____

_____

_____

_____

_____

_____

_____

_____

_____

Loving Father, daily walking on water with You is certainly exciting, and knowing that each step is secure in You and will find its ultimate destination smoothly, makes it an adventure. It is so comforting to know that You see the end from the beginning and have everything that pertains to my life held safely in Your hands of love! Every day is a new treasure to behold and a gift from You, loving Father. Thank You, Father, that every day is a new beginning! I love You!

289

PROVERBS 8:35 AMP

"For whoever finds me [Wisdom] finds life
and draws forth and obtains favor from the Lord."

My Child,

The classroom of life is always on the move. A little of this and a little of that, all combine together to make the whole. Despise not the seemingly insignificant parts, for what seems insignificant may many times be the key part. Take each day in stride, as allotted, with praise and thanksgiving. Restore joy when depleted, singing to Me with joy. Do not resent the small inconveniences that arise, but see them as open doors in another direction. There are no vacuums or empty spaces in My Kingdom. All things work together to form the whole. Be at peace and rejoice.

You Are Doing Well!
Your Loving Father

Loving Father, there is such peace in knowing that life is a continuous learning process, a little of this and a little of that all combine together to make the whole. You have said, "Respond to those around you with open arms of acceptance and love. Relax in My Spirit. Refrain from much ado over nothing. Rely on Me in all things and all shall be as it should be. Draw from the rivers of life that are flowing through you. As they flow out to others, you partake too. Rely on Me for every breath you take. Be more aware of My moment by moment Presence with you."

Father, teach me, I pray, to be more aware of Your moment by moment Presence with me!

_____

_____

_____

_____

_____

_____

_____

_____

_____

_____

_____

_____

_____

_____

290

PSALM 16:8 AMP
"I have set the Lord continually before me;
because He is at my right hand, I shall not be moved."

My Precious One,

Happy is the one who trusts in and truly relies on My leadings, for he shall feed peacefully on the dew-laden, tender grasses each morning, and be at peace the rest of the day. Allay your self-styled worries and anxieties. Once again, be My lamb who perfectly trusts in My guiding and protecting hand. Let Me bring things about, and do not fret in the meantime. Stand tall in My Spirit. The grass often seems greener on the other side, but bloom where I have planted you, for there the soil is perfectly mixed for your growth. Rejoice, for I am cultivating, feeding, and watering the plot in which you reside, daily and faithfully.

I Love You,
Your Father

Father, once again, I give You my worries and anxieties so that I can walk peacefully with You and follow Your leading.

Loving Father, You also said, "Continue on the course I have given you. The blind follow the blind, but you shall walk with your eyes wide open and drink in the glories of My Kingdom. Wrestle not with the whys and the wherefores. Walk with Me day by day, basking in My love for you. The whys and the wherefores shall take care of themselves. Basic trust! It all boils down to basic trust. Do you trust me in all things? If so, be at peace in all things." Help me Father, to always remember to be Your lamb, who perfectly trusts in Your guiding and protective hand starting each day peacefully feeding on the dew-laden tender grasses, and being at peace the rest of the day.

291

PSALM 30:12 AMP

"To the end that my tongue and my heart, and everything glorious
within me may sing praise to You and not be silent. O Lord my God,
I will give thanks to You forever."

My Child,

Eliminate waste, hurt, fear, and all negatives. Replace these with love and faithfulness. Counteract the negative by the positive. Speak life. Be a proclaimer of My peace. Establish My love. Surrounded by My angels, you shall go forth unafraid. You have let go of the overwhelming forces of fear and rejection and have looked to Me for your worth and abundance. I shall carry you forth with ease and simplicity and it shall be known to My Glory, that all is well with your soul, for I have established it. My love overshadows you, protects you, and carries you forth into uncharted territory. Strong, immovable, and filled with My power are those who stand in My grace and proclaim the Divine Providence and sustaining power of their God!

You Are Precious to Me,
Your Loving Father

Father, life is so pure and simple when I remember to speak life, live in Your peace and love, and look to You for my worth and abundance. Whenever I let any of the negatives creep in, life becomes complicated. You have said, "Bring forth the positive and shun the negative. Liken your walk with Me as a kangaroo child, tucked in its mother's pouch, jostled up and down, but protected and safe. Be on the alert! Let not the negative come up to rob you of your peace. Walk in the positive. Reflect my love and my peace." Thank You Father, for teaching me always to live and speak positively!

Loving Father, all is well with my soul as I stay in Your Presence, always listening for Your direction and Your Words of life!

_____
_____
_____
_____
_____
_____
_____
_____
_____
_____

292

PSALM 31:21 AMP

"Blessed be the Lord!
For he has shown me his marvelous loving favor."

My Child,

The world says, "Three strikes and you are out." I say unto you, "Whither thou goest, I will go with you." From the crown of your head to the soles of your feet shall My Spirit be with you, abide with you, and rest upon you. Enter into each day with expectancy to see Me in every event. Faithfulness is a virtue obtained as one stands in the face of unfaithfulness. Love is a virtue obtained as one stands loving in the face of unlovingness. One becomes sweet as they respond with sweetness in the face of anger. One becomes content when one stands strong in the presence of discontent. Destiny fulfilled is the greatest joy, for it brings together faithfulness, love, contentedness, and wisdom—all the gifts of My Spirit brought together by living in My Presence.

My Favor Is upon You,
Your Loving Father

Beloved Father, thank You for the beauty of Your love and the gifts of Your Spirit! How can I bless You today?

_____

_____

_____

_____

_____

_____

_____

_____

_____

_____

Loving Father, living in Your Presence is the joy of my life and the reason for my life! Your wonder and beauty is everywhere I look. Just now, the whole sky is filled with Your sunset, row after row of wispy clouds in the shape of rainbows across the sky reflecting Your crimson light! Your light is reflected in the faces of Your people! Your beauty is everywhere I look. Precious Father, Your love permeates Your creation! Daily I see destiny fulfilled in my life and in the lives of others. Precious Lord, I love You!

293

SONG OF SOLOMON 2:16 AMP
"My Beloved is mine and I am His!"

My Child,

Fortify your stand of faith. (How do I do that, Lord?) As you are doing, spending time in My Presence. Come forth in such a way that those that know shall say, "Among My treasures she was found, and her heart rejoiced at the gentle sound of My voice, for to hear My voice was her choice." The pathway lies ahead of you, and together we shall walk, talk, sing, and enjoy the blessings each day brings. For within each day, My treasures are found. Not one day shall fall to the ground; all shall be blessed with My very best. So, go forward now, My little one, unafraid and knowing full well, that I your God, your faithful Friend, know the beginning from the end.

You Are My Treasure!

I Love You

Dear Father, my faithful Friend, I love walking, talking, singing, and enjoying the blessings of each day with You. Truly each day is filled with Your treasures, whether through the smile of a Heart Friend, the music of shared laughter, or surprise from Your heart, each day has Your seal of blessing upon it! I love You so much, Father!

Precious Father, my heart does rejoice at the gentle sound of Your voice, for to hear Your voice is always the choice of my heart!

_____

_____

_____

_____

_____

_____

_____

_____

_____

_____

_____

294

PSALM 31:1 AMP
"I will bless the Lord it all times;
His praise shall continually be in my mouth."

My Child,

There are times and seasons. Winter is the time of seclusion and rest, reflection, healing, preparation, storms, stretching, and watching for the wave. Spring brings expanded vision, cleanup from the storms, renewed hope, and new vision, spotting the wave. Summer is implementation, riding the wave in the joy of fulfillment. Autumn brings change and time to catch the new wave. Each season in the spirit has its new challenges. Cling to Me in every thought, word, and action. Rejoice in each season.

I Am with You Always,
Your Loving Father

Father, truly Your Word is like a rock to me. What do You want me to learn from Your Word today?

_____

Loving Father, thank You for the beauty, blessing, and revelation of each season. You have said, "Stand straight and tall, with your back to the wind and your shoulders thrown back, with determination to finish the course with distinction. Let your steadfastness and determination be known to all. Do not let up your stance of faith, faith in My Word to you, for My Word is like a rock to you that cannot be moved or swayed. Steady on, My child. The best is yet to come!"

EPHESIANS 2:14 AMP
"For He is [Himself] our peace
(our bond of unity and harmony)."

My Precious Child,

It is My peace that sustains you and makes life worthwhile. When it flickers, you flicker. It is a treasure more precious than silver and gold, and must be maintained at all times, at all cost. See to it that you remain in My peace. When it flickers, sit in My Presence. It is, and always has been, the barometer of My life within you. As you seek Me and My heart, you shall continue to find Me, and be a transmitter of My peace and My love. Continue on, My child, with favor surrounding you. It is My favor that opens doors and My peace and love that allows you to go through those doors, bringing fulfillment and joy.

I Am Your Peace, My Child,

Your Loving Father

Loving Father, Your favor truly surrounds me with Your peace and Your love. When in doubt, You have said to follow Your peace, for You are peace, and to follow Your heart, for truly Your Presence is the barometer of Your life within me. Truly Your peace sustains me and makes life worthwhile. It is a treasure more precious than silver and gold.

Beloved Father, here I am, seeking Your heart and Your peace in a greater way than I have known before, that I might more fully become a transmitter of Your peace and Your love.

_____

_____

_____

_____

_____

_____

_____

_____

_____

_____

_____

296

2 CORINTHIANS 3:12 AMP
"Since we have such [glorious] hope,
(such joyful and confident expectation),
we speak very freely and openly and fearlessly."

My Precious One,

The measure of a person is their ability to love and stand in faithfulness and truth. Simple words, but impossible without My guiding and sustaining Spirit empowering. Treasures from My heart shall continue to become a part of Your life and bring you joy. Hope is your gift to them. Bask in the Glory of My love and that Glory and love will continue to be poured out on them without measure. Praise paves the way to success as you walk in My Spirit, which is love.

You Are Precious to Me,

Your Loving Father

Beloved Father, here I am basking in Your Presence with praise and love for You singing in my heart!

_____

_____

_____

_____

_____

_____

_____

_____

_____

_____

_____

Loving Father, thank You for trusting me with the treasures from Your heart, Your beloved people. Each treasure that You have sent my way has become a treasure to my heart, and they bring me such joy and pleasure. Hope is the gift that You gave to me, and it is such joy to pass it on. Every person that I meet is a new gift from You from Your vast Treasure Chest. You have said that eventually the world would be my family, that You have created our hearts to be big enough to hold the world. I believe that, Father!

297

HEBREWS 13:1 AMP
"Let love for your fellow believers continue
and be a fixed practice with you [never let it fail]."

My Precious Child,

Liberally bless My people. Swathe them with your love, which is My love, and the awareness of My Presence. Let them know that My heart reaches out to them. Out of the ash heap shall rise my Phoenix (a beautiful lone bird which lived in the Arabian desert for 500 to 600 years, then consumed by fire, rose renewed from the ashes, to start another long life). You shall lift Me up with joy and show the way—My way of hope and faithfulness with the ability to stand, unmoved by the world and outside pressures, by hearing My Word and standing! Stand steady, My Child, and faint not, but see Me in the midst of all trauma. Start now to rejoice, for the victory is now and you shall see the victory of your God as you take pleasure in Me.

I Take Pleasure in You, My Child,
Your Loving Father

Wonderful Father, I love to bless Your people, to let them know how much You love and treasure them! Thank You for teaching me to stand, unmoved by the world and outside pressures, by hearing Your Word and staying in Your Presence, seeing You in the midst of trauma. It has been a long, long road, but one in which You have been faithful to me, and now I can readily see the victory in every struggle and trial.

Loving Father, I take such pleasure in You, too, not only spending time in Your Presence, listening to Your heart and learning Your ways, but also being in Your Presence, all through the night and all through the day. My heart is listening with loving anticipation!

_____

_____

_____

_____

_____

_____

_____

298

PROVERBS 11:18 AMP

"He who sows righteousness (moral and spiritual rectitude in every area and relation) shall have a sure reward [permanent and satisfying]."

My Child,

Shower your love on others with no fear of lack of return, for I return double and refill your reservoir to overflowing. In the past, you have looked to others for that refilling and they could not. Only I have the power to refill. Look to Me and give as I lead, following the anointing I give and as my Word directs. See your reward in Me, not in others. Be My bond slave. I will reward you openly and without reservation. Go forward this day with the assurance that you can never be hurt again, for your reward does not come from people; your reward comes from Me. The rewards are great to the one who blows not his own horn, but lets Me blow it for him. Lay down your horn. Continue to see Me as your provider in all things. Together, we shall walk new ground and see new vistas of splendor, for more is available when people are no longer your source. Let us proceed.

I Love You,
Your Father!

Wonderful Father, what new ground and wonderful vistas of splendor are we going to walk together in today?

_____

_____

_____

_____

_____

_____

_____

_____

_____

_____

_____

Loving Father, many times You have said that I am to love Your people with no expectations, simply to love them with Your love, that my expectations are in You! Thank You, Father, that You are my provider in all things. In years past, I couldn't figure out why the more I loved, the emptier I became, because I hadn't learned yet that only You have the power to refill. Thank You, Father, that people are no longer my source, but You, the Creator of the Universe, are my source! Father, I just realized why I feel so loved today, not only by You, but by those around me—because they love me with no expectations, for love's sake, because You are their source too! What a wonderful way to live!!!

299

PSALM 145:20 AMP
"The Lord preserves all those who love him."

My Precious Child,

Ease on down the road. As each grain of sand of the hour glass falls, so shall each step be taken, one by one. It is not the big blast, but the continual pressing in that builds the strong foundation. Be not afraid of the slow start. Rest in My preparations and My love for you. Step by step, day by day, resolve to walk in what I have given you to walk in, and more will be added. Be not pressured nor grieved over lack of action. It is there. Remain in My peace for you. Do not let oppression knock on your door, for all shall go as I have planned. Remain unmoved by outside pressures. Simply move as I lead, step by step. Remain agile and alert. Be at peace, My child.

All Is in My Loving Care,
I Love You!

Beloved Father, it is so comforting to know that all shall go according to Your plan. I can simply remain unmoved by outside pressures and move as You lead, step by step. It is the continual pressing in that builds the strong foundation, to simply resolve to walk in what You have given me to walk in and that more will be added, step by step. Help me Father, to always remain agile and alert and at peace! I love You!

Loving Father, my heart reaches out to You for strength and wisdom.

300

MATTHEW 21 :22 AMP
"And whatever you ask for in prayer,
having faith and [really] believing, you will receive."

My Child,

Wave from afar as you traverse this road, intent upon the fulfillment of My Word to you. Wave from afar to the demands upon your time, that try to steal away your time with Me. Wave from afar to the negative advice from well-meaning doubters. Wave from afar to their like-minded cousins, defeat and dismay, for unto you I give the gifts of straightforward trust, faith, and understanding. Portends of doubt and gloom cannot touch you. Blessings and fulfillment are your portion.

I Love You, My Child,
Your Father

Loving Father, I am snuggled next to Your heart, intent on what You have to share with me today!

_____

_____

_____

_____

_____

_____

_____

_____

_____

_____

_____

Beloved Father, just thinking of You causes my face to smile with great joy! You give such wonderful gifts; promises fulfilled, straightforward trust, faith and understanding, and blessings beyond measure! How wonderful to simply wave from afar to defeat, dismay, doubt, and demands that try to steal away my time with You! I love You, Father!

301

1 CORINTHIANS 1:9 AMP
"God is faithful (reliable, trustworthy, and therefore ever true
to His promise, and He can be depended on)."

My Child,

I raise a standard before you to walk in. Walk in My ways unflinchingly. Cry aloud saying "My God is an awesome God. Nothing is too difficult for Him!" You will find within your heart a new openness to respond with love, unfeigned, free to receive without restraint. Laughter comes with freedom. Be free! Stand aside and watch Me work. Say not to yourself, "The weight is too heavy," but say to yourself, "My God is faithful." Go forth this day with a song in your heart and a bounce in your step, for My faithfulness is your life and your song!

Be Free My Child, Be Free!

Your Loving Father

My Faithful Father, forgive me for saying "the weight is too heavy," for truly, "My God is faithful," and Your faithfulness is my life and my song. What freedom, to be able stand aside and watch You work and bring such wonderful things to pass, that cause my heart to sing! Laughter is such a wonderful gift from You! No wonder it is such a precious gift, since it comes with freedom, which is also a gift from You. I love You, Father!

Father, there is a song in my heart and a bounce in my step when I am aware of Your Presence! Here I am, joyfully in Your Presence, listening with all my heart!

LUKE 6:37 NKJV
"Judge not, and you shall not be judged.
Condemn not, and you shall not be condemned.
Forgive, and you will be forgiven."

My Child,

Stand back, survey, and forgive. Doing so is a testament of My Spirit residing and acting in you. Daily cleanse your heart of all the built up debris of the day, that it not pile up, surround, and overpower you. Every negative word spoken is evidence of debris retained. Go forth this day, determined to be My clear channel of love, free from the bondages of self. Lay down your life before Me. See it as a sacrifice unto Me, to be broken as bread, to bring forth My perfect will. Minister life to those around you! Build up their hearts, and they shall see the Glory of their God.

You Are Precious to Me!

Your Loving Father

Father, forgive me for negative words spoken. Cleanse my heart I pray. Help me to always speak positive, uplifting, and encouraging words.

_____

_____

_____

_____

_____

_____

_____

_____

_____

_____

_____

_____

_____

Loving Father, what a clear word picture to always remember, that when I speak negative words or hear others speak negative words, it is evidence of unforgiveness and debris retained. You have said, "Forgiveness is the key to cause the enemy to flee. Stolen ground is his to grab. He'll always take a stab. Release his hold by being bold to stand in forgiveness and say, 'I refuse to be offended this day!'" Father, I am determined to be a clear channel of Your love, free from the bondages of unforgiveness and self, a sacrifice unto You, to build up others' hearts and minister life to those around me. I love You, Father!

303

2 CORINTHIANS 5:7 AMP
"For we walk by faith...not by sight or appearance."

My Child,

Stages, the victory comes in stages, like climbing stairs. Be not fainthearted, but march straight ahead undaunted by the passing scene. Mysteries unfold as you spend time with Me. Triumphant and glorious shall be the days ahead, filled with the Glory of My love. Restore the walls that have been broken down around people by My love and acceptance. For they shall see in you restoration by My hand of love, and it shall draw them toward the warmth, light, and truth of My love.

I Love You, My Child,
Your Father

Beloved Father, thank You for giving me such a love for Your people! It is so exciting to see Your unconditional love and acceptance bring healing and joy to their lives. Often, they say to me, "You live such an interesting life!" And Father, it is true, every day walking with You is an adventure and a joy. And at the same time, there has been such a visible progression of restoration in my life by Your hand of love. Thank You, Father, that each one of us who love You become word pictures of Your faithfulness, restoration, and Your unconditional love!

Loving Father, thank You for speaking to my heart with such love and acceptance!

_____

_____

_____

_____

_____

_____

_____

_____

_____

_____

_____

_____

_____

_____

_____

304

PROVERBS 4:12 AMP
"When you walk, your steps shall not be hampered
[your path will be clear and opened]; and when you run,
you shall not stumble."

My Child,

In times past, I have said to you, "Go forth, conquer the land, and lay hold of the promises I have given you." Today, I say, "Struggle not with inconsistencies!" Let Me do the choreography and pursue not easier ground, but flow with Me as I lead. You shall not miss out and I will not allow your foot to stumble. Straight are the pathways laid out by Me. Be at peace and watch the scenario unfold. So shall you see wonders beyond imagination, and My Spirit shall rejoice over you and with you.

I Direct Your Steps!
Your Loving Father

My Father, speak to my heart today as I rest in You.

Loving Father, thank You that no matter what is going on around me I can trust You. Thank You for continuing to impress upon my heart that I shall not miss out, that You will not allow my foot to stumble, and that as I flow with You, Your Spirit rejoices over me and I shall see wonders beyond my imagination. Truly, You have taught me, Father, that it doesn't matter how old we get, You will fulfill Your promises to us in Your time and in Your way. That knowledge brings such peace to my heart!

305

PSALM 19:8 AMP

"The precepts of the Lord are right, rejoicing the heart;
the commandment of the Lord is pure and bright,
enlightening the eyes."

My Child,

Line upon line, precept upon precept, I have led you, opening unto you marvels and promises of My Kingdom. Laid out before you is My plan of the ages, witnessed by those who would but see. Be not afraid of my reluctance to go forward in areas of concern to you. Worry not that the day seems as the night to your soul. Worry not that much of your life seems filled with questions and concerns, for My Word to you is yea and amen, and My love for you is constant and true. My plan for you goes forth unabated by times and seasons, for the times and seasons are all created by Me, for you. So be at peace, knowing that I have created for you, a panorama of blessing and purpose in your life, to bring forth My will in all its fullness. You are precious to me, My Child.

I Love You.

Beloved Father, truly You have led me line upon line, precept upon precept, which has brought forth a panorama of blessing and purpose for my life. Patience has been Your main theme to me as the years have gone by, to know that all will be fulfilled in Your time and in Your way. One thing I know, You love me and I can trust You in every area of my life, and in the lives of those I love!

Father, thank You for Your love that is constant and true! Thank You for teaching me of Your all-encompassing love as You speak to my heart!

_____

_____

_____

_____

_____

_____

_____

_____

_____

_____

_____

_____

~⊚ 306 ⊚~

PSALM 55:22 AMP

"Cast your burden on the Lord, [releasing the weight of it]
and He will sustain you; He will never allow the [consistently]
righteous to be moved (made to slip, fall, or fail)."

My Beloved Child,

Now go forth under the strength of My protection, showing forth the magnitude of My love and support toward you. Joy comes forth as the morning sun over the mountains, filled with expectation for the new day. Release the heaviness that has built up. Release unto Me all the byproducts of those burdens—weariness, trials, tribulations, joylessness, sorrow, and despair. Sense my Presence, My Child, and know its power. Come through the gates with singing and into My courts with praise. Serve your Lord with gladness, thanksgiving, and lightness of heart. Once again, be My peacemaker and joy-giver. Let the world major in distractions and destruction, but you major in trust and love, praise and fullness of joy.

I Will Never Forsake You!
Your Loving Father

~⊚

Loving Father, thank You for speaking to my heart and being my source of joy, gladness, and peace!

_____

_____

_____

_____

_____

_____

_____

_____

_____

I love You, my Father! You speak to me with such gentle love and care. I release unto You the heaviness that has built up, including all the byproducts of those burdens, especially of weariness of heart, choosing instead the strength of Your protection and the magnitude of Your love and support toward me.

307

1 JOHN 4:16 AMP
"God is love, and he who dwells and continues in love
dwells and continues in God, and God dwells and continues in him."

My Beloved One,

I love you, My child. Know this and rejoice. All else is secondary. Rejoice, and be glad, for My Spirit hovers about you, is in you, and enlightens you. The past is past! The present is now and is My gift to you. Savor each morsel of My present and Presence. Be captivated by its gloriousness. Be enraptured by the preciousness of the present. The future will hold its own gloriousness, but the present holds all you need to be catapulted into the future. Be estranged from the past, captivated by the present and confidently secure about the future. It is all yours, but "now" is My precious gift to you, to be enjoyed and treasured. My Spirit continues to encourage and make known the precious present. Be enlightened, encouraged, and enhanced!

You Are My Treasure!
Your Loving Father

Beloved Father, thank You for the precious gift of Your Presence and the preciousness of Your present! Long ago, You said, "Struggle not! Be at peace! My plans for you shall unfold as beautifully as the rose from bud to full bloom. It does not struggle. It lets the sun warm it into full bloom. Lift up your petals to Me for My warmth, and rejoice." What a beautiful word picture to teach me to be captivated by Your present, and confidently secure about the future, all held safely in Your protective hand!

Loving Father, thank You for Your encouragement and love as day by day, I live in Your present and Presence, listening to You, as You speak to my heart!

_____
_____
_____
_____
_____
_____
_____
_____
_____
_____
_____

308

HEBREWS 10:38 NKJV
"Now the just shall live by faith."

My Child,

Revel in the completeness of all I have created for you to experience, that you might proclaim My faithfulness to a dying world. Have you not tasted of the death that is the everyday portion of the world? I have said, "The just shall live by faith and rejoice in God their Father, through Jesus their Lord." Faithfulness is the key; My faithfulness to you and your faithfulness to Me. Rejoice in the quiet days of reflection. Rejoice in the hectic days of service, and rejoice in the days of shared love. They all are by My hand, none better than the other.

I Am Always with You,
Your Loving Father

Father, thank You for the quiet days, the hectic days, and our days of shared love! Thank You, Father, for always being there to speak to my heart!

_____

_____

_____

_____

_____

_____

_____

_____

_____

_____

_____

_____

Loving Father, You have said, "Every step that you take has been prepared ahead by Me. Have you not found it to be so? Carry on with confidence and assurance in My guiding hand. Go forth with joyful anticipation. Many shall know of My loving dealings with you and many shall rejoice to know of My love for them through you." Thank You, Father, for the completeness of all You have created for me to experience, that I might proclaim Your faithfulness to a dying world, that they too might know the preciousness of Your love for them!

309

1 CORINTHIANS 13:13 NKJV
"And now abide faith, hope, love, these three;
but the greatest of these is love."

My Precious Child,

Dramatic weeks, months, and years have made you transparent, sincere, and trusting in Me. The weeks and the years have passed, forming within you a trilogy of faith, hope, and love. Within your heart beats the rhythm of My heart, a steady beat that only grace can give. You have depended on My grace to carry you through and thus extend that grace to others, knowing that grace can turn failure into success, death into life, and sorrow into joy. My grace has been sufficient for you and shall continue to uphold you and make a way for you. See, I have made a way for you through the midst of the storm, through the desert place, and through every trial and tribulation that has come your way. Amidst all you have seen and heard has been My abiding peace and love. My hand covers and protects you and gives you life and stability. Be at peace and rejoice with contentment and confidence in the outcome. You shall declare the Glory of God in thought, word, and deed. Continue to prepare as My hand of deliverance works in your life.

Your Faithful, Loving Father

Precious Father, what a beautiful overview of all You have been to me, done through me, and done for me through the many years that we have walked together! Long ago You said, "Rejoice and be glad, for I have placed within you My Spirit to lead you in all things. Rejoice in My guiding hand and know that, **I Will Not Fail You**! Build not walls of protection, but be vulnerable and transparent. Bring forth My light and My joy to a needy world!" Thank You, Father, for Your faithfulness and love!

Father, thank You for continuing to cause me to grow by Your Spirit of love, as You speak to my heart!

_____

_____

_____

_____

_____

_____

_____

_____

_____

_____

310

MARK 11:22 AMP
"Have faith in God, (constantly)."

My Child,

Through the years, My Spirit has lifted you up and shown you a marvelous way of contentment and peace through the length of your days. I have blessed you in all of your ways. Through the years, My Spirit has comforted you and lifted you out of the mire. Now, your feet shall dance and your heart rejoice. You have come through the midst of the fire. So rejoice and sing, let your praises ring, for My Spirit has caused you to see that no matter what the circumstance, My love for you will always be the source of your strength, full and free. Do you believe this? (Yes, Father!) Never doubt the power of My love and direction in your life. It will never become less. It will only become more.

You Are Precious to Me, My Child,
Your Loving Father

Father, my heart sings to You a song of love and thankfulness, as I enjoy Your Presence as You speak to my heart.

_____

_____

_____

_____

_____

_____

_____

_____

_____

_____

_____

_____

_____

Loving Father, thank You for the confidence You give! Your Spirit has caused me to see that no matter what the circumstance, Your love will always be the source of my strength and direction for my life! Long ago, You said, "Keep your focus on the road I have mapped out for you, not on the available side roads!" Thank You, Father, for Your faithful guidance and direction in my life! I love You!

311

PSALM 64:10 AMP
"The uncompromisingly righteous shall be glad in the Lord
and shall trust and take refuge in Him."

My Beloved Child,

Stranger than fiction is the stream of your life, fashioned by your Father's hand to bring forth My handiwork in due time. Breakneck speed is not My way. Be at peace, My Child, as I fashion your life in My image, complete in every way. The ravages of time shall not harm you, but shall enhance you. So, fear not the passing of time. Time is your friend, as it works within you treasures to be enjoyed and beheld. You are My treasure, transformed and changed into My image. Rejoice and be glad in My Spirit of truth coming forth in your life. Fear not, each moment of each day is protected by My hand.

You Are My Treasure!
Your Loving Father

Loving Father, through the years You have continued to say, "Time is your friend," and those words have been such a comfort to my heart as the years have come and gone, forming within my heart a "love song" for You and Your people! Yes, breakneck speed has not been Your way, as You have continued to fashion my life in Your image, complete in every way. Many times You have said, "Stranger than fiction is the stream of your life, fashioned by your Father's hand to bring forth My handiwork in due time." And so it has been Father, to Your delight and to mine! I love You!

Father, I trust and take refuge in You, as You continue to speak to my heart!

_____

_____

_____

_____

_____

_____

_____

_____

_____

_____

_____

_____

_____

_____

~•~ 312 ~•~

ISAIAH 54:2 AMP
"Enlarge the place of your tent,
and let the curtains of your habitations be stretched out."

My Child,

Stability and contentment go together to bring you to a place of fulfillment and confidence. In contentment and peace shall my promises come forth. Bridge the gap from hoping to knowing through joy, thanksgiving, and trust. Trials have come and gone, but each one has left a deposit of strength, resourcefulness, and faithfulness within you. You've gone the extra mile with a smile, and with words of encouragement to many. They have seen your struggle to survive, and yet they have seen My Glory about you. The struggle has been great, but the reward shall be greater. Secure in My love you have been, able to see Me in every occurrence, willing to lay down your life, if need be, knowing I have laid down My life for you. The struggles have weighed you down and caused you to pull in the corners of your tent pegs, but now I say, "Open up the tent. Let the sun stream in, and I shall expand the tent pegs of your life to magnify My Name."

I Am Forever with You, My Child,
Your Loving Father

~•~

Father, thank You for Your contentment and peace, and thank You, Father, for speaking to my heart!

_____

_____

_____

_____

_____

_____

_____

_____

Loving Father, I love seeing You in every occurrence and I love that each trial has left a deposit of strength, resourcefulness, and faithfulness within me. You are so faithful, Father! Thank You for helping me to expand the tent pegs of my life, letting the sun stream in! I give to You all the struggles that have weighed me down, releasing them like dust in the wind. I love You, Father!

～ぐ 313 の～

1 CORINTHIANS 9:24 AMP
"So run [your race] that you may lay hold [of the prize]."

My Beloved Child,

Feast your eyes on the prizes coming your way. Some will be the desires of your heart resurrected; some the fulfillment of dreams past; some seem to be the figment of your imagination, and some the cry of your heart. You shall sit in amazement as you see the multitude of blessings coming your way. See the mystery of times past come into focus. See the answers to questions asked, revealed. Expectation shall be high as you walk through this appointed time. Fluctuations, renovations and revelation shall be the order of the day, as you draw ever closer to the fulfillment of Words spoken.

You Have Been Faithful!

I Love You!

Loving Father, my expectations are high as I walk through this appointed time! You said, "You have walked and talked My Word to you. Now, you shall revel in the fulfillment of that Word. Stay along the path that I have mapped out for you to follow. The light shall shine ever brighter to help you to see the destination." Thank You, Father, for being with me as I walk through the fluctuations and renovations that bring forth the revelations, as I draw ever closer to the fulfillment of Your Words spoken.

Father, I love the way You "turn the lights on" and suddenly give revelation as You speak to my heart! Each day with You truly is a feast in Your Presence!

_____
_____
_____
_____
_____
_____
_____
_____
_____
_____
_____
_____
_____

≈ 314 ≈

1 JOHN 5:4 AMP
"For whatever is born of God is victorious over the world;
and this is the victory that conquers the world, even our faith."

My Precious One,

My strength has prevailed in your life to make you strong and resilient. Measure not physical strength with strength of character and strength of resolve. The heavens declare the victory of one who has walked the weary miles and prevailed. With a song in your heart and in your mouth, you shall continue to march forth, but with flags of victory flowing in the wind as you walk, for it shall be a walk of victory, not one of struggling to remain upright to prevail. Sincerity of heart has kept you straight on target. Now the shout of victory shall lead you forth and cause your heart to burst forth with song and rejoicing.

I Am Proud of You, My Child,
Your Loving Father

≈

Father, You fill me with delight and wonder as You speak to my heart!

_____
_____
_____
_____
_____
_____
_____
_____
_____
_____
_____
_____
_____
_____

Loving Father, through the years You have said so many wonderful things to my heart that have kept me delighted and encouraged, reveling in Your love and beauty! Long ago, You said, "Go forth, and My Spirit will shine through you and people will see and respond to My Spirit within you. It will shine out of your face and it will light the way before you. I will give the guidance that you have asked of Me and you will be as a small child holding My hand, walking through an unknown place, filled with the delight and the wonder of all the new things I will open before you." And so it has been, dear Father! I love You!

315

Psalm 145:18 AMP
"The Lord is near to all who call upon Him,
to all who call upon Him, sincerely and in truth."

Dear One,

Ministry is a Covenant with Me. You receive from Me and then give it out. Receive and give, receive and give. So life is a Covenant. Receive life from Me and give it to others. Receive and give. Receive life; give life. Receive life; give life through your words, through your prayers, and through your actions. Life is tangible. You can see life and you can transfer life. Only I can create life. Only I can give life. You must receive life from Me, and then you can pass it on. Receive and pass on! Receive and pass on! But, receiving life is a commitment, and thus, the Covenant.

You Are Precious to Me!
Your Loving Father

Loving Father, You have taught me that in order to walk in a Covenant Relationship with You, or with others, I must walk in love, faithfulness, honor, trust, joy, and committed communication. Relationship means communication! That I must stand firm in faith, believing You for the unbelievable, the impossible and the inconceivable, helping others to fulfill their destiny. Thank You, Father, for the blessing of being in Covenant with You, that I might receive life from You and then pass it on to others!

Beloved Father, thank You for Your Covenant of love and life! Thank You for anointing me to pass this on to Your treasures! I Love You, Father!

_____

_____

_____

_____

_____

_____

_____

_____

_____

_____

_____

_____

316

PSALM 37:5 NKJV

"Commit your way to the LORD, trust also in Him,
and He shall bring it to pass."

My Child,

You have struggled long and hard to come into this place. You still feel inadequate to the task, but all you need is within you to complete and fulfill the tasks at hand. Your destiny is sure and secure. Struggle not to fulfill that destiny, but start each day with Me securely in the place of authority and love over your life. Take each day as it comes, rejoicing in Me and free to move, love, and be refreshed by Me. The enemy would love to make you feel pressured and inadequate. Refuse to be moved by him. When anxiety arises, "Come Away My Beloved." Let Me calm your inner being, moment by moment. Remember, running in place does not accomplish the goal but a calm and unrushed, step by step progression towards the goal. Be not pressured. Each day will have within it that step or steps, moving forward with confidence and peace.

I Will Not Fail You!

Your Loving Father

Father, today I commit my way to You, Lord, confident that we shall prevail, for my adequacy is in You! Thank You, Father! I love You!

_____

_____

_____

_____

_____

_____

_____

_____

_____

_____

Thank You, loving Father, that my destiny is sure and secure in You and You will fulfill that destiny in Your time, in Your way, through me. I don't have to feel rushed and pressured; I can move in a step by step forward progression toward the goal, with confidence and peace. You have said, "Struggle is not necessary for success. Indeed it is a hindrance. Set your will, give your will to Me, and be at peace, confident that we shall prevail!"

~ 317 ~

"O Lord of hosts, blessed (happy, unfortunate, to be envied)
is the man who trusts in You [leaning and believing on You,
committing all and confidently looking to You,
and that without fear or misgiving]!"

My Beloved Child,

Divine strategies have come into play. Strong leadings shall continue to come your way. Influences shall guide you each day as My Spirit moves upon you. Be that standard bearer of truth. Walking a tight rope is not My way. Be open and let the chips fall where they may. Be established in My love. That is trust and forbearance; trust in My ability to work all for your good and forbearance to know I will protect you as you give out grace to others. You are to be a standard bearer of forbearance and grace. It is by My hand that you shall stand and show forth My love and acceptance, total acceptance in humility and truth.

You Are Precious to Me!

Your Loving Father

Loving Father, You have created Your people to walk in truth, patience, grace, humility, and loving acceptance, being established in Your love and trusting You to protect us as You guide us each day. Help me, Father, to stay off the tight rope and simply walk in your peace, straightforwardly with love! I love You, Father, and I love Your ways!

Father, I treasure this time with You as You speak to my heart!

_____

_____

_____

_____

_____

_____

_____

_____

_____

_____

_____

_____

318

ISAIAH 40:31 NKJV
"But those who wait on the LORD, shall renew their strength;
they shall mount up with wings like eagles,
they shall run in not be weary,
they shall walk and not faint."

Precious One,

Be as the eagle in flight and see as from above, looking down with eagle eyes. Fly above the smog and pollution. Be set free from religiosity. Fly high in the sky. Rely on My ability to bring the air currents for you to catch. Be released and set free. Let your world be from sea to sea, not from tree to tree. Open your eyes that you might see the mighty catch I have for thee. Be not astounded at what I shall bring as you take wing.

Fly Free My Child, Fly Free!
I Love You!

Father, speak to my heart as we fly together in joy and freedom!

_____

_____

_____

_____

_____

_____

_____

_____

_____

_____

_____

Loving Father, years ago You gave me a dream in which I was flying like an eagle on the back of a large eagle. It was the most exhilarating experience! I knew that someday You would say, "Come fly with Me," and I would be like an eagle in flight with You, flying with freedom, seeing with eagle eyes, flying from sea to see, not from tree to tree, high above the smog and pollution, seeing with Your eyes! Today is the day! I love You, Father!

319

ISAIAH 12:2 AMP
"I will trust and not be afraid,
for the Lord God is my strength and song."

Precious One,

Just sing your song all the day long, through the late-night hours, into the new dawn. The bird truly sings for the pure joy of singing praise to its Maker and Friend. The world beats a path to the door of one who has found peace within. (Lord, I don't feel like I have peace within.) Then sing with abandon. My peace will return and turn the rain into sunshine. Be lifted up and into higher realms of praise. Be set free from the pull downward. Fly high in the heavenlies, where the songs of angels are heard and one can see the panoramic view. Fly high in the sky. Fly above the problems and remain unruffled in My mantel of peace.

Sing with Me, My Precious One!
I Love You!

Loving Father, I want to be that bird that truly sings for the pure joy of singing praise to its Maker and Friend, flying high in the heavenlies, joining in with the songs of angels! Father, when my heart sings to You, it brings a smile to my face, laughter rings from my voice, and peace returns, turning the rain into sunshine. And then I can truly say, "I will trust and not be afraid, for the Lord God is my strength and song!" Thank You, Father, for being faithful to remind me! I love You!

Father, in Your Presence there are no problems, for You have my life safely in Your hand! Thank You, Father, for lovingly speaking to my heart!

_____
_____
_____
_____
_____
_____
_____
_____
_____
_____
_____

SONG OF SOLOMON 2:14 AMP
"Let me see your face, let me hear your voice;
for your voice is sweet, and your face is lovely."

My Child,

Seasons of change have weaved the tapestry of your life; here a valley, there a mountain high. But in each place, a touch of the Master's hand makes the valleys the same as the mountains, touched and sustained by love, each moment, a gift of grace. The style has changed, but the message remains the same: "See My face of love and grace reflected in this place. Struggles cease with full release, when the spirit knows you cannot fail along this trail. My love has made it so."

I Love You, My Child,
Your Father

Father, Your peace envelops me with such joy! I love Your Presence!

Loving Father, Your words are so beautiful; they bring tears of joy to my eyes! It is so true that struggles cease when my heart remembers that I cannot fail along this trail, for Your love and grace have made it so. I can look at the tapestry of my life and see that You have caused each moment to be a gift of grace. I love You, Father!

321

JOHN 15:8 AMP
"When you bear (produce) much fruit,
My Father is honored and glorified."

My Precious Child,
Straight words of love, I speak. (Lord, they speak straight to the heart.) You
have listened, blossomed, and bloomed. The beauty is real and the fragrance is
sweet. The path you have trod has been no small feat. Now, with words of love
straight from your heart, you shall impart insight gained only from traveling
the road of the trusting heart, listening intently, My words to impart. See Me
reach out to hearts poised to receive. See Me restore hearts that mourn and
grieve. Among my treasures I will be found, and their hearts will leap at the
gentle sound of My voice resounding clear as they hear, "I love you," with
clarity and grace. Hear Me comfort, exhort, and impart just the right things that
will warm their hearts. You will see, hear, know, and sense My Presence, as My
seed you sow.

You Are My Treasure, I Love You.

Loving Father, my prayer has always been to see, to hear, to know, and to sense Your Presence, every moment of every day! Thank You, Father, that You are found among Your treasures, and our hearts do leap at the gentle sound of Your voice! Thank You, Father, for helping me to continually hear Your loving voice with more clarity, that I might hear just the right words to bring comfort, to exhort and impart just the right things that will warm their hearts, bringing healing and restoration!

Father, thank You for always speaking straight words of love to my heart! The beauty of those words is real and the fragrance is sweet. I love You, Father!

_____

_____

_____

_____

_____

_____

_____

_____

_____

_____

JAMES 2:13 AMP
"Mercy [full of glad confidence]
exults victoriously over judgment."

My Child,

Fiery darts from the enemy have sought to derail you and throw you off track. But a humble heart stays on track. Respect and love go hand in hand, the foundation of My plan. Respect others' place in Me and love them as I love them, but steer clear of strife and division. Take your stand to remain on neutral ground, forbearing and releasing blessing to each. It's a mystery to be told; a truth that cannot be bought or sold. In My Presence, one can simply be unafraid of human frailties. Seek My heart, and you will see confusion leave. Strength of purpose standing strong, rejoicing in My Presence all the day long. Seek the Giver of all things. Seek the peace, My Presence brings.

Stay in My Peace!
Your Loving Father

Father, thank You for helping me to steer clear of division and strife. Thank You for the peace Your Presence brings!

_____
_____
_____
_____
_____
_____
_____
_____
_____
_____
_____

Loving Father, the wisdom and beauty of Your words and Your heart set me free, to be released from the fiery darts of the enemy. I love Your way—staying humble, with respect and love, forbearing and releasing blessing, unafraid of human frailties, rejoicing in Your presence!

323

1 PETER 2:9 RSV
"That you may declare the wonderful deeds of him
who called you out of darkness into his marvelous light."

Dear One,

The race goes well for the strong of heart. Make sure your heart is strong. Resilience still brings forth the most strength and stamina, for resilience is a guard against injury. Minister love and acceptance. Let go of critical judgments. Speak the positive, creative word that builds and creates. Leave behind the critical word that causes others to balk and protect the status quo. It may seem like creative criticism to show the way, but it blocks the way. Simply speak the positive, uplifting truth in love that creates and causes miracles to take place. Don't make comparisons. Be My light bearer. A light bearer does not make judgments, does not criticize. A light bearer brings forth light and radiates that light with joy, enthusiasm, and love. Seasoned veterans and seasoned warriors call forth light. My light shall overcome the darkness! Be my light bearer!

I Love You,
Your Father

Loving Father, thank You for causing me to be strong and resilient; teaching me to simply speak the positive, uplifting truth in love that creates and causes miracles to take place. When I start to make comparisons, please stop me! I would much rather speak the positive, creative word that builds and creates, than the critical word that tears down and blocks the way. Father, may I always minister Your love and acceptance with joy and enthusiasm!

Father, thank You for the light of Your Presence! Help me Father, to always declare Your wonderful deeds, leaving the opposite, critical judgments unspoken!

_____

_____

_____

_____

_____

_____

_____

_____

324

EPHESIANS 6:18 AMP
"Pray at all times [on every occasion, in every season] in the Spirit,
with all [manner of] prayer and entreaty."

My Precious One,

Out of sight, out of mind—it is the way of the world, but not the way of My Kingdom on Earth. My Spirit goes out to heal at any moment of any day, to My faithful ones, who hear the call to love and pray, opening the way for My Spirit to move. You are a candle lighter that I use to spark hope, light, joy, and enlightenment into the lives of others. It only takes a spark get a fire going. You are a fire starter for My people. Bask in My Glory. It gets the fire burning hotter in your soul, attracting others to partake with exuberance and joy.

Listen to My Heart, My Precious One,
Your Loving Father

Father, here I am, basking in Your Glory, loving Your Presence, with exuberance, to hear You speak to my heart!

Loving Father, I love being Your candle lighter, sparking hope, joy, and the deep knowledge of Your wonderful, healing love into the lives of Your precious people! Thank You, Father, for daily causing the fire to burn hotter in my own soul, as I love and pray and watch Your Spirit move in the most magnificent way. I love You, Father, with all my heart!

325

"Trust in, lean on, rely on, and have confidence in Him at all times,
you people; pour out your hearts before Him.
God is a refuge for us (a fortress and a high tower)."

Dear One,

Secret places of My abiding Presence you shall find as you persistently come into My Presence with love and devotion. I have carried you in My arms of love. I have kept you secluded away in the protective place of My love. The Heavens proclaim the Glory of God. You shall proclaim, along with the Heavens, the Glory and protective love of your Father and God. Sweet communion shall be the order of the day, and your heart shall be bursting to say, "My Lord and my God, you have shown me the way to life and liberty."

You Are Precious to Me.
Your Loving Father

Loving Father, such sweet communion we do have together, and it seems that there's a perpetual smile on my face just thinking about You! My Lord and my God, You have shown me the way to life and liberty, abundant and free, causing my heart to soar on the wings of Your love! Your protective love is always there for me! I love abiding in Your Presence! I love You, Father!

Father, right now there is the biggest smile on my face as I sit in Your Presence, listening for You to speak to my heart, and as I speak my heart to You!

_____

_____

_____

_____

_____

_____

_____

_____

_____

_____

_____

_____

326

2 CORINTHIANS 3:12 AMP
"Since we have such a [glorious] hope,
(such joyful and confident expectation),
we speak very freely and openly and fearlessly."

My Child,

Be bold, be strong, be confident. Shine forth My light. Be brave, for I am confident in you. I have made you bold. I have made you strong. I have made you brave. I have made you confident to do My will. My Presence will become more precious to you as you continue to step out in faith. I will stretch you, and you will grow in grace, truth, and freedom; freedom to think and know My will and My good pleasure in your life. The walls of self-imposed restrictions shall continue to come down with a thud, and in their place will be the fragrance and beauty of My heart and My Spirit in your every action and thought. Measure each day by the Glory of My Presence.

I Am with You!

Your Loving Father

Father, thank You for teaching me to measure each day by the Glory of Your Presence! Loving Father, thank You that You are here to speak to my heart!

_____

_____

_____

_____

_____

_____

_____

_____

_____

_____

_____

Loving Father, thank You for making me brave and strong; that even as You stretch me, I will grow in grace, truth, and freedom. Father, I am so thankful that the walls of self-imposed restrictions shall continue to come down with a thud, and in their place will be the fragrance and beauty of Your heart and Your Spirit in my every thought and action! Thank You, Father, for Your confidence in me! I love You!

PSALM 119:160 AMP
"The sum of Your word is truth."

Precious One,

Struggles come when one doubts My ability to carry them through to completion. (When we feel like we're losing ground and it depends on us to be good enough.) Rest in My ability to accomplish it through you. Put to flight all worries and struggles to maintain the status quo. We shall overcome the status quo and go forth to greater victories. Truth sets the captives free, that they might be all they were created to be. The sky is the limit, when truth is walked in and believed. Truth burns away the clouds that the sunshine might shine through the dimness and proclaim victory. Struggles abound outside of victory's light. It actually seems like night in the light of day when the enemy has his way. But the way of truth received always causes the heart to believe.

Trust Me, My Child,

I Love You!

Loving Father, forgive me for trying to be "good enough." When I start struggling, I'll know that I'm not resting in Your ability to accomplish and carry through to completion all You've proclaimed through me. I will remember that, "Struggles abound outside of victory's light," and You have proclaimed victory in every area of my life! I love You so much, Father!

Father, thank You for putting all worries and doubts to flight as I peacefully come into Your Presence and listen to Your heart!

_____

_____

_____

_____

_____

_____

_____

_____

_____

_____

_____

_____

328

2 CORINTHIANS 3:17 AMP
"Now, the Lord is the Spirit, and where the Spirit of the Lord is, there is liberty (emancipation from bondage, freedom)."

Dear One,

Struggle not! Restrain yourself from apparent stress. My Word to you is freedom in the midst of hardship and pain. Rise above the shadows. Come into My marvelous light, above the clouds and shadows. Be restored in my abundance of joy and freedom of heart. Be not bogged down with the transitory. See Me in every moment of every day. Carry not the burden of the immediate. Be not driven by the immediate. Stand strong in My Presence. Be not dismayed, but abound in the joy of being. I am with you! You are sustained to bless and to be a blessing. Set into place are the foundation stones which are truth, faithfulness, and love!

I Am with You, My Child!
Your Loving Father

Father, may I always stand strong in the peace of Your Presence, not bogged down by the transitory, but continually restored in Your abundance of joy and freedom of heart!

_____

_____

_____

_____

_____

_____

_____

_____

_____

_____

_____

Loving Father, long ago You said, "A picture is worth a thousand words. Be a picture of My faithfulness and love. Let Me paint the picture clearly in your life; a picture of Me, seen through thee!" Since that day I have talked about and deeply felt, the importance of being "A word picture of Your love"! Father, I love the way You bring together two words from Your heart, years apart, one the exhortation and one the understanding; the Foundation Stones of being a blessing; truth, faithfulness, and love!

ISAIAH 3:10 AMP
"Say to the righteous that it shall be well with them,
for they shall eat the fruit of their deeds."

My Beloved One,

Time and time again I have uprooted you and placed you on a new trail, and you have rejoiced at the newness and awesomeness of My Plan. Now I do a new thing in your life that shall outshine all the other paths that you have taken. You shall see such beauty on this new path and your heart shall rejoice at the ability to take it all in and respond with joy. Bask in the warmth of My smile and know as never before My ability to create and re-create. Seasons of change have formed your existence in Me. Change has brought forth the formation of the fruit, and trust has caused it to ripen. Now, the fruit shall bring forth the change and gladden your heart.

You Are Blessed!
Your Loving Father

Thank You, Father for the grace to love change! I do love the warmth of Your smile and the fascination of watching Your ability to create and recreate. How wonderful to know that seasons of change have formed my existence in You. That change has brought forth the formation of the fruit, and trust has caused it to ripen, but most fascinating of all, is to know that it is actually the fruit that shall bring forth the change and gladden my heart!

Father, You bring such beauty and joy to my life! Thank You for being not only my loving, Heavenly Father, but my Faithful Friend! Thank You for lovingly speaking to my heart!

_____
_____
_____
_____
_____
_____
_____
_____
_____
_____
_____

330

PSALM 37:5 AMP
"Commit your way to the Lord
[roll and repose each care of your load on Him]; trust (lean on, rely
on, and be confident) also in Him and He will bring it to pass."

Precious One,

Restoration of what has been lost has come at a great cost. But the fulfillment foretold, has made you bold. See the future through My eyes of love. Blessing is cumulative. Watch it unfold with more blessing than your heart could hold. But now, the Master Plan set forth, nothing shall close the open doors. Kick up your heels! Laugh with Me! The time has come! You are set free!

Be Free My Child, Be Free!

Your Loving Father

Beloved Father, once again I commit my way to You, trusting in and leaning on You, and confident that You will bring to pass all that You have promised! You have never failed me! You are faithful and I love you!

_____

_____

_____

_____

_____

_____

_____

_____

_____

_____

_____

_____

_____

Loving Father, I love to laugh with You, and with others too! Thank You for the gift of seeing the future through Your eyes of love, so that I can be bold as I watch it all unfold. Thank You for the restoration of what has been lost, and thank You that Your blessings are cumulative. And, yes, it has come at a great cost, but with You at the helm of my ship, it is always worthwhile! I love You, Father!

331

PROVERBS 11:30 AMP
"The fruit of the [uncompromisingly] righteous is a tree of life."

My Dear One,

Passages of time clear the way for new beginnings and new openings in the Spirit. Time is your friend and brings forth the blessings spoken of. There are many passages of time in the growth of a tree before it ever sets fruit. Even when it flowers, the flowers fade and fall off, making way for the fruit. So it has been in your life. Lasting fruit takes time. Fear not because of time. It is your friend. Milestones along the way refresh and bring to mind the promises. Resist not the parameters of time. I say again, "Time is your friend."

You Are Blessed!

Your Loving Father

Loving Father, every time You say, "Time is your friend," it brings peace to my heart and a smile to my face! Thank You for milestones along the way that refresh and bring to mind Your promises! The most important promises to my heart have taken years to be fulfilled and yet they have always come to pass through Your love and faithfulness! Thank You, Father, that I can trust You! I Love You, Father!

Father, thank You that all the passages of time in my life are safely in Your arms of love, waiting for Your time to come forth to the joy of Your heart and the absolute delight of mine! Thank You for keeping me on track as You speak to my heart!

332

PHILIPPIANS 3:1 AMP
"Delight yourselves in the Lord
and continue to rejoice that you are in Him."

My Precious One,

I will lead you today with delight! Let the fresh breezes of My Spirit breathe through you and bring delight and joy to your soul. Your cares shall evaporate in the joy and pleasure of My Presence. Recapture the fragrance of fun. Be the Pied Piper, who sings and dances along the trail of blessing, leading others in the joy and fragrance of My love, freedom, laughter, and joy. No good thing do I withhold from My loving, joyful, trusting children.

I Delight in You, My Child!

Your Loving Father

Precious Father, You are the joy and delight of my life! Thank You for the pleasure of Your Presence as You speak to my heart!

Loving Father, You bring such delight to my soul! At the same time You said that I was to "play" until further notice, I said, "Father, how can I play with no playmates? My friends are all workaholics!" You have taught us all the freedom, laughter, and joy of recapturing the fragrance of "fun" with You, singing and dancing along Your trail of blessing! And then You said that our lives were always to retain that sense of joy and fun, no matter what we were doing for the rest of our lives! Thank You, Father, that no good thing do You withhold from Your loving, joyful, trusting children!

❧ 333 ❧

EPHESIANS 2:10 TLB
"It is God himself who has made us what we are
and given us new lives from Christ Jesus; and long ages ago, he
planned that we should spend these lives in helping others."

My Beloved Child,

Picture-perfect, My love for you. Green pastures, skies of blue. Quiet pools, be not concerned. My love for you will see you through. Streams in the desert have watered your soul. They have poured forth refreshing, to complete and make you whole. Seek not to conform or control. Just give forth that others might be made whole. My heart has always been, that you be that treasured friend. Bask in the warmth and glow of My love, positioned in the assurance of My gifts from above. Now is the time, be not afraid. I hear and have heard every cry you have made. As you give forth all that you are and have by My hand, I bring you into My plan, complete and able to stand.

Love As I Have Loved You,
Your Loving Father

Loving Father, the wonderful unexpected gift of Your love and learning to love with Your love, is that You bring wonderful friends my way that You've also taught to love with Your love. It becomes an ever-growing, ever-expanding, exciting circle of Your love that never ends; like a pebble tossed into a pond, causing the circles to grow larger and larger, unendingly. Thank You, Father, for the overwhelming marvel and wonder of your wonderful love!

Father, it's only the beginning, I know, of experiencing and knowing the beauty and fathomless joys of Your love. I treasure beyond measure our communion together, as You speak to my heart!

_____

_____

_____

_____

_____

_____

_____

_____

_____

꧁ 334 ꧂

"The Heavens declare the Glory of God;
and the firmament shows and proclaims His handiwork."

My Beloved One,

Symbols, spiritual symbols, are in abundance to see. When your eyes are open to see, everything you see proclaims Me! Miraculous, you say, filled with wonder each day as the Heavens proclaim the Glory of God. So too, the earth proclaims the same. You have heard it said, and yes you've read, such things are true. But now, I show them in abundance to you. Today shall be transformed in every way, as you hear and see a world that proclaims Me! It is your destiny to see Me!

Precious One,
I Love You!

Beloved Father, I am in awe, not only of the beauty of Your love, but of the beauty of Your creation! The fresh breezes of Your Spirit do breathe through me and bring delight and joy to my soul! I love You!

Loving Father, it is so exciting to see You wherever my eyes look: the dew sparkling like diamonds on the roses; the glory of the brilliance of the sunset that covers the whole sky; double, full rainbows of promise across the sky in front of my house, so close you feel like you could touch them; wispy clouds across the sky looking like rainbows as they catch the bright pink fuchsia glow of the sunset. These are just some of the wonders I've beheld in the last few days, of the earth and heavens proclaiming Your Glory! Truly everywhere I look, I see the Glory of Your Kingdom proclaiming You!

335

1 JOHN 3:18 AMP
"Little children, let us not love [merely] in theory or in speech but in deed, and in truth (in practice and in sincerity)."

My Precious One,

Unfolding before you are scenic vistas of beauty and grace. Magnified before you is the purpose of your life and very being. Seek Me daily, that I might lay out before you plans and areas for concern and prayer. The magnitude of all that I have for you is vast. It will take much stamina and praise, much time with Me face to face. Strategic plans I have for you. Listening is the key. You must remember to just be. Be that fountain of hope and peace, love and joy coming forth from My heart. Pour forth on all alike.

Seek Me Daily My Precious One,
Your Loving Father

Loving Father, the magnitude of all that You have for me to fulfill must include being that fountain of hope and peace, love and joy, bringing forth Your heart of love, and pouring it out on all alike. But that is not just who You have called me to be, it is who You have called all of your people to be, a reflection of Your love. Father, grant me stamina, I pray, that I might fulfill Your strategic plans as I spend much time with You face to face, listening to You as You speak to my heart, remembering just to be!

Precious Father, my heart sings to You with praise, joy, and gladness for all You have planned and are bringing to pass in my life and in the lives of Your people. Speak to my heart I pray, that I might know Your plans, and areas for concern and prayer. I love you Father!

~336~

ROMANS 8:28 NKJV

"And we know that all things work together for good to those who love God, to those who are the called according to His purpose."

My Child

The fulfillment of your heart and dreams comes hidden and unseen. Then in the fullness of day, suddenly eyes see what was there all along, but hidden from view. Hope fulfilled is the hope of all who dream. The wise man seeks My plan, then stands unmoved by the passing scene. (Many have stood unmoved by the passing scene, only to see the plan changed and rearranged. But nothing can take away the growth that standing proclaims.) The human heart was created to beat with the strength of My love. It seeks to know the strength of My love. And in the fulfillment of that knowledge found, it continually seeks for higher ground. Be alert as you climb that mountain high, as you are tempted to groan and sigh, that every crest and level taken requires trust and faith, that you feel not forsaken.

Stand in Faith, My Child,

I Love You

~

Beloved Father, speak to my heart I pray, as I walk with You today!

_____

_____

_____

_____

_____

_____

_____

_____

_____

_____

_____

Loving Father, You have said, "The travel has been long and arduous, but the fulfillment is great. Your destiny is charted and mapped with the utmost of care. You shall see, and we shall be delighted together. Continue to explore and examine the mingling of the various paths and byways by which I have brought you, discerning each clue and bright jewel of hope and expression of My everlasting love toward you. The picture is becoming brighter and clearer. You shall see the whole picture with nothing lacking, and we shall rejoice together." When I am tempted to groan and sigh with every crest and level taken, I will remember, victory requires trust and faith!

337

1 TIMOTHY 1:5 AMP

"The object and purpose of our instruction and charge is love,
which springs from a pure heart and a good (clear) conscience
and sincere (unfeigned) faith."

My Beloved Child,

Sincere praise lifts up the heart into realms of Glory, My Presence, and it proclaims My goodness. Shallow praise rings hollow in the heart and the ears, and proclaims emptiness and futility. Lasting gifts of My Spirit come forth through sincere praise and thanksgiving, brought forth from a trusting, loving heart. Seek to walk with steadfast abandon to My heart and will. Shallow ways bring forth shallow deeds. My ways of faithfulness and love bring forth My will upon the earth.

I Love You!
Your Father

Loving Father, may my ways always be pleasing to You and bring joy to Your heart! May I always walk with steadfast abandon to Your heart and will, and may my ways of faithfulness and love help bring forth Your will upon the earth! But most of all, I pray that my love always springs forth from a pure heart, a good clear conscience, and sincere unfeigned faith!

Father, my heart reaches out to You with praise and thankfulness.

_____

_____

_____

_____

_____

_____

_____

_____

_____

_____

_____

_____

_____

_____

_____

_____

338

PSALM 40:6 AMP
"You have given me the capacity to hear and obey."

My Precious One,

Singleness of mind and faith in Me has been, and always is, the key to a walk with Me. Struggles abound, but the sound of My voice is enough to stop the enemy of your soul in his tracks and bring forth My victory. Soundness of heart and mind come forth through a firm commitment to listening to and obeying that inner witness of My love and heart toward you. Be lifted up this day from the muck and mire that tries to close in on you, for My hand of blessing is upon you and forever clears the way, as you come forth with praise and thanksgiving. The earth rejoices at the sound of one rejoicing in their King.

We Shall Prevail Together!

Your Loving Father

Loving Father, my heart sings to You with such gratefulness and joy, thanksgiving and praise! My heart listens for the sound of Your voice today!

I Love You Father, and rejoice in You with my whole heart! Your gentle, loving voice brings peace to my heart. Thank You for Your hand of blessing that clears the way before me, disbursing the muck the mire that tries to close in, making it inconsequential, like ashes in the wind.

339

PSALM 42:8 AMP
"Yet the Lord will command He is loving-kindness in the daytime,
and in the night His song shall be with me,
a prayer to the God of my life."

Precious One,

Free fall into My arms. The forces of evil surround you for the kill, but My power is greater. Have I not said that, "I have put you in a safe place surrounded by My love"? My love is a shield to you to bring you through to victory. Nothing shall stay My hand of victory in your life. I have commanded it and it shall come forth. Go forth in faith and trust like a child, with a loving, powerful Father, who leads, guides, and protects, saying, "This is the way, walk ye in it." Go forth with freedom, tenacity, and joy. I am with you!

You Are Safe in My Arms!

Your Loving Father

Loving Father, truly You have put me in a safe place surrounded by Your love. I can trust You and can "free fall" into Your arms of love, for over and over again You have protected my life, shielding me from harm and bringing me through to victory! So I can live transparently with the faith and trust of a child, because I have a loving powerful Father, who leads and guides and protects me, saying, "Go forth with freedom, tenacity, and joy, for I am with you!" I love You, Father!

Father, You are my song in the day and all through the night! My heart sings to You with love!

_____

_____

_____

_____

_____

_____

_____

_____

_____

_____

_____

_____

_____

340

"I am my beloved's [garden] and my Beloved is mine!"

My Precious Child,

It is a lifestyle of listening and walking, listening and talking, basking in My love and giving it forth with joy. I send you forth this day to play in My Garden of Life, fit and secure in My love. Many will come into this garden with you to bask in My love and play with you in My Presence, for in My Presence is fullness of joy. In this Garden is every good thing for your development, enhancement, and advancement, nothing lacking. It is a Garden of hope, for I place within each heart that enters, the knowledge of My love and care and from that knowledge springs freedom. Linger in My Garden each day. Let Me teach you how to play. For in My Garden, every action and reaction is led by My heart and sets you apart as a precious child of My heart. Through you, I can impart My heart, for you have come apart from the racing, humdrum ways of empty days into the Garden of My joyful praise. Stay in this Garden all of your days.

Your Loving Father!

Father, I am listening intently as You speak to my heart in Your Garden of Love!

_____

_____

_____

_____

_____

_____

_____

_____

_____

_____

_____

Loving Father, I love Your Garden of Life! Nothing in life is more rewarding and wonderful than this lifestyle of listening to You and walking, listening to You and talking, basking in Your love, and giving it forth with joy! Such wonderful treasures from Your heart You send into this Garden with me, that we might bask in Your love together, learning to play with You in Your Presence, with freedom and joy, together, being word pictures of Your love in all we say and do. I love You, beloved Father!

341

JOHN 10:14 AMP

"I am the Good Shepherd; and I know and recognize My own,
and My own know and recognize Me."

My Precious Child,

Relax and fret not, for My Word shall come through. Continue to wait upon My Word with regularity. Do not let our relationship take second place in your priorities. Come to Me with expectancy and I will respond. My little lambs run and jump and play gleefully, but they are always aware of My Presence. They know I am their Shepherd and they obey instantly when I call, because they recognize My voice clearly. Practice My Presence continually. Relax, and enjoy My Presence.

I Am Always with You!
Your Loving Father

Loving Father, it is so true that as I relax and fret not, having laid down the heavy loads that were not mine to carry, trusting You to safely carry me through in all things; so much more is accomplished of lasting value! Singing and dancing, laughing and playing gleefully with the other lambs and with You, simply enjoying Your Presence together, is one of the pure joys of life! But the greatest joy of life is practicing Your Presence continually with great expectancy as You speak to my heart!

I love You, Father! Here I am once again, excited to hear Your loving voice and Word to my heart.

_____

_____

_____

_____

_____

_____

_____

_____

_____

_____

_____

_____

_____

_____

342

"It is better to trust and take refuge in the Lord
than to put confidence in man."

My Precious One,

There is peace in the midst of the storm, as you draw on My love to keep you warm. As you rest in My arms, you will know exactly which direction to go. So fear not, My little one, you shall not fail. Your train shall not derail, but will keep moving joyfully down the track. Be content to know My promises given, their fulfillment this side of Heaven. You've known in your heart; you've known each fulfillment is sure. Trust is not an issue here. Hope deferred has once again caused weariness to set in. But be encouraged! You know you will win! Release the tendency to rely on others to lift up your heart and cause you to sing. Look to Me first for My peace and confidence to bring. Let Me be the one you call out to, to give you strength and peace in all you say and do.

Drink in My Peace!

I Love You

Father, I am calling out to You today to give me strength and peace, for just a word from You lifts up my heart and causes me to sing!

_____

_____

_____

_____

_____

_____

_____

_____

_____

_____

_____

Loving Father, forgive me when I call out to others to give me strength and peace instead of You! And Father, forgive me for allowing hope deferred to cause weariness to set in, for I do know that I will win; that Your promises are true and that I shall not fail. It is so comforting to know that as I rest in Your arms, You will lovingly show me exactly which direction to go and that my train shall not derail, but will keep moving joyfully down the track. I will call out to You, Father, to give me strength and peace, to lift my heart up and cause me to sing. My confidence is in You!

⚜ 343 ⚜

PSALM 139:1 AMP
"O LORD, you have searched me [thoroughly]
and have known me."

My Child,

Painstakingly I have formed you and taught you and brought you to this place of total surrender and grace. You have been patient in this place of pruning and grooming, bringing you forth to this new day of revelation, provision, and new vision. Your cup shall overflow with new manna for the journey and you shall say, "My God has prepared me well." You have been fashioned by My hand of love to stand the test of time, because you are Mine. And now, My precious singing dove, you shall more fully reflect My love, in everything you say and do, which is My perfect will for you.

You Are Precious to Me,
Your Loving Father

Loving Father, You have truly, painstakingly, formed me and taught me through "patience"! In the beginning, You said, "The spirit of anxiety and the spirit of anticipation often causes physical man to be out of balance. Patience is the key, one of the keys to My Kingdom. Be not impatient, lest the key turn on an empty lock. Worshiping Me, and getting to know Me, My life, and My Parchments, shall not only relieve the spirit of anxiety and desire, but is the only way to My way." Thank You, loving Father, for all of the pruning and grooming through the years by Your hand of love, to help me stand the test of time! I love You, Father!

Thank You, Father, for new revelation, new provision, and new vision!

Thank You, Father, for lovingly speaking to my heart!

_____

_____

_____

_____

_____

_____

_____

_____

_____

_____

_____

_____

344

ECCLESIASTES 9:1 AMP
"The wise and their works are in the hands of God."

My Precious One,

The scenery is changing, My child, along this, your pathway, chosen by Me. (Father, I keep seeing a mountain stream, gurgling with joy, but in an isolated place in the mountains.) This has been a place of beauty, peace, and fellowship with Me. Once again you will come down the mountain into the excitement and activities further down the mountain. But for now, continue to bathe in the wonderment and beauty of this appointed time of quiet in My Presence. Let Me take care of the rest of your life. It is safe in My hands and shall come forth to your joy and to My Glory. But for now, rejoice in the now, in the magnitude and the absolute beauty of the now that I have created for you to bask in and enjoy.

I Treasure this Time with You!
Your Loving Father

Father, thank You for this place of beauty, peace, and fellowship with You. Thank You, that my life is safe in Your hands, as I continue to have precious fellowship with You!

_____

_____

_____

_____

_____

_____

_____

_____

_____

_____

_____

Loving Father, I can see it is not necessary to worry about what we are going to do with the rest of our lives, for You, loving Father, have a plan to bring fulfillment and destiny to each of our lives when we place them in Your capable and loving hands, to our joy and to Your Glory! That the times of quiet in Your Presence are times of wonderment and beauty, to bask in and enjoy with You, preparing us for more active times ahead, not one more important than the other. Father, I am so glad that I am on Your pathway, chosen by You!

345

ROMANS 15:13 NKJV
"Now may the God of hope fill you with all joy
and peace in believing, that you may abound in hope
by the power of the Holy Spirit."

My Child,

Be satisfied with who you are, where you're at, and where you're going, knowing that I hold all things in My hands. Your growth is in My hands and all it requires is a willing and dedicated heart, walking with My faith and My love, moving along with My joy. A joyful heart is a peaceful heart, filled with trust and love, motivated by a desire to walk in My righteousness, not your own. Fulfillment and trust walk hand in hand. Trust in My mighty hand to move on your behalf. Have faith and win.

Trust Me, My Child!
Your Loving Father

Loving Father, long ago You said, "The time has come to lean on My promises with tenacity. I shall not fail you. Stretch out your heart to receive the abundance of My love for you. Trust in being is your song. Let Me orchestrate. You sing the song and through that song My Spirit shall go forth." Father, You have always said that I am simply to be the reflection of who You are and Your love, and You will do what needs to be done in and through me. As I totally trust You with my life, You will bring forth the fulfillment of Your destiny for me in Your time and in Your way! I trust You, Father!

Father, thank You for the hope and peace You give as I daily walk in Your loving Presence and listen to You speak to my heart!

346

PSALM 57:7 AMP
"My heart is fixed, O God,
my heart is steadfast and confident!
I will sing and make melody."

Dear One,

I sing a song of love to you, My child. You fit next to My heart, causing your heart to sing. Listen for the words being close to My heart brings. The music and the lyrics ring clear, proclaiming My love. Struggle not. Simply rest your head on My heart. Heart to heart, your ears shall hear breathtaking words of beauty, love, and peace. Be a reflection of Me, that the world might see and hear with clarity My heart of love for them. Treasure My people as I do.

I Love You, My Child,
Your Loving Father

Father, my head is resting on Your heart, listening for the beautiful words and music that only Your heart can bring, heart to heart, causing my heart to sing!

_____

_____

_____

_____

_____

_____

_____

_____

_____

_____

_____

Loving Father, no wonder my heart sings such beautiful songs of love to You, because I hear them as You sing them to me! The music and the lyrics all proclaim Your love; truly breathtaking words of such beauty, love, and peace! Father, You have taught me to treasure Your people. They bring such joy and blessing to my heart. Teach me to treasure them even more!

347

MATTHEW 10:8 NKJV
"Freely you have received, freely give."

My Child,

I charge you this day, "Know the hearts of My people!" Study them and love them for who they are. That love will loose their lives from fear and doubt. That love will set them free. Be a messenger of My love, joy, freedom, and truth. Restore their confidence through Me. Help them to see their potential in Me. Be a standard of love, freedom, and joy. Every time you hug each one and smile at each one, you impart these precious elements of My heart. It is a package deal!

Love As I Love You!

Your Loving Father

Loving Father, long ago You said, "You are called to be filled with compassion for the uncompassionate ones, to love the unloved, to serve the unserved that none have turned and looked toward, to speak a word about My Son with them. But I know that you will, because of your love for Me. Look unto your left and look unto your right, for they are there, and they are hurting and dying. Be those eyes for others that cannot look Me full in the face, that they might see Me through your eyes." O Father, those words make me cry and I know they are Your heart for Your people. My answer is YES!

Father, thank You for teaching me to love Your people, those that already know You and those who don't. Thank You for loving Me with Your all encompassing, healing, restoring love but especially for teaching me to "know the hearts of Your people"!

_____

_____

_____

_____

_____

_____

_____

_____

_____

_____

_____

_____

348

ZECHARIAH 7:9 NKJV
"Show mercy and compassion, everyone to his brother."

Dear One,

I have surrounded you with prayer and love. When one strikes out who feels neither, respond with compassion, for My truth will win out and My compassion shall rule and bind up hurts and fears. Reach out, unafraid of repercussions. Reach out and love, and let Me take care of the results. Proceed with caution, but proceed with love and acceptance for the one who feels none. I am with you, My Child, to bring healing and wholeness. Let Me lead, and together we shall see miracles abounding, love and joy surrounding your life at every turn.

Love Heals!

Love As I Love!

Father, thank You for being with me to bring healing and wholeness to those that have experienced neither, but whom You love so passionately! May I love them the same way!

_____

_____

_____

_____

_____

_____

_____

_____

_____

_____

_____

_____

_____

Loving Father, You have said, "Confidence! Confidence in Me is the key! It is the key to the understanding of all things permanent. Stand secure in My plan. Let Me play it through you, step by step. The miraculous shall be to you, the reality of life. Enjoy each piece as it appears to complete the whole; a continual transformation, bringing forth beauty and restoration. Trust Me to bring it forth to completion. Continue to be My tool of restoration and transformation." Father, truly You have surrounded me with prayer and love. Thank You for giving me compassion, love, and acceptance for those who strike out and feel none. Thank You for binding up their hurts and fears, bringing healing and wholeness!

349

PSALM 27:14 AMP
"Wait and hope for and expect the Lord; be brave and of
good encourage and let your heart be stout and enduring."

My Child,

*Perilous times cause frustration and anxiety in the lives of those with no hope.
I have set before you a course of action to bring hope and love to many on the
trail of hopelessness. Continue to strengthen hearts with the freedom of love and
hope. Continue to lift up weary arms with the promise of Spring within their
hearts, bringing direction and fulfillment where there was disillusionment and
fear. Release unto Me all weariness and weights. My heart for you has always
been, walk with Me and win. March forth, dear child of My heart, unencumbered, flying free, following My lead.*

You Are Blessed!
Your Loving Father

Loving Father, You also said, "You will be as a silver streak (redemption and restoration) calling forth the lame, the deaf, and the blind into the safety of My love; calling them into their destinies, one by one, lighting fires of destiny within their hearts. Stragglers along the way will find out that it is a brand new day for them too. Straight and narrow paths they, too, shall walk down, proclaiming to one and all, it is because of God's blessing, love and call." Thank You, Father, for setting for me a course of action to bring hope and love to those on the trail of hopelessness with the freedom of love, direction, and fulfillment, where there was disillusionment and fear!

Father, I release all weariness and weights to You so that I can fly free with You, unencumbered, listening to Your heart, following Your lead!

_____
_____
_____
_____
_____
_____
_____
_____
_____
_____
_____
_____
_____

350

ISAIAH 30:15 AMP

"In quietness and in [trusting] confidence shall be your strength."

My Child,

Measure your progress by your peace. Be not in a rush to accomplish all that is set before you. Let the pieces fit together. Don't force them together. You shall see order and discipline descend and take up residence. Let time bring forth perfection in every way. The days all are numbered and assigned. Take them one at a time with joy. Blessed assurance is yours that much is prepared and shall come forth. Rise above the seeming indecision and frustration. Rise above the negative aspects and let My Spirit reign once again in your heart and mind. Be still and know that I am God. Among the many joys of My Kingdom is the ability to enjoy the quietness and peace that I give. Let the tranquility and beauty of My creation be a soothing, healing ointment to your soul.

Be At Peace, My Child!

For I Love You!

Loving Father, the quietness and peace of Your Presence fills my heart! It is a soothing, healing ointment to my soul!

_____

_____

_____

_____

_____

_____

_____

_____

_____

_____

Thank You, Father, for reminding me to measure my progress by my peace; to always remember that time is my friend and that it brings forth perfection in every way. Such peace comes from knowing that my days are numbered and assigned, that I can take them one at a time with joy! Truly, Father, peacefully trusting You with confidence is my strength!

351

PSALM 31:24 AMP
"Be strong and let your heart take courage,
all you who wait for and hope for and expect the Lord!"

Precious One,

Some give a song, some give the Word, but it is all by My Spirit. Worry not as to the giving, for I am with you to bring forth the very best. The strength of My Word never varies. It is like a metal stake placed into concrete, immovable and unchangeable. Be at peace and rejoice, for My promises shall come forth unhindered, unhurried, and unyielding. You can set your heart on that. You shall be blessed, you shall bless, and you shall bring forth blessings to others as yet untapped. Strength of purpose combined with strength of will—My will—brings forth victory. Be still and know that I Am God. I bring forth strength and will of purpose.

I Am Always with You!
Your Loving Father

Loving Father, You have said, "Stand your ground, the ground gained through struggle and determined resolve. Let not up your stance of faith, and let Me continue to lead you on to higher ground of accomplishment. Hang on to victories won and lay the groundwork for even higher achievements in My Name. *(How do I lay the groundwork, Lord?)* Stay in My Word, listen astutely to My guiding voice, and let your heart sing in the joy of your salvation!"

Father, thank You for bringing forth strength and will of purpose in my life! My heart is encouraged and sings as I enjoy Your Presence and listen for You to speak to my heart!

_____

_____

_____

_____

_____

_____

_____

_____

_____

_____

_____

_____

352

SONG OF SOLOMON 4:15 AMP
"You are a fountain [springing up] in a garden,
a well of living waters, and flowing streams."

My Child,

My peace is upon you, it is in you, it is through you, and you shall know in ways beyond your understanding how deep that peace runs like a river within you. (Father, I had a vision of a deep, hidden underground river in a cave-like area.) *Wells are drilled to tap these underground rivers. They have to go through many layers of different density of rock to reach it and then it erupts in a gushing fountain for all to see and be bathed in. So shall your peace be to all who come in contact with it. They shall be bathed by it as by the Spirit who gives life. It is a peace that produces life and cleansing in you, and in them. There is a joyfulness to a gushing, gurgling fountain of water. There is a continuous constancy to it that brings peace. Rest in that peace. Let your life continue to be carried along by that peace.*

Remain in My Peace, My Child,
Your Loving Father

Father, thank You for leading me by Your peace as You speak to my heart with love!

_____

_____

_____

_____

_____

_____

_____

_____

_____

_____

_____

_____

Loving Father, no wonder life is such a process, as day by day, year by year, You patiently lead us through the many layers of density of rock in our lives to fully release the fountain of life within each of us! What joy, when that peace that is released, becomes a gushing, gurgling fountain of life within us that splashes on everyone around us! I love You, Father!

353

ROMANS 5:5 AMP

"Such hope, never disappoints or deludes or shames us,
for God's love has been poured out in our hearts
through the Holy Spirit Who has been given to us."

My Child,

Be patient and see the fulfillment of all your hopes and dreams. A dreamer dreams big and has the courage to say all he expects to see displayed. I have placed within you gigantic hopes and dreams, and you have proclaimed them without fear. So carry on, dear Child of My heart, and you will continue to play a part, brought forth by My very own hand, a wonderful part of My Master plan. You are like the little tugboat that said, "I can!" And you will proclaim by every thought, word, and deed, every thought of My heart that fulfills the need. Be strong and alert, proclaiming My Word; having counted the cost, pursuing the lost, and bringing them to Me, helping them to see, who they were created to be. So step out with pride, with Me at your side, never missing a beat, as each step we complete.

Continue Dreaming Big, My Child,
I Love You, Your Father

Loving Father, long ago You began giving me promises, and one by one they came to pass, building within my heart the courage to dream big! You said, "Glimmers of My blessings you have you seen and reveled in. Now go forth with My promises resounding in your heart, for the fulfillment is sure and the foundation has been laid with soundness. The ship of My provision for you has set sail, and will find safe and sure harbor." And so it has been, dear Father! You are always faithful to Your Word!

Faithful Father, thank You that You always have new dreams for me to believe for, with You and through You! Thank You for patience to see them through to their fulfillment with You!

_____

_____

_____

_____

_____

_____

_____

_____

_____

_____

354

ISAIAH 30:18 AMP

"Blessed (happy, fortunate, to be envied) are all those who [earnestly]
wait for Him, who expect and look and long for Him
[for His victory, His favor, His love, His peace, His joy,
and His matchless, unbroken companionship!]"

My Precious One,

Blessed, blessed, I say, are My people entrusted with My Word. They are like a well watered spring, bringing forth bubbling, life-giving enthusiasm and life from My heart. They shrink not back during trials, but forge ahead and make headway even when others say, "Too bad." Go forth now with confidence and ever-growing faith in My ability to see you through to victory in every circumstance, and to confirm and make known My propensity to My people. Together we shall continue to rejoice and see fruit spring forth in every season of life.

The Blessings of My Heart Are with You!

Your Loving Father

Loving Father, may I always see through Your eyes, hear through Your ears, and think with Your Heart!

_____

_____

_____

_____

_____

_____

_____

_____

_____

_____

Wonderful Father, every day, walking with You is a treasure to behold. You're teaching me that even the trials of life hold such beauty, that those who see and hear Your heart need never fear, for You are always there. Every moment of every day, is a gift from You, when seen through Your eyes. Everywhere I look, there are precious gifts given through hearts that love You! Thank You Father!

355

MATTHEW 5:8 NKJV
"Blessed are the pure in heart,
for they shall see God."

Precious One,

The words of My Spirit shall ring forth with clarity that shall let you know the where and the when to move into action. Words alone do not convey the Spirit of My love. Actions and words work together to bring freedom and the resolution to love. Lift up before Me others, that I might bestow upon them the reality of My love, that they might know that I Am what I Am; that I reside in hearts, not in cold, stone walls. Bless them, continually understanding their vulnerability. Love with My love, which opens the heart to My Spirit. Blessed are the pure in heart, for they shall know God's ways. Walk in honesty and walk in truth.

Love As I Love You!

Your Loving Father

Loving Father, the joy of my day is when You bring those to my door or through the phone that just need a word of encouragement, love, and wisdom from Your heart! More and more the vastness of the reality of Your love is settling in on me and causing my heart to sing, as You continue to show me the wonderment of all You have in store, and have done in and through Your love for me!

My Beloved Father, thank You for teaching me Your ways as You speak to my heart!

_____

_____

_____

_____

_____

_____

_____

_____

_____

_____

_____

_____

_____

_____

356

MATTHEW 6:33 NKJV
"But seek first the kingdom of God, and His righteousness,
and all these things shall be added to you."

My Child,

Walk with a light, sure step. I have fashioned for you a pathway that you shall traverse with joy and thanksgiving. Blessed assurance is yours, My child, for I have given it to you. You shall know heart peace as few have known, heart rest that shall bring you joy. Listen with your whole heart. There is much I have to tell you, much for you to learn and know. The time IS now. Open up your heart to receive. Abundant blessings go to the listening heart. No good thing shall be withheld from you. Respond with alacrity and delight and I shall respond to you with fullness of joy. Have you not heard? Have you not seen the rewards I have stored up for you? There is much to be done, much to experience and know. Seek my Kingdom and all these things shall be added unto you.

Listen with Your Heart, My Child,
Your Loving Father

Loving Father, I have always wanted to ask you about…

_____

_____

_____

_____

_____

_____

_____

_____

_____

_____

_____

_____

Wonderful Father, You are so willing to share Your wisdom and Your heart with Your people, and yet we spend our time doing other things, rather than spending time in Your Presence, listening to Your heart. I can see that I've always tried to be so grown-up, simply letting You share with me what You want to share. But now, I truly want to be like that small child who asks about everything, because Father, You have said, ask, seek, and knock, that everyone who asks receives, and he who seeks finds, and the door will be opened to those who knock! There is much You have to tell me, much for me to learn and know! Truly, the time is now!

357

PSALM 105:3 AMP
"Glory in His holy name;
let the hearts of those rejoice, who seek and require the Lord
[as their indispensable necessity]."

Precious One,

Your heart shall overflow with the goodness of My Spirit to you. Think not of past sorrows. Look to the immediate future with joy and anticipation. My heart reigns within your heart. (Lord, this whole year has been difficult.) *Yes, but hearken unto the sound of birds singing. Make way for the promise of spring. Listen, for I shall make of you a singing heart, a singing spring of living waters, bubbling up with joy and thanksgiving, giving forth of My Spirit. You shall see coming forth to you an abundance of blessings from My heart. Give ear and listen to the coming of My Spirit through you. Stand forth in the radiance of My smile. I shall lift you up and speak through you words of life!*

I Delight in You,
Your Loving Father

Loving Father, I'm learning that the most difficult times bring forth the most growth and blessing. That when I come through a difficult test and trial, You always have a wonderful blessing and time of refreshment at the other end. You are such a wonderful, loving God! No wonder You say to love others the way I would like to be loved, because that is how You love me, and I am so grateful! Truly, my heart is overflowing with the goodness of Your Spirit to me.

Wonderful Father, I am listening with anticipation as You speak to my heart words of life.

_____

_____

_____

_____

_____

_____

_____

_____

_____

_____

_____

~358~

ISAIAH 40:29 AMP
"He gives power to the faint and weary, and to him who has no might
He increases strength, [causing it to multiply and making it to abound]."

My Child,

I have made you stable and secure. Faint not within your spirit from the strain, but mount up as on eagle's wings and begin to soar again in the Heavenlies, unfettered by the strains and restraints of earth. Begin to fly again, My child, and worry not over the details of this life. Leave the details in My hands. They are inconsequential to you. I have them well in hand. I will handle them. You simply fly with freedom, grace and trust in My ability to see you through each appointed junction and upheaval in the road. Worry not, I say again, but begin to fly again with peace, joy, and abandonment to My love and protection over you. Be at peace and remember, I am your Creator, the perfector and director of all things pertaining to you. I have said in the past that you will not miss My best for you. By My power, it is yours to enjoy.

Fly with Freedom, My Child!

I Love You

Father, right now I just need to rest in Your arms and listen to Your beautiful voice of comfort, love, wisdom, and peace. I love You, Father!

Faithful Father, the words that You spoke long ago, that I would not miss Your very best for my life, have brought peace and comfort through the years. But when I get faint and weary, I forget to mount up as on eagle's wings that I might once again soar in the Heavenlies, unfettered by the strains and restraints of earth. Thank You for reminding me to leave the details in Your hands and simply fly with freedom, grace, and trust in Your ability to see me through each appointed junction and upheaval in the road. Thank You, Father, for not only increasing my strength, but for causing it to multiply and making it to abound!

359

PSALM 57:2 AMP
"I will cry to God Most High,
Who performs on my behalf and rewards me
[Who brings to pass His purposes for me
and surely completes them]!"

My Child,

Make of your heart a resting place. Come often to the well to be refreshed and refurbished, for the needs shall be great. Maintain an unruffled spirit. I have said, "The desires of your heart are the desires of My heart, for I put those desires there." Continue on, rejoicing on the way. Nothing shall deter your steps. Be assured, be sustained, and be confident of this very thing, that what I have begun, I shall complete. A storehouse of treasure have I placed in your heart. Continue to fill that storehouse with the treasure of My Word.

Rest in Me,
Your Loving Father

Loving Father, every day I am more aware of the storehouse of treasure that You have placed in my heart. It keeps coming out of my mouth in the most amazing ways, delighting me with such joy! Long ago, You said, "The desires of your heart are the desires of My heart, for I put those desires in your heart in the first place." I have depended on those words, Father, through the years! Thank You, Father, that I can be confident of this very thing, that what You have begun in my life You will complete, to my joy and to Your Glory!

Father, thank You for bringing refreshment and restoration to my heart as I drink in Your peace, as You speak to my heart!

360

2 TIMOTHY 1:9 NKJV
"Who has saved us and called us with a holy calling,
not according to our works, but according to His own purpose
and grace which was given to us in Christ Jesus before time began."

My Child,

My blessings have been as a sprinkle, sprinkled as the blood of purification to make you a living sacrifice worthy of your calling. Much has been in preparation. You have called upon Me and I have answered your cry. Revealed from the beginning of time has been My plan for you. Do not let down the intensity of your search and desire to walk in the fullness of My Spirit. Let the weak and weary take the side roads. You take the main road, the shortest route, but not the easiest, the road that My warriors take. Strengthen, strengthen, I say, by drawing on My strength, My wisdom, and My peace through My Word and My Spirit. You shall not know the disillusionment of defeat, but always the joy and delight of victory!

You Are Victorious in Me!
Your Loving Father

Beloved Father, this is how I intend to live every day of my life, drawing on Your strength, Your wisdom, and Your peace, through Your Word and Your Spirit, as You speak to my heart!

_____

_____

_____

_____

_____

_____

_____

_____

Loving Father, it's been the journey of a lifetime and I know it's only begun. You have said, "Everything that comes into your life is filtered through My love! Stalemates are broken when you come into My Presence. Simple, straightforward answers are My way, every day. Settled in your heart, each day, the simplicity of My Way! Listen closely each and every day as I speak to your heart!"

361

PSALM 119:50 AMP
"Your Word has revived me and given me life."

My Faithful Child,

Look out over the vastness of all that is before you. It is limitless. See, the times and the days, weeks and years, are culminating into a time of richness and focused fulfillment and blessing. Continue on in your quest to know My Word and to understand it by the power of My Holy Spirit. The days ahead are rich and full; full of the knowledge and character of My Word to you, and through you. Reach out your heart and mind to drink deeply, and I shall make of you a water fountain of life—abundant life—in My Name. Refreshed you shall be and restored, filled with My Glory, peace, faithfulness, and love. See it come upon you and transform you, making of you a servant in whom I am well pleased. Continue on, My child, and know that the door is open wide and the fulfillment is sure. Strain not to fulfill My dreams in you. Take the land step by step.

You Are Precious to Me,

Your Loving Father

Loving Father, thank You that I shall fulfill Your dreams for me, and for Your refreshment and restoration. Thank You for helping me to know You and Your Word with understanding by the power of Your Holy Spirit. You also said, "Remain steadfast and alert, ever ready to be a hearer and a doer of My Word to you. Strengthen your inner spirit with praise and thanksgiving. Enter in with abounding joy!" Thank You, for making me a water fountain of life, in Your Name! I love You, Father!

Precious Father, My heart reaches out to You to drink deeply, as You speak to my heart!

_____

_____

_____

_____

_____

_____

_____

_____

_____

_____

_____

362

PROVERBS 28:20 AMP
"A faithful man shall abound with blessings."

My Faithful Child,

As you continue to know My gifts and blessings to you, the skies will become bluer and the flowers brighter and you will never be bored or lonely, for I am always there, opening new doors of delight to your heart. Strength, strength of character, fortitude, resilience and the knowledge of My love and heart, are all gifts I have bestowed upon you in abundance. I have given you strength of will, that will to do My will in the face of all obstacles and temptations. I have given you fortitude to stand in the midst of the storm and resilience to rejoice and sing praise to Me in the midst of the storm. The knowledge of My heart shall increase, and you shall know beyond the shadow of any doubt the abundance of My love. Stand in amazement at what I shall do.

You Have Been Faithful!
I Am Proud of You

Loving Father, my heart sings to You a love song! You are my song!

_____

Precious Father, You also said, "It's been a time of strengthening, body, soul, and spirit. A time of seeing Me in everything. It's a time of separating the precious from the vile. A time of learning what is permanent and what has been a trial. Secluded you have been. It has been part of the plan. You have strengthened your resolve. You have found order from above. You have lightened your load. And now you will see what it really means to be free, to skip and laugh and let the world know you are free as a bird wherever you go. Free to love, laugh, and sing. Princess of everything! Confident to let the world know, I am with you wherever you go. Your song of life shall continue to be, 'This is what it is really like to be free'!"

363

PSALM 40:3 AMP
"And He has put a new song in my mouth,
a song of praise to our God."

My Precious One,

Skip lightly, joyfully, gracefully, but resolutely, for strong and secure shall you be with every step you take and every decision you make, as we go forward, as the future becomes the present and My promises to you become the fulfillment of your dreams and wishes. Sure, secure, and sound shall every step be, orchestrated and directed by My heart of love toward you. Your heart shall sing and your praises ring in exhilaration and joy, pure joy.

Sing and Dance with Me, My Child!
Your Loving Father

Loving Father, You have put a new song in my mouth and in my heart! It sings through my life every moment of every day and it says, "God loves you, you are so precious to Him! Let Him fill your life with meaning, destiny, and song! Let Him protect and bless you all through the night and all through the day long. His hope, love, and peace will see you through, and bring such freedom and joy to you!" Father, my heart is so filled with exhilaration and love for You!

Father, Your love fills my heart with a "Heart Song" of love for You!

_____

_____

_____

_____

_____

_____

_____

_____

_____

_____

_____

_____

_____

_____

~~ 364 ~~

LUKE 10:20 NKJV
"Rejoice because your names are written in heaven."

My Child,

Your ways are written in My book of life, created by My hand, formed by My love. Never reject as inadequate your ways. I simply add to them elements to enhance and delight your soul, to balance out the beauty of My creation. Each element of your being is created by My hand and is a necessary part of the whole. Enjoy each facet of your being. Honor not one above the other. Reject not parts of your being, created lovingly by your Father and Creator. Be confident in the functioning of each facet of your being, for I have placed it there to create a beautiful picture to reflect My love. Precious in My eyes are those who awake to the sound of My voice, at any age, to know that everything about them is precious in My sight, part of the reflection of My love. Each facet is to be drawn together in unity to create a symphony of praise. Each life is created to be a symphony of praise, all of their days.

You Are Formed by My Love,
You Are Precious to Me

~~

Father, You bring so much joy and music to my heart! My heart is listening to hear the music of Heaven so that I can sing it back to You!

Loving Father, it's the desire of my heart to awake every morning to the sound of Your voice speaking to my heart. Many mornings I wake up singing the Psalms, and when that happens, such joy fills my heart. I want my whole being to be a symphony of praise to You, reflecting Your love, every moment of every day, every day of my life!

ᔐ 365 ᔐ

"O come let us sing to the Lord; let us make a joyful noise to the Rock of our salvation! Let us come before His presence with thanksgiving; let us make a joyful noise to Him with songs of praise!"

My Precious Child,

Built within the fiber of your being, is the purpose and plan for your life. Day by day it comes forth, many times unheralded and unobserved, but now you shall see it come forth speedily, with delight, as you see clearly what has been there all along. You have prepared. You have been faithful. You have seen Me in everything. My heart sings for you, My child, for you have heard My call and answered it. The days, the months, and the years are all coming together to form the "Heart Song" of your life. Mysteries shall come to light. Every day is a testament of My love. Now it comes forth as the rising sun over the mountains, proclaiming the new day! Rejoice and be glad, My little one!

I Love You!

Your Father

Loving Father, I can't imagine not walking daily with You, for every day is a testament of Your love! My desire is that others might know the joy and delight, peace and wonderment of knowing You, the Mighty God and Creator of the Universe. And yet You are our loving Father, who created each of us for intimate and loving friendship. You love us individually, as if we were Your only and most precious and valuable creation. Father, I long for Your people, Your treasures, to know, that they too can hear Your loving heart and voice to their hearts, proclaiming the absolute beauty and wisdom of Your heart to them! Thank You Father, for Your Love!

Precious and Beloved Father, You are my "Heart Song"! I will always cherish each loving moment of every day with You, as You speak to my heart!

Rosalie Willis Storment began writing down every precious word that God spoke to her heart in the early 70's with the desire to draw closer to God, which was the inspiration for this book—conceived as a way to acquaint readers with the very personal side of God's love.

Rosalie is the founder and director of *A Company of Women, International*, a family of women's ministries coming together in the unity of God's love, and established in 1996. This ministry is a network of worldwide "Heart Friends" whom God has called to take His love to the nations. An important part of *A Company of Women* is the *PraiseNet* and International Prayer Network, through which all can pray together regarding needs, and rejoice in shared victories, while connecting hearts around the world.

Also a musician, Rosalie has written and copyrighted the music, word for word to all 150 Psalms, from *The Amplified Version* of the Bible. It takes about twelve hours for her to sing them straight through. The first CD has been produced in Nashville, Tennessee, and is titled "The Psalms," which includes twelve Psalms. The CD is available through Praise Publishing.

Rosalie currently has three other titles in the market place; *A Walk With Jesus, Walking On With Jesus,* and *The Singing Bride.*

Frequently speaking at retreats and conferences, Rosalie has a true devotion in life to encourage others in their pursuit toward a personal and intimate relationship with God. For additional information on conferences, scheduling speaking engagements, or to write the author, please address your correspondence to:

Rosalie Willis Storment
P.O. Box 324
Post Falls, ID 83877-0324

E-mail: rosalieacw@gmail.com
Website: www.rosaliewillis.com
Website: www.acompanyofwomen.org
Praise Publishing: 208-773-8411

PraiseNet International Prayer E-mail Network:
praisenet@acompanyofwomen.org